MW01092574

Compassion's
COMPASS

Compassion's
COMPASS

Strategies for Developing Insight, Kindness, and Empathy

Wilson C. Hurley

Foreword by His Holiness the Dalai Lama

ROWMAN & LITTLEFIELD

Lanham • Boulder • New York • London

Executive Editor: Mark Kerr
Associate Editor: Courtney Packard
Sales and Marketing Inquiries: textbooks@rowman.com

Credits and acknowledgments for material borrowed from other sources, and
reproduced with permission, appear on the appropriate pages within the text.

Published by Rowman & Littlefield
An imprint of The Rowman & Littlefield Publishing Group, Inc.
4501 Forbes Boulevard, Suite 200, Lanham, Maryland 20706
www.rowman.com

86-90 Paul Street, London EC2A 4NE

Copyright © 2022 by The Rowman & Littlefield Publishing Group, Inc.

All rights reserved. No part of this book may be reproduced in any form or by
any electronic or mechanical means, including information storage and retrieval
systems, without written permission from the publisher, except by a reviewer who
may quote passages in a review.

British Library Cataloguing in Publication Information Available

Library of Congress Cataloging-in-Publication Data

Names: Hurley, Wilson C., 1955– author.
Title: Compassion's COMPASS : strategies for developing insight, kindness, and
    empathy / Wilson C. Hurley.
Description: Lanham : Rowman & Littlefield, [2022] | Includes bibliographical
    references and index.
Identifiers: LCCN 2021025453 (print) | LCCN 2021025454 (ebook) | ISBN
    9781538141823 (cloth) | ISBN 9781538141830 (paperback) | ISBN
    9781538141847 (epub)
Subjects: LCSH: Compassion. | Mindfulness (Psychology) | Kindness. | Insight. |
    Meditation. | Compassion—Religious aspects—Buddhism.
Classification: LCC BJ1475 .H87 2022 (print) | LCC BJ1475 (ebook) | DDC
    177/.7—dc23
LC record available at https://lccn.loc.gov/2021025453
LC ebook record available at https://lccn.loc.gov/2021025454

∞™ The paper used in this publication meets the minimum requirements of
American National Standard for Information Sciences—Permanence of Paper for
Printed Library Materials, ANSI/NISO Z39.48-1992.

Contents

THE DALAI LAMA

FOREWORD

All major religious traditions have the potential to bring about inner peace. They achieve this through the practice of such virtuous qualities as love, compassion, forgiveness, and self-discipline. Since over one billion of the world's seven billion human beings don't believe in religion, I believe that common sense, common experience, and an acceptance of scientific discovery can become the basis for practicing compassion and tolerance.

I am concerned that our present education system is not adequate for developing these essential qualities for our happiness. I hope that more people will pay attention to the education of our hearts as well as our minds.

Compassion's Compass: Strategies for Developing Kindness and Insight, by Wilson C. Hurley, explains how to develop basic human values such as patience, mindfulness, and kindness without touching any particular religious belief. It is accessible to all regardless of age or belief. I commend the author for his hard work and hope that readers will find this book helpful.

2 December 2019

Preface

This book has been written for a general audience as well as for helping professionals. The main body of the text is for everyone, with short sections, inserted intermittently as text boxes throughout, specifically for helping professionals. The appendix, "A COMPASS Handbook for Helping Professionals," contains more detailed sections focused on challenges that contribute to compassion fatigue and ways to overcome them. All the main exercises of COMPASS that are mentioned throughout the book are included again at the end of the handbook.

Acknowledgments

I dedicate this book to my teachers and parents, all of you, and to future generations.

This book would not have been possible without my teachers, both Eastern and Western. Particularly, I am indebted to His Holiness the Fourteenth Dalai Lama, who took time from his busy schedule to write the foreword. He is an inspiration for me and for millions around the world, and a living example of compassionate insight. With the help of two friends, John Cerullo and Geshe Dhargye, I was able to bring this book to the attention of Geshe Ngawang Sonam, who serves in the office of His Holiness the Dalai Lama. Geshe Ngawang Sonam took the time to read the book, offer helpful suggestions, and present it to His Holiness. His Holiness's foreword speaks directly to the need for secularized approaches to self-regulation and compassion development. His clear and eloquent message promotes basic human values of tolerance, kindness, and peace. I also am indebted to my many teachers, especially Gyumed Khensur Losang Jampa Rinpoche and Sermey Khensur Lobsang Tharchin Rinpoche, who kindly instructed me over the past 40 years in the vast and profound teachings of the Tibetan mind training tradition. It is their guidance and example that led me to write this book.

There are so many to whom I feel gratitude. I am grateful to my wife, Sharon, who has patiently stayed by my side as I have worked on this. Several friends offered support through being advance readers, including Dr. Lorne Ladner, Peter J. Delany, PhD, Dr. Michael Sanger, Dr. Carly Hunt, Eric Treider, Ingrid Czintos, and Maureen Sullivan. Thomas Pruzinsky, PhD, helped me develop the initial model for the COMPASS approach to compassion training and wrote a brief passage for the introduction to this book about empirical validation of other similar compassion training programs. Jeremy Lehrer read early sections of the book and made helpful suggestions. Several other friends also contributed to sections of the book, including Dr. John Tedeschi, Dr. Lorne Ladner, Peggy DiVincenzo, LPC, LMFT, Erika Neil, LCSW, JD, Kimberly Hoskins, PsyD, and Eric Propst, PsyD. I am indebted to Thomas Pruzinsky,

PhD, Rachael D. Goodman, PhD, and Dr. Carly Hunt for designing and implementing three formal pilot studies of COMPASS and to Dr. Clara Hill and Alex Hilert, who offered their expertise. I am also grateful to those who participated in the pilots, to my students who have tried the exercises, and to everyone who has given me feedback and encouragement over the years. Also, I am indebted to John Cerullo, Mark Kerr, Courtney Packard, Jehanne Schweitzer, Jo-Ann Parks, and everyone at the Rowman & Littlefield Publishing Group for bringing this work to fruition.

Without the pioneering efforts of mindfulness practitioners such as Jon Kabat-Zinn, Sharon Salzberg, Jack Kornfield, Tara Brach, Kristen Neff, Christopher Germer, and many others, much of the material in the section on the foundational mindfulness practices of COMPASS would not be available. Without Tibetan and Western scholars of Tibetan Buddhism such as Thubten Jinpa, Professor Robert Thurman, Artemus Engle, and many others, we would not have access to the rich treasury of Tibetan literature. I also want to acknowledge Dr. Lorne Ladner for his pioneering work in bringing a Western psychological perspective to the Tibetan mind training tradition in his book *The Lost Art of Compassion*. This, together with the efforts of many Western and Tibetan scholars, writers, and researchers has led to a blossoming in empirically validated compassion training approaches, most notably Cognitively Based Compassion Training and Compassion Cultivation Training. I am also indebted to the work of Dr. Charles Figley and others who have written extensively on compassion fatigue, its causes, ways to assess it, and ways to prevent and treat it. I am grateful to all of you and delighted that the life-giving tradition of Tibetan mind training is becoming more widely understood and used around the world.

CHAPTER 1

Introduction

Minding Your Inner Troll

It seems that we all have an inner troll of sorts. It's the persistent, obsessive focus on me and mine that drives our thoughts, feelings, and behaviors both day and night. We might notice our inner troll when it makes us irritated at a slow-moving driver, or when we get upset at our spouse for not catering to our every whim. Sometimes it seems to be our only focus as we perseverate on "what about me?" With our constant devotion to it, you would think it would bring us some sort of comfort or pleasure in return. Instead, it increases our fears of loss, insecurities about what life holds for us, anger and hurt at being unnoticed or disregarded, and a myriad of other maladies. Research is emerging that indicates a relationship between heightened self-focus and heart disease, increased anger, dysphoria, and social isolation. And yet we protect this inner troll as if it were our best friend.

In fact, it seems that modern culture has become deranged in its infatuation with big egos, narcissists who boast their way to prominence. In the age of selfies and social media, millions chirp about themselves to a deaf audience too consumed with itself to notice. In a desperate attempt to connect and feel valued, people take excessive measures to gain likes on social media, posting and trawling the internet into the wee hours and even forgoing sleep. All of this is to no avail because in the end we are still left feeling empty and disconnected. This is the legacy of the inner troll.

On a more ominous note, selfish impulses threaten to ruin the planet we share. For example, big money interests support the denial of climate change and seek to plunder public lands. The poor keep falling deeper into poverty while becoming more marginalized while the rich amass yet greater fortunes and influence governments to protect them rather than the majority of the people. Government leaders pulled by self-interests not only cater to big-money interests but turn a blind eye to environmental devastation and use their citizens' tax money to develop the military instead of addressing basic human needs.

Tips for Helping Professionals

Empathy and Compassion

Compassion, which is the empathic wish that others be free from suffering, is an essential motivator for helping professionals. Doctors, nurses, teachers, police, firefighters, social workers, psychologists, counselors, and many other types of helping professionals become more effective and productive when their compassion is strong and intact. Research also indicates that clients have better outcomes when treated compassionately. Empathy is our ability to know how another is feeling and to consider what their situation and experiences are like for them. Compassion includes empathy and goes an extra step: reacting with care. It is a courageous state of mind that protects both us and our clients.

Section 1 of the appendix, "A COMPASS Handbook for Helping Professionals," discusses the benefits of empathy and compassion for helping professionals in more detail.

This book seeks to impart a methodology to stop this madness through offering a systematic approach to developing our human potential for compassionate insight. The ancient approach presented here has been secularized for modern consumption. Research is emerging that supports its effectiveness in enhancing empathy, self-compassion, compassion for others, resilience, and well-being. The strategies, origins, legacy, and research connected to these techniques will be discussed in the pages that follow, but in order to make it work for you, you must try it. Regular use increases its effectiveness.

It is hoped that, as more people become familiar with these age-old strategies for compassion development, there will be efforts to impart them to future generations by including them in school curricula, training for public servants, and for public use. In many ways, compassion is the thread that stitches together the fabric of society. From the schoolteacher who spends their own scarce resources to provide positive learning experiences for their students, to the police officer who goes out of their way to deescalate a dangerous situation so that no one is harmed, people who choose compassion over hate and intolerance each day make this a better world. Compassion is medicine that heals the ills of hatred, fear, selfishness, and alienation. Like fuel, it moves us toward humanitarian activities, lifting ourselves and others into well-being. Imagine a world in which people are universally trained in compassionate insight, in which tolerance and understanding replace fear and hatred. It would be a safer and happier world and one more likely to survive for future generations. Who would not want to be part of such a world?

The strategy that will be described in this book is called COMPASS, which is an acronym for Compassion and Analytical Selective-Focus Skills. Selective-focus skills suggest contemplations that can help us to generate and enhance compassionate insight. These skills are practiced within the context of cultivating mindful awareness and self-compassion. There is an "emotional logic" to these exercises in that one step produces a basis for cultivating the next. These techniques have been piloted with social workers and therapists-in-training. Details of these pilot studies as well as related research are included below. Each chapter contains exercises for you to try. These exercises are also compiled sequentially for easy use at the end of the appendix, "A COMPASS Handbook for Helping Professionals." The appendix contains detailed sections focused on challenges that contribute to compassion fatigue and ways to overcome them. Brief textboxes are also inserted throughout this book that provide helpful tips for professionals about ways to recognize and overcome compassion fatigue while enhancing compassion resilience.

My Journey to Find COMPASS

As a young man, my interests were mostly hedonistic. I was training to be a jazz musician at the University of California at Santa Cruz (UCSC), which my friends and I humorously referred to as "Uncle Charlie's Summer Camp." This title was well deserved because the campus was set amidst a redwood forest, bordered by the Monterey Bay. Students in my area of the campus could eat outside under a gorgeous blue sky and gaze at the bay while we discussed whatever our hearts desired. It was a perfect scenario, and yet I found that there was a gnawing sense of internal dissatisfaction growing within me that I did not fully understand.

Now, I can look back on those days with a better understanding of what was wrong. It was 1978, the last phase of the hippie movement was still strong, and people were still living by the mottos "sex, drugs, and rock and roll" and "if it feels good, do it." Like most people in my generation, I was raised in a culture of narcissism in which the pursuit of happiness was primarily seen as an effort to satisfy one's own needs and wishes. As I pursued happiness in this way, my desires and self-focus were growing stronger and my sense of well-being and contentment was losing ground. As a result, while surrounded by an idyllic environment, my internal experience was one of discontent.

I didn't know it at the time, but my direction was about to change. One day, as I was exiting a required class that I abhorred, a friend looked at his watch and said, "We still have time to check out that Tibetan Lama over at Oaks College." This was the first I had heard about it, but together, we dashed across campus to find a crowded room of students eagerly listening to a jolly Tibetan monk, Lama Yeshe, describing his culture and way of life. He had been invited by Jan Willis, a religious studies professor, to be a visiting professor for a semester and teach a class on Tibetan Buddhism. I became fascinated with his views of life and later sought him out during office hours in order to make a connection. When I told him of my newly forming attempts at learning how to meditate, he drew into meditation himself for a few moments. Then, as he emerged from his absorption, he said, "You're very lucky," and sent me to his own teacher, Kyabje Song Rinpoche, for instructions.

Later, after I had received instructions from his teacher, I met again with Lama Yeshe, who asked me what my parents would think about my study of Buddhism. I told him that my mother would probably be okay with it, but that my father was very scientific. He slapped his hands together debate-style and said, "Buddhism is a science." Lama Yeshe's statement had a profound effect on me and has continued to guide my spiritual study and practice over the years. Rather than imposing a sense that reason must be abandoned in the pursuit of spirituality, it made me feel comfortable applying research and logic to my spiritual path. In fact, I was to find that this acceptance of reason, logic, and scientific method is common among Buddhists.[1] For example, His Holiness the Dalai Lama says, "If scientific analysis were conclusively to demonstrate certain claims in Buddhism to be false, then we must accept the findings of science and abandon those claims."[2]

As I pursued my studies and practice of Tibetan Buddhism more deeply, I also began working and going to graduate school at the Catholic University of America in Washington, DC, in order to train as a clinical social worker. It was as if I were living two lives: one as a deeply committed spiritual aspirant and another as an engaged social worker. Since the latter pursuit was entirely secular, I formed a habit of hiding my spiritual side for fear of public censure and rejection. However, I couldn't help but notice an overlap between the principles I was learning in my Buddhist studies with the empirically validated approaches to helping people in my social work studies.

For example, social work practice is rooted in systems theory, in which the interdependence of the person and their environment is emphasized.[3] The sense that everything is dependent on something else is also a keystone to Buddhist philosophical thought. Therefore, as I read about systems theory, I easily saw the correlations with Buddhist tenets. Also, social work ethics emphasize the dignity and worth of people, service, social justice, and other humane principles that dovetail well with Buddhist principles of compassionate service to others. Western psychological theories like cognitive restructuring, ego psychology, and depth psychology also resonated with ideas I found in Buddhist texts on the mind and its functions.

Therefore, I began to weave together a working model combining aspects of these two different approaches to understanding reality.

This was well before the flood of research emerged on the psychological benefits of mindfulness meditation, which is a simple strategy derived from an ancient Buddhist practice for cultivating meditative stability and insight. A supervisor at a mental health clinic where I worked became aware of my interest in meditation and asked if I would introduce the practice to staff and children at a camp program run by the clinic. So, during the summer of 1985, I introduced my fellow staff members and the camp children to a basic meditation on mindfulness of breathing. A staff psychologist did informal pre- and post-assessments of the intervention and observed that this exercise had a noticeable impact on the camp climate, and that counselors and children seemed much calmer than in previous years.

During those years, in my free time I was transcribing and editing taped lectures on a practice called "training the mind" by a Buddhist teacher who had become my spiritual guide.[4] The mind-training practice emphasizes setting one's attitude each day by attempting to overcome self-focus and to cultivate compassionate insight. This was especially poignant for me because my job required me to embody compassion constantly, often in the face of the most tragic situations imaginable. I was working with children in poverty, living in chaotic and often dangerous situations. Some of them had been severely abused physically, sexually, and/or emotionally. Some had witnessed their parents succumb to substance addiction, incarceration, victimization by an abusive partner, or death by murder or suicide. The children would enter the program where I worked each day hungry for attention, nurturance, safety, and affection. They would often act out their neediness, anger, and fearfulness aggressively. It was a constant challenge for me to maintain my emotional balance, so I began to rely heavily on my meditation practice and contemplations on compassion when I had time off from work.

From there, I entered the Fairfax County Public School System for 12 years as a school social worker in programs for children with emotional disabilities. The school system was emphatic about remaining secular, so there was less opportunity to work with staff and children using meditative strategies, which were still seen as primarily spiritual in nature. However, I kept seeing the need for self-regulation and mindfulness when witnessing the problems that arose in staff and student functioning due to stress and conflict. As in my previous job, many of the children I worked with came from tragic situations, which led me to rely on my meditative practices to rejuvenate myself each day. I would practice mental-training techniques in the morning before going to work, and then again upon my return home. When I exited the school system in 2001 to start a private mental health practice, I once again was able to introduce clients to meditative strategies, especially because research was starting to emerge showing the benefits of mindfulness practice.

Along with basic mindfulness practice, I began to introduce the concept of mental gardening to some of my clients. This concept accords with research emerging in the fields of cognitive behavioral therapy and positive psychology. Basically, the mind tends to amplify the thoughts and feelings on which it focuses. Some mental states are conducive to well-being while others increase experiences of distress. By consciously cultivating a positive focus and weeding out afflictive mental states, internal well-being is strengthened. For example, perhaps we find that our minds are agitated and upset after a challenging day at work. We then find ourselves focused on a memory of a troubling interaction that increases internal feelings of anger. By consciously shifting our focus to a contemplation on kindness, we can change our emotional state and regain equilibrium for a while.

On the surface, mental gardening might seem to clash with the form of mindfulness practice widely researched and propagated by Western mental health professionals. The point of divergence seems to lie in the emphasis in the latter approach of allowing mental events to arise without hindrance or mental judgment. This approach calls for us to merely place our attention on the breath and present moment, accepting whatever comes up within mindful awareness. In contrast, mental gardening emphasizes topics for contemplation and a selective focus of awareness.

However, I have noticed personally and with clients that both approaches can be helpful within specific contexts. Buddhist meditation manuals suggest different objects of focus depending on what mental factors are causing difficulty. For instance, if your attention is scattered, it is suggested that you focus on the breath. If you are overcome by anger, loving-kindness contemplation is recommended. If your mind is depressed, texts say that you should contemplate uplifting topics or focus on an image of light. Such flexibility in approaching meditation allows you to choose whatever focal object fits your mood and circumstances.

So, in developing COMPASS, I chose to use both an accepting approach and a selective-focus approach. The COMPASS exercises start with a basic mindfulness of breathing exercise in which self-compassion and self-acceptance are emphasized. This is conducive to helping the mind settle, which provides a stable basis for pursuing the contemplations that follow. Then, within the context of mindfulness, selective-focus exercises are suggested that aid in the development of compassionate insight.

I did not arrive at this approach on my own. A friend, Thomas Pruzinsky, PhD, worked closely with me to develop the COMPASS exercises. Tom is a professor in positive psychology at Quinnipiac University in Connecticut. Like me, he is an earnest student of Tibetan Buddhism, and he noticed parallels between that tradition and emerging research in the field of positive psychology. We were originally intent on writing a paper together on the mind-training practices of Tibetan Buddhism when the tragedy at Sandy Hook took place on December 14, 2012. Adam Lanza entered an elementary school and randomly killed 26 people, most of them young children. This event horrified and sickened us both, as it did the rest of the world.

The tragedy at Sandy Hook provoked a sense of urgency to the work Tom and I were doing. The sense that "Rome is burning" took hold of us both. While consulting with Tom, I decided to ask my social work students at George Mason University if they would be willing to try out the emerging exercises and offer candid reactions, working out a system where they could give their feedback anonymously. They agreed, so I started leading them through short exercises at the beginning of each class. The results and procedures used are documented in a paper called "Enhancing a Positive School Climate with Compassion and Analytical Selective-Focus Skills (COMPASS)."[5]

COMPASS was well received, and several symposia followed. For example, the American Psychological Association hosted a symposium titled "Cultivating Compassion—Empirically Validating Tibetan Buddhist Mind-Training Techniques" that included a presentation on COMPASS in the organization's August 2014 national conference. The audience, which filled the room past capacity, seemed to have a very positive response. The National Association of Social Workers accepted a similar symposium solely dedicated to COMPASS at their national conference that summer (July 24, 2014) titled "Courage to Serve in the Face of Suffering: Clinical Perspectives on Compassion and Self-Compassion." In these and other public presentations, it became clear that people felt a deep connection with the COMPASS approach to compassion development.

Tom and I began working with Dr. Carly Hunt, who was then a graduate student in counseling psychology at the University of Maryland, and with Rachael Goodman, PhD, LPC, an associate professor in the Counseling and Development Program at George Mason University, to devise ways to study COMPASS more empirically. We conducted three small pilot studies of COMPASS, two at George Mason University and a third at the University of Maryland. The first formal pilot was conducted at George Mason University on January 25, 2015, and consisted of a three-hour presentation on COMPASS with breaks for participants to fill out questionnaires. Feedback from the seven participants indicated "increased positive emotions (e.g., empathy, compassion), decreased fear of compassion, and positive anticipated increases in empathy and compassion."[6] Similar feedback was given by participants in the second pilot at George Mason University on May 31, 2015. Feedback was elicited from participants in these pilots about both their positive and negative experiences with the training and the exercises, which will be explored later in the book. Some participants mentioned enhanced interest in developing compassion and commented on the importance of training in empathy and compassion as a support for providing effective counseling.[7]

The third formal pilot study, conducted at the University of Maryland's on-campus Psychotherapy Clinic and Research Lab, was more complex.[8] Following a two hour COMPASS training with pre- and post-mindfulness assessments, six therapists-in-training were randomly assigned one of three possible tasks between client sessions: (1) listen to a recording of a one-minute COMPASS-based centering exercise on mindfulness and kindness, (2) listen to a reminder of their supervision instructions, or (3) prepare as usual. They completed measures after each session and completed the study with a 30-minute focus group. Therapists changed significantly in terms of mindfulness (i.e., curiosity and de-centeredness) and meditation self-efficacy after attending the COMPASS workshop. In terms of pre-session preparation, therapists evaluated sessions as more effective after the meditation intervention than after the preparation as usual condition. Further, they noted that pre-session meditation exercises led to a positive state of being and increased self-care and reflection. They also suggested that longer, at-home practice might ultimately be more helpful to them than pre-session exercises. Further research investigating the optimal mode and amount of COMPASS training in the context of clinical practice is indicated.[9]

While these pilot studies were small, their outcomes, nonetheless, dovetailed with the findings of larger, better-funded studies on the effects of compassion training being conducted at Stanford and Emory using two other approaches derived from Tibetan mind-training traditions.[10] Thomas Pruzinsky, PhD, who has studied and written on these two approaches, made the following observations:

> Over the last fifteen years there has been a great deal of scientific attention devoted to the study of compassion all of which has direct relevance to the practice of COMPASS. Two widely utilized and highly studied forms of compassion training are Cognitively-Based Compassion Training (CBCT) and Compassion Cultivation Training (CCT). CBCT was developed and empirically validated at Emory University.[11] Compassion Cultivation Training (CCT) was developed and empirically validated at Stanford University.[12]
>
> The Emory and Stanford programs have the following core characteristics in common with COMPASS:
>
> 1. A systematic approach to compassion training, which includes learning and practicing a series of specifically defined subcomponents of the skill of compassion.

2. These skill training programs were developed by scholars with deep academic knowledge as well as extensive practical experience in the Tibetan Buddhist contemplative tradition of mind training (*Lojong*). These mind training techniques are, essentially, a highly sophisticated form of positive psychology intervention developed and mastered over multiple centuries.
3. Each of the programs have been secularized such that they do not require any specific knowledge of and/or belief in the Tibetan tradition.
4. Each of these compassion training methods have been taught in a wide variety of secular contexts.

Additionally, both CBCT and CCT, have been empirically evaluated using rigorous methodologies including considerable research assessing the neurophysiological effects of compassion training. While COMPASS has not yet had the benefit of this specific kind of empirical evaluation, it has consistently resulted in a range of positive psychological and social benefits over the course of decades that the author has taught these methods in a very wide range of settings. Therefore, it is very reasonable to extrapolate the range of positive findings regarding the efficacy of CBCT and CCT to COMPASS.[13]

It is hoped that more rigorous empirical study of COMPASS techniques can be done in the future. Meanwhile, they have been introduced to staff at the Association of State and Territorial Health Officials (ASTHO) as methods to help them cope with stress and compassion fatigue related to their efforts addressing the opioid epidemic and the COVID-19 pandemic.[14] I also have continued to introduce COMPASS exercises in various training opportunities and to my social work students at George Mason University each year as a self-care strategy to guard against compassion fatigue and burnout. I weave them into the curriculum so that they resonate with the agenda of the direct practice class content. The feedback that I receive from students and other helping professionals has always been positive and welcoming. Personally, I continue to use these exercises each day and have found them to be central to my self-care. They have supported me through more than 35 years of direct social work practice and renew me each day. I hope you will find them equally helpful.

Tips for Helping Professionals

Compassion Fatigue

Compassion fatigue is a condition that can affect helping professionals who work with intense, troubling, or draining client situations. It can manifest as a sense of fatigue, emotional depletion, anxiety, depression, dread of work and of clients, work avoidance, and a variety of related problems. In some people, it is brought on by exposure to client trauma and manifests as secondary traumatic stress (STS), which mimics the symptoms of post-traumatic stress disorder (PTSD). In others it might take the form of vicarious trauma, which impacts the cognitive schema of helping professionals who listen repeatedly to client accounts of traumatic events, having a negative impact on the professional's view of themselves, their world, and their sense of meaning. Many helping professionals might also suffer from burnout, which is brought on by excessive caseloads, facing intense and complex problems each day, and other stressors in the work environment.

In the pages that follow, we will discuss ways to combat factors that can contribute to compassion fatigue. A more detailed description of compassion fatigue can be found in section 2 of the appendix, "A COMPASS Handbook for Helping Professionals."

An Overview of COMPASS

In order to systematically cultivate and strengthen compassion, the COMPASS approach offers a step-by-step process with three main divisions and subcategories as follows:

Chapter 2: The Foundation Practice of Mindfulness. Exercises include

- a foundational exercise of mindfulness practice in which one spends a few moments focusing on breathing,
- a section on acceptance and self-compassion, and
- mental gardening and self-care.

Chapter 3: Core Practices for Developing Compassion describes the logic for COMPASS practices to develop compassion that involve brief contemplations that can be introduced individually or in combination. These core compassion skills follow an "emotional logic" in which one skill sets an emotional tone conducive to the development of the next step. This part of the book begins with sections on "What's in It for Me?" and "Selecting a Focus," after which the core compassion skills are explained. These core skills are as follows.

Chapter 4: Equanimity: a contemplation on how everyone is equal in not wanting to suffer and in wanting to be happy, safe, and respected. This sets a universal backdrop for the steps that follow.

Chapter 5: Gratitude: a contemplation on the help one has received from others both directly and indirectly and developing a wish to repay such help by "paying it forward."

Chapter 6: Kindness: contemplations on forgiveness and on wishing well-being for oneself and for others.

Chapter 7: Compassion: developing the wish that oneself and others be free from suffering and its causes.

Chapter 8: Giving and Taking: an exercise to strengthen compassion that entails an imagined taking on of hardships for the sake of others, reduction of self-centered fear, enhancement of compassionate courage, and a giving back of well-being.

Chapter 9: Activation: formulation of a decision to engage in direct work toward helping others.

Chapter 10: Goal-Focused Compassion: developing one's own internal goals for putting compassion into action.

Chapter 11: Core Practices for Developing Analytical Insight. These final methods are cognitive strategies for identifying and undermining cognitive distortions about self-image that might become obstacles to one's compassionate goals. Such distortions include overly negative as well as overly positive self-assessments based on circumstances. For instance, if we have encountered several challenges within a brief period, we can start to feel helpless, and think of ourselves as a failure. This distortion about who we are further saps our energy. Conversely, if we have experienced several successes in a short period of time, we might start to develop an attitude of superiority, which can interfere in our ability to access empathic concern. Such distortions in self-concept can be dispelled in three steps:

1. Identifying distorted self-concepts.
2. Analyzing and debunking them.
3. Reidentifying with one's compassionate goals.

Appendix: A COMPASS Handbook for Helping Professionals

The book's final section is designed as a manual for helping professionals to provide a quick reference on COMPASS strategies. It is a more detailed discussion of points made in brief text boxes inserted throughout the book as tips for helping professionals about compassion, its benefits for staff and clients, challenges that helping professionals often face, compassion fatigue, and ways to cultivate resilient compassion. All the main exercises of COMPASS are included in sequential order at the end of the appendix.

The chapters that follow will take each of the above divisions and elaborate on them, adding research, logic, and procedural suggestions that will enable the reader to try them out and impart them to others.

Notes

[1] Tibetan Buddhist monasteries are actively engaged in incorporating Western science into their curricula. See Chen, J. (2018, July 26). For life's big questions, Tibetan Buddhist monks and nuns try a scientific approach. *Stat News.* https://www.statnews.com/2018/07/26/tibetan-buddhist-monks-and-nuns-try-a-scientific-approach/

[2] Dalai Lama XIV. (2005). *The universe in a single atom: The convergence of science and spirituality.* Morgan Road Books.

[3] Germain, C. B., & Gitterman, A. (1980). *The life model of social work practice.* Columbia University Press.

[4] Tharchin, Sermey Khensur Lobsang. (1999). *Achieving Bodhicitta: Instructions of two great lineages combined into a unique system of eleven categories.* Mahayana Sutra and Tantra Press.

[5] Hurley, W. (2014). Enhancing a positive school climate with Compassion and Analytical Selective-Focus Skills (COMPASS). *IISTE Journal of Education.* http://www.iiste.org/Journals/index.php/JEP/article/view/11589

[6] Goodman, R. D., Hunt, C. H., Pruzinsky, T., & Hurley, W. (2015). *Brief mindfulness-based compassion training: A multi-method approach to assessing positive psychological outcomes and potential barriers to future practice among therapist trainees.* Unpublished grant proposal.

[7] Goodman, R. D., Hurley, W., Pruzinsky, T., & Rietschel, C. H. (2016, April). Development of COMPASS: Mindfulness-based compassion training research. Paper presented at the meeting of the American Counseling Association, Montréal, QC.

[8] Hunt, C., Goodman, R. D., Hurley, W. C., Pruzinsky, T., Hilert, A. J., & Hill, C. (2015). *Assessing the effects of a mindfulness workshop and pre-session centering exercises for therapists: A pilot study.* Unpublished.

[9] Hunt, C., Goodman, R. D., Hilert, A. J., Hurley, W., & Hill, C.E. (2020, November). Assessing the effects of mindfulness and compassion-based, pre-session centering for therapists. Poster presented at the annual Mind and Life Contemplative Research Conference; and Hunt, C. A., Goodman, R. D., Hilert, A. J., Hurley, W., & Hill, C. E. (2021). A mindfulness-based compassion workshop and pre-session preparation to enhance therapist effectiveness in psychotherapy: A pilot study. *Counselling Psychology Quarterly.* https://www.tandfonline.com/doi/full/10.1080/09515070.2021.1895724

[10] For example, see Jazaieri, H., McGonigal, K., Jinpa, T., Doty, J. R., Gross, J. J., & Goldin, P. R. (2014). A randomized controlled trial of compassion cultivation training: Effects on mindfulness, affect, and emotion regulation. *Motivation and Emotion, 38*(1), 23-35. https://doi.org/10.1007/s11031-013-9368-z

[11] See www.compassion.emory.edu/cbct-compassion-training/research.html

[12] See http://ccare.stanford.edu/research/current-research/

[13] Pruzinsky, T. (2020). Personal communication. For a comprehensive summary and integration of the neurobiological efficacy of compassion training see Calderon, A., Ahern, T. H., & Pruzinsky. T. (2018). Can we change our mind about caring for others? The neuroscience of systematic compassion training. In L. Stevens & C. C. Woodruff (Eds.), *The neuroscience of empathy, compassion and self-compassion* (pp. 213-234). Academic Press.

[14] Hurley, W., Farfalla, J., & Pless, V. (2020, August). Fighting compassion fatigue during public health epidemics. *ASTHO Brief, Exploring critical issues in state and territorial public health.* https://astho.org/ASTHOBriefs/Fighting-Compassion-Fatigue-During-Public-Health-Epidemics/. See also www.compassmethods.com.

CHAPTER 2

The Foundation Practice of Mindfulness

Have you ever noticed your mind settle for a moment just to take in where you are, what's around you, and what you are doing, thinking, and feeling? Such moments are brief experiences of mindfulness. Many people take trips into the wilderness just to allow themselves to unravel from the anxieties and demands of daily living so that they can enjoy the present and let themselves be. Such immersions into mindful moments have a healing effect on the mind and body. Researchers have begun to study an ancient method for cultivating such experiences of calm, present-focused awareness by simply noticing the breath.

As you are reading this, take a moment just to notice your breath, the rise and fall of your chest and abdomen, the feel of the breath entering and exiting your nostrils. Notice the shapes and colors within your field of vision, the sounds around you. Tune into your sense of smell, taste, and touch, the experience of your senses. Do you notice how this simple exercise draws you out of your thoughts and into the present moment for a while? It seems so simple, yet the effects over time are profound.

Studies on mindfulness practice have shown that it thickens cortical areas associated with attention and sensory processing, and that it might slow down the thinning of these areas brought on by aging.[1] It seems that the process of repeatedly conveying one's attention to the breath and the present moment exercises the brain and enhances neural networking. It is helpful to think of this as like an athlete in training. At first, working out takes effort, especially if the athlete has been on vacation for a while. But once the athlete begins a routine of workouts, his or her muscles begin to thicken and become more defined. The same is true for regions of the brain associated with focusing attention and regulating our emotions. As we work them out, they respond by becoming more robust.

Mindfulness practice has been shown to increase positive affect and enhance the functioning of the immune system.[2] Also, its use has been linked to a reduction in anger, anxiety, and depression.[3] This is of particular importance in this context because anger, anxiety, and depression can disrupt the development of compassionate insight. It is difficult to feel compassionate when one's mind is in an afflicted state. Anger, anxiety, and depression also contribute to a host of psychological and physiological maladies.

For example, high levels of anger have been linked to heart disease and premature death.[4] Anger also impacts individuals, families, and communities in negative ways. It tends to distort our perceptions of people, causing us to see only negative qualities in them. It also frequently leads to saying or doing harsh things that can fracture relationships. We have all watched with horror the increase in mass shootings, terrorism, and random hate crimes that have besieged our nation and the world. Where does it come from? In a simple word, anger.

I recall a talk given in April 2017 by Scarlett Lewis, the mother of Jesse Lewis, one of the children who died at the hands of Adam Lanza in the shootings at Sandy Hook. She said that as she processed the terrible tragedy on the day of the shooting, she had a choice: to let Adam Lanza's hateful act destroy her life as it did her child or to use it to go forward and produce some meaning from the tragedy. She realized that the terrible actions of Adam Lanza began with an angry thought. She has now dedicated her life to promoting a program of Social Emotional Learning (SEL) for schoolchildren and founded the Jesse Lewis Choose Love Foundation to honor her son.[5] She said that the inspiration for her name "Choose Love" for the SEL program came from her child Jesse, who as he stood by his teacher that frightening morning and watched her shot down, instead of choosing fear or hate, turned to his classmates and yelled "run" as the shooter's gun jammed. Jesse chose love in that moment, his last moment, and by doing so saved nine of his classmates who were able to run from the classroom and survive.

From an internal point of view, this choice is partly psychological and partly physical. We are all equipped with an HPA Axis, which stands for Hypothalamic-Pituitary-Adrenal Axis. In lay terms, this is known as the flight/fight response. It is a survival system that reacts to perceived threats. Humans and animals have similar systems, but humans can trigger it with a thought. Luckily, there are parts of our nervous system that can turn off the HPA Axis because, without them, we would be locked into a perpetual state of fear and reactivity. By choosing love and our higher emotions, we can repair some of the damage that the HPA Axis does to our bodies and minds, and we can mold a life based on a higher purpose and meaning. Jesse, whose life ended tragically and too soon, also died a hero because he chose in his last moment to act with courage and love.

Anxiety and stress are closely related to fear and anger in being triggers of the HPA Axis and in being problematic realities of modern living. They permeate most of our lives from waking, through the day, and into the night. Many of us experience disrupted sleep, digestive problems, and difficulty concentrating due to relentless worries and the anxiety and stress they cause. The hustle and bustle of daily life seems to be intensifying as our ability to connect electronically increases. Subjectively, anxiety and stress hamper our ability to enjoy our lives and function optimally. Objectively, they deplete us emotionally and physically. From the common cold[6] to the ravages of cancer,[7] anxiety and stress have been shown to compromise our immune systems.

There is also a link between anxiety and depression.[8] Many people who experience anxiety early in life succumb to depression as they approach adulthood. There are high comorbidity rates of people who experience both anxiety and depression. Both problems are associated with hyperarousal of the nervous system due to repeated triggering of the HPA Axis. Sufferers of comorbid anxiety and depression are more likely to engage in substance abuse and to contemplate suicide. In addition, depression has been linked to a thickening of blood platelets,[9] resulting in increased risk for heart attack and stroke.

In brief, anxiety, anger, and depression afflict body and mind, leaving us depleted and making it difficult to function. There are

advanced ways to bring such problems into the service of developing compassionate insight that will be explored later in this book.
But in the beginning, mindfulness practice can help us to manage
and reduce them. In one study, teachers reported better academic
functioning and fewer anxiety symptoms in children introduced to
mindfulness practice.[10] Researchers on depression have found that
training clients with a history of depression in mindfulness-based
cognitive behavioral therapy decreases rates of relapse.[11]

The latter finding may be worth discussing a bit because it has
led to a theoretical shift in the field of cognitive restructuring. A
major principle of cognitive restructuring comes from the observation that our thoughts influence our emotions. For example, if we
think depressive thoughts, our depression will worsen. If we think
catastrophic thoughts, our anxiety will grow. If we think angry
thoughts, we will experience intensifying anger. Therefore, traditionally, cognitive behavioral therapists help their clients identify
and challenge destructive patterns of thought using logic to talk
back to their thoughts and debunk them. This can help reduce
afflictive emotions, but it can also lead to an internal debate in
which one thought chases after another in a cycle of internal dialogue. Mindfulness practice breaks this cycle by focusing the attention on the breath and present moment, thus centering awareness
nonconceptually.

Think of it as the difference between being stuck in traffic and
watching a traffic jam on TV. When we are stuck in our thoughts,
they begin to define how we feel, who we think we are, and how
we view our world. It's like being in a traffic jam where we feel
that we have no choice but to be defined and hemmed in by the
traffic around us. When we focus our attention on the breath and
present moment, we can stay aware of our thoughts, but it's more
like watching them come and go than being defined by them. This
is more like watching a traffic jam on TV with the option of changing the channel. We can learn from what passes through our minds
without being defined by it.

I heard of a humorous example of how we can become fused
and stuck on a thought when I was a counselor at a therapeutic
summer camp. A colleague told me of an incident that occurred
when they were returning from a trip to a community pool. He said

that a counselor of a toddlers' group, holding a nail in her hand, approached one of the camp directors. Holding out the nail, she said in an accusatory tone, "Look at this! Do you know what this is?" The director replied calmly, "A nail." The counselor said, "Yes, I found it under that tree where a child could have stepped on it!" The director said calmly, "Thanks for picking it up. By the way, you might want to tend to your group right now." As the counselor regained her composure and turned to see what had become of her group of children, she was able to see that the toddlers were running in different directions across the wide-open playground behind her. In that moment, it sounded as though she had become stuck with her anxiety, stress, and anger all focused on the danger posed by the nail. The camp director, whose mind was not fused to the worry about the nail, was able to keep track of the bigger picture. We can do a similar thing for ourselves with mindfulness practice.

In Acceptance and Commitment Therapy (ACT), this process is called de-fusion.[12] De-fusion describes the ability to become unstuck by gaining a perspective on our thoughts and emotions like a spectator watching marchers go by in a parade. Normally, when less observant, we are in a state of fusion with our thoughts and emotions, rising and falling with them. Mindfulness practice allows us to de-fuse from thoughts and develop a calm central awareness from which we can assess and respond. Dialectical Behavioral Therapy (DBT) refers to this calm central awareness as "wise mind."[13] We can slowly develop an observing awareness that is less and less thrown off kilter by the rise and fall of thoughts. Both ACT and DBT utilize mindfulness practice and they are both empirically validated approaches to mental health treatment.

If we can learn how to center ourselves in mindful awareness, disturbing thoughts have less influence over us and therefore there is less of a tendency to succumb to anxiety, depression, and anger. An analogy can be made of open awareness being like the sky and thoughts/emotions being akin to clouds coming through. During a major storm, it might seem like we will never see the sky again, but once the storm passes through, we can realize that the clear blue sky was there all along, even during the storm. By focusing on the sky instead of the storm, we can gain some calm in knowing that the storm is temporary. Similarly, by developing our center within mindful awareness, we can better weather the fleeting storms of our thoughts and emotions.

Western mindfulness instructor, Michele McDonald, coined the acronym RAIN, which stands for Recognize, Accept, Investigate, Non-identification. This is a helpful principle to keep in mind during sessions of mindfulness practice. Within mindful awareness, it is possible to recognize whatever comes up with acceptance rather than resistance, allowing it to enter our awareness with gentleness while we investigate it. This investigation is not like an inquisition, but rather an inquisitiveness about the things that arise during meditation. Rather than identify with the thoughts and emotions that arise, which would only strengthen their intensity and allow them to define us, the reminder of non-identification helps us see them as passing reactions to causes and circumstances. They do not define our identity, but instead, remind us of how we have reacted to the situations we have encountered. The stance of non-identification helps us let go of thoughts and feelings as they pass through our awareness without letting them consume or define us.

Unchecked, rumination and identification with our thoughts can be addicting, increase likelihood and duration of depression, and increase our stress levels. Rumination has been linked to increased risk of alcohol abuse, eating disorders, and cardiovascular disease. It intensifies negative thinking and impairs problem-solving abilities.[14] Therefore, mindfulness practice is being used by a growing number of psychotherapists as a preferred intervention for their clients who suffer from anxiety, stress, anger, and depression. One simplified version of the practice is to notice the breathing and label distracting thoughts as "thinking" before returning one's attention to the breath. Such an approach disrupts rumination and brings the awareness back to the present moment.

Viktor Frankl (1905–1997), the great neurologist and psychiatrist who survived the Holocaust and went on to write on the importance of finding meaning in life, noted in his account of his experiences in a concentration camp how our freedom comes through our ability to choose how to respond to what happens to us.[15] We can choose how to view it, understand it, integrate it, and then how we act. Mindfulness practice gives us a strategy to increase the gap between stimulus and response, so that instead of just reacting, we can respond from a place of consideration and awareness. This is a particularly important skill in the field of anger management. In one study, training adolescents in mindfulness practice significantly reduced levels of angry ruminating and acts of aggression.[16] Similar findings are emerging from other studies as well.[17]

Personally, as a social worker, I frequently resort to a few moments of mindful breathing when flooded by anger or anxiety when working with difficult client situations. It has a calming effect and pulls me out of automatic thoughts and behavior, allowing a crucial gap in which I can assess and respond mindfully rather than from a place of fear or anger. Once anger has hijacked our sympathetic nervous systems, it takes a while for our parasympathetic nervous system to fully put on the brakes and return us to equilibrium. Mindfulness practice is a useful strategy that can help us in the process of regaining higher-level functioning when anger has taken hold.

Stress management is critical in reducing anger and depression. Jon Kabat-Zinn and others have demonstrated beyond a reasonable doubt that mindfulness practice is an essential tool for reducing anxiety and stress.[18] The key is to develop a regular practice in which you set aside a few minutes at intervals during the day for practice. Sessions do not have to be lengthy. In fact, many meditation traditions suggest that we start with short periods of practice to keep it focused and in order to feel comfortable returning to our practice again and again.

It can be useful to think of stress and anger as being like a bucket filling with drips of water from a leak in the roof. At first, the bucket contains the leaking water without a problem. But when the bucket becomes full, even a single drop causes the water to overflow; it can no longer be contained. Similarly, throughout our day, things occur that cause us stress and frustration, particularly when something gets in the way of our goals and wishes. If we start out well rested and at ease, we can often handle such obstacles without a problem. But when we start to feel tired and overwhelmed, like an overfull bucket, even a small obstacle can send us over the top. Stress, anger, anxiety, and depression slowly take up room until we can feel the tension in our muscles and throughout our bodies. Therefore, it is essential that each day we take stock of our stress and frustration levels and reduce them, emptying our stress and anger bucket routinely.

Two useful exercises that can help in this process are called progressive relaxation and the body scan. Progressive relaxation is often done while lying down. You simply tense individual muscle groups for a moment and then let them relax. You can start with your forehead, tensing those muscles and then relaxing them. Afterward, do the same with the muscles around your eyes; often people store tension there. Then move to your jaws where stress sometimes leads to teeth grinding. The neck and shoulders come next. If the back of the neck is too tight, it can restrict blood flow, causing headaches. So tense and relax your neck, shoulders, arms, hands, and fingers. Then do the same with muscles in your chest and back, especially the lower back and abdomen, where so many of us hold our stress. Eventually include your legs, feet, and toes until your whole body becomes relaxed, like Jell-o.

You can combine progressive relaxation with self-suggestions, repeating phrases silently to yourself like "my muscles are feeling warm, loose, and relaxed." You can also follow it with the body scan, which is like progressive relaxation except that you merely mentally scan your body from head to toe and then from your feet back up to your head. As you do so, imagine that you are breathing in calming relaxation into each part of your body as you scan it. Then imagine that any tension or discomfort in that part of your body goes out with your exhale. As you do these exercises, you might feel drowsy or want to take a nap. This is usually a sign that you have successfully turned down the volume of your fight-or-flight system. These are useful exercises to try before sleep, but also useful for helping you regain equilibrium after a stressful day or week.

The Tibetans often employ visualization with their meditation practices. One of my teachers taught me two visualization exercises that can be used to reduce tension, stress, and anxiety.[19] They can be done while sitting with your back upright. In the first, you imagine a vase atop your head made from light. Inside it is liquid light, the consistency of melted butter. You imagine that the liquid light has the ability to heal and restore well-being. Visualize that the vase

Tips for Helping Professionals

Regaining Equilibrium

All of us need regular sleep, good nutrition, and exercise to keep good physical and mental health. However, stressors throughout the day can throw us into disequilibrium. When we encounter stressful situations, they impact our sympathetic nervous systems, provoking fight/flight responses in our HPA Axis (hypothalamus, pituitary, adrenal axis). This is good for a quick burst of energy in a crisis, but if it is triggered repeatedly, we start to burn out and are flooded with too much adrenalin and cortisol. Over time, this chronic stress depletes us and can compromise our digestive, immune, cardiovascular, and nervous systems. Therefore, it is essential for helping professionals who work with stressful client situations to develop a healthy routine for regaining equilibrium each day.

Mindfulness and other stress management strategies are essential in this process. Section 3 of the appendix, "A COMPASS Handbook for Helping Professionals," details ways to develop a positive daily routine for regaining and maintaining equilibrium.

overflows and that the liquid light begins to descend through your body, healing and dispelling your stress and worries, filling you up from head to toe with the healing elixir. A second visualization is to imagine a small round ball of healing light in your heart area and imagine that it emanates soothing light throughout your entire body, dissolving your stress, worries, and tension and filling you with well-being.

Sometimes people report feeling an immediate reduction in their feelings of stress with such practices, but others may have to practice consistently over time before noticing some relief. As mentioned before, the secret is repeated practice over time. Progressive relaxation, body scan, and the visualization practices mentioned above are a bit different from traditional mindfulness of breathing exercises in that they target stress, anxiety, worries, and frustration for reduction rather than just taking a more observing and accepting stance toward whatever arises during practice. Therefore, they fit into the mental gardening approach of working with your thoughts and feelings. It is possible to combine these approaches. One way to do so is called the four foundations of mindfulness.

In the four foundations of mindfulness, one sits in an upright position and begins by noticing the breath without altering it. If the breath is short, just notice that it's a short breath. If it's a long breath, just notice that it's a long breath. Awareness of the body is the first foundation of mindfulness. Notice the whole body as you breathe, imagining that you are calming the body and bringing it to peace. You can join this with the body scan, gradually scanning each part of your body as you breathe, breathing in calm and breathing out tension. Wherever your feel discomfort in your body, you can pause, breathing in well-being to that part of the body, releasing the discomfort, and imagining that it goes out with the exhale.

As your body starts to relax, you can shift your attention to notice the second foundation of mindfulness, which involves bringing your awareness to your feelings. As you maintain awareness of your breathing, notice the activities within your mind, letting them start to settle and bringing them to peace. You can imagine breathing in joy and breathing out your sorrow. Focus your attention on the present moment as you breathe, letting go of the past without anticipating the future. Just let yourself be fully present with your breath.

As your feelings start to settle, you can shift your attention to your awareness, concentrating your mind as you breathe. States of mind are the third foundation of mindfulness. As you breathe, notice the clear nature of your awareness. Like the sky, untainted by the clouds that move through it, your awareness remains clear and lucid, no matter what thoughts and feelings pass through it. Concentrate your mind on the breath and present moment while liberating it from chasing after the various impulses and thoughts that arise.

As your awareness focuses on the here and now, you can notice the fourth foundation of mindfulness: mental objects, the things that appear to awareness. While maintaining mindfulness of your breath, you can notice the thoughts and contents of your internal dialogue that arise while you are meditating. Label them "thinking" and let them go, returning to your breath. Notice how they arise, stay awhile, and then fade away. Without becoming enmeshed in them, remember the RAIN approach of recognizing, allowing, investigating, and not identifying with whatever arises. You can also notice that the thoughts floating through the mind are mental in nature, thus allowing them to dissolve back into awareness like waves collapsing back into the ocean. Maintain your focus on the breath and let go of everything else for now.

The practice of the four foundations of mindfulness need not take a long time. In fact, short, sweet sessions are much more effective, safe, and rewarding than long, arduous ones. Four or five minutes is fine at first. Some research is emerging showing that meditation can provoke distressing experiences as well as peaceful, uplifting ones.[20] There is even some research emerging on instances of serious mental health issues arising in people who have preexisting conditions, especially when they try to force themselves into long, arduous meditation retreats.[21] So, in order to keep the practice safe and helpful, start with short sessions and consult with someone experienced in meditation practice. Also, if you suffer from a mental health issue, consult with a mental health professional with some training in mindfulness practice about how best to tailor your meditation practice to meet your mental health needs.

One useful way to think about the effort involved to develop an effective mindfulness practice regimen is the analogy of brushing your teeth. If you brush your teeth only just before visits to the dentist, it is doubtful that it will be of much use in preventing cavities. But if you brush for a couple of minutes a few times each day, you will gain the protective benefits that come from regularly brushing your teeth. The same is true of caring for your mind with a regular routine of mindfulness practice. A few minutes a few times each day is all that's needed in order to start experiencing its benefits. It also helps you look forward to your practice if you stop sessions when they are going well rather than trying to extend them.

If you want to make your sessions more conducive to enhancing concentration, a simple addition to the strategies mentioned above is to count your breaths. This is done by silently counting "one" with your first outbreath, then "two" with your second, and so on until you reach "ten." Then begin again with a count of "one" as you breathe out and continue to count each breath until reaching ten again. You can repeat this a few times and then stop. Doing this regimen regularly helps to clear and focus your mind. It can be helpful before starting a project, or in the case of COMPASS exercises, before you consider a topic of contemplation.

In summary, research on mindfulness practice is revealing benefits to both physical and mental health when it is practiced briefly, properly, and regularly. Exercises like progressive relaxation and body scan can be practiced in conjunction with mindfulness of breathing to reduce stress and tension. Mindfulness practice is used within the context of COMPASS to calm and focus the mind before beginning contemplations conducive to the development of compassionate insight. A simple exercise of the four foundations on mindfulness can be practiced as follows:

1. Mindfulness of body:

    - Begin by noticing your breath as it leaves your nostrils and returns, noticing if it's a short breath or a long breath.
    - Be aware of your whole body as you breathe.
    - Breathe in calm and breathe out stress.
    - Let your body start to calm and settle.

2. Mindfulness of feelings:

    - As you notice your breath, also notice your feelings.
    - Be aware of the present moment as you breathe.
    - Breathe in joy and breathe out sorrow.
    - Let your feelings start to settle.

3. Mindfulness of awareness:

    - As you notice your breath, also notice your awareness.
    - Focus your awareness on the present moment.
    - Notice the clear nature of your awareness, freeing it from worries.
    - Concentrate your awareness on your breath.

4. Mindfulness of mental objects:

    - As you focus on your breath, notice thoughts come and go.
    - Notice the changing and impermanent nature of thoughts.
    - Let disturbing thoughts and feelings fade away.
    - Let go of thoughts and return your focus to your breath.

Acceptance and Self-Compassion

When Tom Pruzinsky and I first presented COMPASS at a conference in Amherst, Massachusetts, a participant who had trained with Jon Kabat-Zinn, the founder of Mindfulness-Based Stress Reduction, reminded us that he teaches a nonjudgmental form of mindfulness. In this approach, one simply allows whatever is experienced to arise within awareness of the breath and present moment without judgment. I like to call this approach to mindfulness an acceptance approach, in which we attempt to just be fully present in an accepting way with whatever is occurring in and around us.

The participant's comment was delivered with the implication that it was a mistake to try to alter mental states using selective-focus skills, and thus to deviate from a stance of mindful awareness without judgment. This led me to contemplate the difference people may experience between attempts to practice mindful self-acceptance and attempts to develop positive mental qualities and reduce afflictive mental states. In Buddhist traditions, practitioners alternate between calm introspection, analysis, cultivating positive mental states, and reducing/eliminating negative mental states. These passive and more active styles of working with one's mind are not seen as contradictory, but as different approaches that can be used by a single person for different purposes.

A calm acceptance of whatever comes up while meditating helps us know and accept parts of ourselves that otherwise might influence us secretly, outside of our awareness. This can protect us from being led astray by emotional reasoning and other cognitive distortions. It enriches us with self-awareness. Awareness can have a transformative effect. As Jon Kabat-Zinn points out, "The real meditation practice is your life and how you conduct it from moment to moment. Mindfulness helps you to take wise and discerning action, which is vitally important if you want to participate in your own healing process."[22]

The wise and discerning action I am suggesting by including selective-focus skills in our repertoire is to sometimes employ methods for cultivating healthy mental states and reducing afflictive ones. These skills constitute a form of self-care and self-compassion. They do not preclude spending periods of time in mindful, nonjudgmental awareness. Rather, they are ways to supplement mindfulness practice with more active methods at times. The process of unearthing the contents of our minds is often challenging. Sometimes people report distressing thoughts and feelings surfacing during meditation sessions. And at times, this can lead to feeling stuck in uncomfortable states of mind. More militant proponents of mindfulness might suggest that it is best to suffer through such discomfort in full awareness without trying to change your mental state, but such a stance can become harsh and even counterproductive at times. It is important to know when a more active approach might be in order.

For example, if a person finds that their mindfulness session is filled with self-denigrating thoughts and feelings of depression and they feel they are unable to get unstuck, it might help to shift the experience by spending some moments reflecting on someone in their life who has been comforting and supportive. By focusing on a positive person, he or she might be able to break through the negative rumination for a moment. This could help the person become unstuck from a round of self-defeating thoughts, allowing more healthy thoughts and feelings to enter the session. This constitutes an act of self-compassion. A combined approach of self-acceptance and self-compassion can form the basis for a safe, supportive approach to working with our minds.

I sometimes think of this as like an artist painting a landscape. After setting up the canvas and paints, the artist takes some time to observe the scene they will paint, noticing the light and shadows, taking in the colors and shapes. Once the artist has a sense of the scenery and of the composition that they want to paint, they begin the more active process of mixing colors and applying them to the canvas. Similarly, as we embark on our inner journey of enhancing compassionate insight, it is important to begin our efforts with calm, nonjudgmental, self-awareness before we begin to purposefully employ selective-focus skills.

By starting the COMPASS exercises with a few moments of mindfulness, we can take stock of how we are doing physically, emotionally, and cognitively. A brief practice of the four foundations of mindfulness helps us to be aware of our physical and mental functioning just as it is in the present moment. An accepting stance allows us just to be as we are and get to know ourselves. A self-compassionate stance allows us to be friendly with ourselves and to regain equilibrium. Equilibrium is an excellent basis for practicing selective-focus exercises.

Self-compassion is a term coined by Kristen Neff, a professor of educational psychology who pioneered research showing the benefits of developing self-compassion over self-esteem. Self-compassion is the ability to be kind, accepting, and caring to yourself instead of harsh and critical. It is based on our common humanity and a recognition that we all have imperfections, fail at times, make mistakes, and encounter life's challenges. In contrast, self-esteem attempts to enhance an ideal sense of self.

Neff observed that self-esteem can contribute to narcissism and that its conditional nature makes it unstable. For instance, if you take pride in your physical or intellectual abilities, that feeling can get dashed upon encountering someone whose abilities surpass your own. In contrast, self-compassion is less contingent on how you compare yourself to others. It has been associated with reduced anxiety and depression as well as a reduction in physical symptoms. People who cultivate self-compassion show enhanced self-care, initiative, happiness, optimism, altruism, empathy, wisdom, ability to cope with adversity, resilience in caretaking, and acceptance of body image. They also have better relationship skills like perspective-taking and forgiveness.[23]

Mindfulness in general has been linked to improved relationships. Advanced contemplators of compassion show evidence of activation of regions of the brain associated with empathic accuracy, which is the ability to accurately comprehend the intentions and feelings of others.[24] Couples also show enhanced communication when practicing mindfulness.[25] Parents practicing mindfulness, who have children with developmental disabilities[26] and autism[27] report more satisfaction with their parenting, a decrease in stress, and more compliance and less aggression from their children. Teens who act out and are introduced to mindfulness practice with their parents have shown better self-control and increased happiness.[28]

Since COMPASS targets the reduction of self-preoccupation and the enhancement of compassionate insight, mindful self-compassion and positive relationship skills are a good place to start. There is a danger of self-punishing thoughts arising in response to one's attempts to reduce self-preoccupation. Anger at or denigration of self can occur when one becomes aware of the extent of one's narcissism, and therefore, starting with self-compassion provides a reminder to be gentle and forgiving toward oneself. Instead of being consumed by guilt at our self-centered ways, it is important to start where we are and grow at our own pace. Positive relationship skills can help in this process by keeping us in connection with others, so we can experience the give-and-take of relationships and practice the development of compassion in real-life situations.

Tips for Helping Professionals

Finding Acceptance and Self-Compassion When Something Goes Wrong

One of the hardest challenges faced by helping professionals is when a case ends tragically. Along with concerns about the client and his or her family, professionals must grapple with worries about their careers, liability, and livelihood. Often this can lead to self-condemnation, especially if we have high expectations about ourselves and client outcomes. One way to reduce this latter part of the problem is to change from a self-esteem model of trying to be the best in our profession to a model based on self-compassion and compassion for others in which we strive to do the best job we can for our clients. With self-compassion, you can forgive yourself for your weaknesses and mistakes while still learning from them. Instead of striving to be the best, you can strive to do your best. Self-compassion is essential for recovering from a client loss and learning how to move forward.

This point is discussed in the context of the tragedy of client suicide in section 4 of the appendix, "A COMPASS Handbook for Helping Professionals."

During pilots of COMPASS, some participants mentioned feeling unworthy or frustrated when they found themselves holding back from certain exercises. Others mentioned having trouble in forgiving harms from their pasts. All such feelings and thoughts can be expected as a normal part of working with our minds. Rather than trying to deny them or push them away, a self-compassionate approach is to simply allow them to be as they are and to notice them within a gentle heart of acceptance. If we are ever going to be able to forgive others, it would be good to start with ourselves.

Some people tell me that when they are alone with their thoughts, they talk with themselves silently to reclaim and heal wounds from their past. For instance, someone who was neglected as a child tried talking to themselves in a nurturing and supportive way and found that this helped soothe a chronic sense of unworthiness. Others who tend to be self-critical report benefit from purposefully changing their internal dialogue to a self-accepting tone.

A useful exercise to help in this process was suggested by a fellow therapist.[29] In this exercise, you imagine someone you care about, with whom you are experiencing some tension, sitting in front of you. As you focus on that relationship, notice the coming and going of your breath and imagine a soft light traveling to them sending them your compassion and then returning to you with the in-breath, extending that compassion back to yourself. I have often used this exercise when troubled about relationships and have noticed it has a soothing effect. It combines caring for someone else with caring for yourself. Clients who have tried it also report a positive experience.

If you would like, you can do the same visualization while breathing, but change the emphasis depending on what you need. For instance, if you have difficulty accepting yourself, you can imagine sending and receiving acceptance with your breath. Or, if you tend toward chronic anxiety, you can imagine sending and taking calm reassurance as you breathe. The point is to bring yourself into calm equilibrium and internal well-being. It is from a stance of clarity and contentment that we become most able to consider the well-being of others.

Mental Gardening and Self-Care

Does happiness come from conditions outside of us, or does it arise in dependence on internal factors? Often, when I pose this question to my clients, they respond "both." Such discussions can become quite philosophical, but the import of the question is to highlight a well-known truth in the field of mental health. Much of our experience of the world around us is filtered through our concepts, memories, and reactions. It is possible to cultivate a stable and satisfying internal life, and it is also possible to fuel internal factors that lead us into despair, chaos, and bitterness. External factors contribute to our well-being or lack thereof, but how we interpret and react to them also plays a major role.

For example, in the spring of my senior year of high school I had a hiking experience in the mountains with my classmates as a part of a wilderness program. It was a special farewell gift from our high school because we were all ready to graduate. My friends were grumbling about the heat, the pace, how tired they felt, and blaming it on the program leaders. I was torn between joining them in the complaints and in trying not to fall. As I balanced from one rock leaping to the next, it suddenly occurred to me, "I can make this hike more miserable by thinking about how many ways I dislike it, or I can focus on ways to make it fun." So I challenged myself, keeping up my speed while focusing on the angles of the rocks and how to line up each step's trajectory. By the end of the hike, I noticed feeling energized and upbeat while I could not help but notice that my classmates seemed drained and grouchy. The difference in our experiences seemed solely based on how we internally processed our hikes.

One way to think about this is to consider our minds as like a garden. If left untended, a garden will become filled with weeds. If nurtured, beautiful flowers, herbs, and plants can be cultivated. Under harsh weather conditions, a garden can be destroyed. But if protected by a greenhouse, it can bloom even in winter. The same is true of our minds. If we pay attention in a caring way to our thoughts, feelings, and reactions, we can cultivate internal factors that bring us closer to well-being. However, if we ignore our internal world and neglect ourselves, we can unwittingly create an internal prison. I have met individuals who have spent their lifetimes gardening their minds with the result of an unshakable fortitude even in the face of adversity.

To put it simply, mental gardening is a process of cultivating positive states of mind and reducing mental factors that bind or cause internal torment. Usually, when I discuss this idea with clients, they come to the same conclusions about which states of mind are conducive to well-being versus which will increase distress. Their responses are also often in accord with research about how different mental states affect body and mind. For instance, almost everyone I have talked with about this has indicated that increased anger will reduce their well-being, which corresponds to some of the research mentioned above about the mental and physical health effects of anger.

Therefore, anger might be considered a "weed" in one's mental garden. However, it is important to discuss this in the context of self-acceptance, because if we denigrate or push away emotions we deem negative, it can create internal conflict, have a detrimental impact on how we feel about ourselves, constrict affect, and submerge aspects of our emotional lives so that they live outside of our awareness. Therefore, mental gardening requires a balanced approach in which acceptance and self-compassion are conjoined with self-care.

Self-care in this context is the process of deciding which impulses and behaviors to cultivate and which to reduce. It is tied to self-compassion because the goal is to care for ourselves. It can be done with acceptance and friendliness. Take, for example, a loving mother who is trying to help her child reduce eating too many sweets. She holds her child in mind with complete affection while seeing that too much sugar could hurt her child's health. Such a stance combines acceptance and care. This combination allows her to be skillful and gentle in how she encourages her child to eat in a healthier way. Ultimately, this is much more effective than a harsh, critical approach.

Like a loving mother, we too can hold our impulsive inner child with acceptance conjoined with care. Our impulses might lead us into behaviors we know are unhealthy, but a compassionate self-awareness can gently coax us back into a healthy direction. This is self-care. Again, it does not have to be harsh or self-critical. Researchers of Motivational Interviewing (MI), an empirically validated strategy for helping clients motivate themselves to fight addictions and follow healthy directions, have found that confrontative approaches to addressing problematic behaviors tend to intensify them. In contrast, a supportive, accepting approach elicits cooperation and progress.[30]

We can apply some of the principles of MI to our internal dialogue. As you listen to your stream of daily thoughts, try to be aware of "change" talk versus "sustain" talk. Change talk considers growth and trying new approaches to issues while sustain talk stays fixed on old, repetitive modes of thought and logic. You can strengthen your motivation by cultivating self-talk focused on change and growth, allowing it to take a central place in your mind. In this context, it means tapping into your natural inclination to become a more compassionate and insightful person.

Edward L. Deck and Richard Ryan founded Self-Determination Theory (SDT), which holds that our natural psychological needs for competence, autonomy, and relatedness cause inherent tendencies for growth within us.[31] Some of us are more extrinsically motivated, which means that we look outside of ourselves for rewards. Some of us are more intrinsically motivated, which means we inwardly feel motivated to develop our capacities. Many of us feel a combination of these two forces motivating change. In the pages that follow, I will mention research on the benefits for developing our capacities for compassionate insight, which I hope will offer both extrinsic and intrinsic rewards for cultivating a friendly approach to internal change through mental gardening and self-care.

In addition to mental gardening, self-care entails setting boundaries. Often, anger and self-centeredness are adaptive strategies for coping with a brutal external world. As you consider developing your compassion and reducing narcissism, it is important to have a strategy for how to deal with harsh external realities of everyday living. Contrary to narcissistic reasoning, "me first" logic is not a helpful survival strategy. In the next section, we will explore this in-depth. But for now, suffice it to say that there are ways to survive and thrive while making your internal world more compassionate.

The central skill of boundary setting is to know when it is necessary. Personally, I can tell when I need to set a boundary by noticing when my wish to be helpful turns into a feeling of fear, anxiety, or resentment. For example, sometimes I have found myself at meetings in which the majority of "to-do" items end up on my plate. As I notice my goodwill shift into dread, I know that it is my responsibility to set a boundary and divest some of my tasks.

Tips for Helping Professionals

Cultivating Self-Care and Healthy Professional Boundaries

A crucial component of self-care for helping professionals is learning how to set boundaries. When you have been saddled with too big a load at work, setting boundaries means to parcel out a reasonable portion of your workload to colleagues and to let your boss know that you are unable to take on additional tasks. When you are depleted and craving unhealthy props like junk food, alcohol, or drugs to feel better, setting boundaries means to hold yourself back from such destructive modes of feeling better and to pursue healthy options like sleep, time with friends, and mind-body exercises. When a friend or colleague is taking advantage of you, setting boundaries means to step back a bit, reassess, and propose a fairer way to proceed.

Section 5 of the appendix, "A COMPASS Handbook for Helping Professionals," discusses the importance of self-care in more detail.

Sometimes, people refrain from setting boundaries because they become angry toward whoever they perceive as taking advantage of them and cannot see a way to express themselves without anger taking over their response. In such cases, it makes sense to spend some time processing the situation, regaining internal equilibrium, and thinking through ways to express your stance. It can help to discuss the dilemma with a trusted friend or confidant. Once you arrive at a stance that seems reasonable, it is usually most effective to state your stance with an I-statement like, "I find that a disproportionate number of these tasks have been assigned to me. I will only be able to accommodate this much. Who is willing to take on the remaining items?"

I find that setting boundaries becomes more challenging when relationships are more personal. This seems due to the connection such relationships have with our core feelings. Resentment in close relationships often follows attempts to support and accommodate someone at a sacrifice to oneself. This can deepen a sense of betrayal if the person does not reciprocate or misuses the support. Therefore, it is important to monitor reciprocity in close relationships and to try to maintain a balance. Sometimes, a "quid pro quo" or "something for something" approach can help. It is a matter of saying, "I will do this for you, if you do that for me."

In cases in which you are feeling continually demeaned and/ or attacked, I think it is important to think through your options and decide whether you want the relationship to continue. If the relationship is clearly detrimental to you, it might be time to look for an exit strategy. Sometimes, people who are hurtful only consider changing their behavior after losing significant relationships. So walking away from abusive relationships can be helpful to both parties.

Keeping healthy boundaries can be compared to a greenhouse in winter: it protects us from harsh external elements that might prevent positive mental states from arising. Mindfulness and stress reduction can be compared to adjusting your inner climate to an optimal level. Mental gardening is the planting and nurturing of positive states of mind through selective focus contemplations and weeding out negative mental states through analysis. These latter skills will be explained in detail in the chapters that follow. To begin this process, a daily practice of mindfulness can help you to gradually experience the dawning of a calm, lucid awareness. Within that peaceful mindfulness, you can begin to add contemplations that open your heart and mind to a wider field of compassionate insight.

Notes

[1] Lazar, S. W., Kerr, C. E., Wasserman, R. H., Gray, J. R., Greve, D. N., Treadway, M. T., McGarvey, M., Quinn, B. T., Dusek, J. A., Benson, H., Rauch, S. L., Moore, C. I., & Fischl, B. (2005). Meditation experience is associated with increased cortical thickness. *NeuroReport, 16*(17), 1893-1897. Cited in *Brief summary of mindfulness research* by G. Flaxman & L. Flook. http://marc.ucla .edu/workfiles/pdfs/MARC-mindfulness-research-summary.pdf

[2] Davidson, R., Kabat-Zinn, J., Schumacher, J., Rosenkranz, M., Muller, D., Santorelli, S. F., Urbanowski, F., Harrington, A., Bonus, K., & Sheridan, J. F. (2003). Alterations in brain and immune function produced by mindfulness meditation. *Psychosomatic Medicine, 65*(4), 564-570.

[3] Tang, Y. Y., Ma, Y., Wang, J., Fan, Y., Feng, S., Lu, Q., Yu, Q., Sui, D., Rothbart, M. K., Fan, M., & Posner, M. I. (2007). Short-term meditation training improves attention and self-regulation. *Proceedings of the National Academy of Sciences, 104*(43), 17152-17156. https://doi.org/10.1073/pnas.0707678104

[4] Kawachi, I., Sparrow, D., Spiro, A. 3rd, Vokonas, P., & Weiss, S. T. (1996). A prospective study of anger and coronary heart disease. The normative aging study. *Circulation, 94*(9), 2090–2095. https://doi.org/10.1161/01 .cir.94.9.2090; and Barefoot, J. C., Dahlstrom, W. G., & Williams, R. B. (1983). Hostility, CHD incidence, and total mortality: A 25-year follow-up study of 255 physicians. *Psychosomatic Medicine, 45,* 59–64.

[5] See Lewis, S. (2013). *Nurturing, healing love.* Hay House. See also https:// chooselovemovement.org/

[6] Glaser, R., Rice, J., Speicher, C., Stout, J. C., & Kiecolt-Glaser, J. K. (1986). Stress depresses interferon production by leukocytes concomitant with a decrease in natural killer cell activity. *Behavioral Neuroscience, 100*(5), 675-678. https://doi.org/10.1037//0735-7044.100.5.675

[7] Spiegel, D. (1996). Psychological distress and disease course for women with breast cancer: One answer, many questions. *Journal of the National Cancer Institute, 88*(10), 629-631. https://doi.org/10.1093/jnci/88.10.629

[8] Anderson, E., & Hope, D. (2008). A review of the tripartite model for understanding the link between anxiety and depression in youth. *Clinical Psychology Review, 28*(2), 275-287. https://doi.org/10.1016/j.cpr.2007.05.004

[9] Musselman, D. L., Tomer, A., Manatunga, A. K., Knight, B. T., Porter, M. R., Kasey, S., Marzec, U., Harker, L. A., & Nemeroff, C. B. (1996). Exaggerated platelet reactivity in major depression. *American Journal of Psychiatry, 153*(10), 1313–1317. https://doi.org/10.1176/ajp.153.10.1313

[10] Semple, R., Reid, E., & Miller, L. (2005). Treating anxiety with mindfulness: An open trial of mindfulness training for anxious children. *Journal of Cognitive Psychotherapy, 19*(4), 379-339. Cited in *Brief summary of mindfulness research* by G. Flaxman and L. Flook. http://marc.ucla.edu/workfiles/pdfs/ MARC-mindfulness-research-summary.pdf

[11] Teasdale, J. D., Segal, Z. V., Williams, J. M., Ridgeway, V. A., Soulsby, J. M., & Lau, M. A. (2000). Prevention of relapse/recurrence in major depression by mindfulness-based cognitive therapy. *Journal of Consulting and Clinical Psychology, 68*(4), 615–623. https://doi.org/10.1037//0022-006x.68.4.615

[12] Hayes, S. C., Strosahl, K. D., & Wilson, K. G. (2012). *Acceptance and commitment therapy: The process and practice of mindful change* (2nd ed.), 240. Guilford Press.

[13] Linehan, M. M., Schmidt, H., 3rd, Dimeff, L. A., Craft, J. C., Kanter, J., & Comtois, K. A. (1999). Dialectical behavior therapy for patients with borderline personality disorder and drug-dependence. *American Journal on Addictions, 8*(4), 279–292. https://doi.org/10.1080/105504999305686

[14] Nolen-Hoeksema, S., Wisco, B. E., & Lyubomirsky, S. (2008). Rethinking rumination. *Perspectives on Psychological Science, 3*(5), 400-424. https://doi .org/10.1111/j.1745-6924.2008.00088.x

15 Frankl, V. (1959). *Man's search for meaning*. Beacon Press.
16 Sharma, M. K., Sharma, M. P., & Marimuthu, P. (2016). Mindfulness-based program for management of aggression among youth: A follow-up study. *Indian Journal of Psychological Medicine, 38*(3), 213–216. https://doi.org/10.4103/0253-7176.183087
17 For example, see Pellegrino, B. (2012). *Evaluating the mindfulness-based and cognitive-behavior therapy for anger management program.* Philadelphia College of Osteopathic Medicine. http://digitalcommons.pcom.edu/cgi/viewcontent.cgi?article=1232&context=psychology_dissertations
18 Kabat-Zinn, J., Massion, A., Kristeller, J., Peterson, L., Fletcher, K., Pbert, L., Lenderking, W. R., & Santorelli, S. (1992). Effectiveness of a meditation-based stress reduction program in the treatment of anxiety disorders. *American Journal of Psychiatry, 149*(7), 936–943. https://doi.org/10.1176/ajp.149.7.936
19 These two visualizations were imparted by Gyumed Khensur Losang Jampa Rinpoche to a small group of clinicians in Centreville, Virginia, 2008.
20 For example, see Orenstein, D. (2017, May 24). Study documents range of challenging meditation experiences. *News from Brown.* https://news.brown.edu/articles/2017/05/experiences, and also Lindahl, J. R., Fisher, N. E., Cooper, D. J., Rosen, R. K., & Britton, W. B. (2017). The varieties of contemplative experience: A mixed-methods study of meditation-related challenges in Western Buddhists. *PloS One, 12*(5), e0176239. https://doi.org/10.1371/journal.pone.0176239
21 Shonin, E., & Van Gordon, W. (2013). Can mindfulness meditation induce psychotic episodes? http://www.edoshoninarchive.com/PDFs/20131226_Shonin_VanGordon.pdf
22 Boyce, B. (2011, February 28). The healing power of mindfulness: Mindfulness: What it does, how to do it, why it works—A discussion with a distinguished panel of experts. *Mindful: Healthy Mind, Healthy Life.* https://www.mindful.org/the-healing-power-of-mindfulness/
23 Neff, K. D., & Germer, C. K. (2013). A pilot study and randomized controlled trial of the mindful self-compassion program. *Journal of Clinical Psychology, 69*, 28-44. https://doi.org/10.1002/jclp.21923
24 Lutz, A., Brefczynski-Lewis, J., Johnstone, T., & Davidson, R. J. (2008). Regulation of the neural circuitry of emotion by compassion meditation: Effects of meditative expertise. *PLoS One, 3*(3), 1-10. Cited in *Brief summary of mindfulness research* by G. Flaxman & L. Flook. http://marc.ucla.edu/workfiles/pdfs/MARC-mindfulness-research-summary.pdf
25 Barnes, S., Brown, K. W., Krusemark, E., Campbell, W. K., & Rogge, R. D. (2007). The role of mindfulness in romantic relationship satisfaction and response to relationship stress. *Journal of Marital and Family Therapy, 33*(4), 482-500.
26 Singh, N. N., Lancioni, G. E., Winton, A. S., Singh, J., Curtis, W. J., Wahler, R. G., & McAleavey, K. M. (2007). Mindful parenting decreases aggression and increases social behavior in children with developmental disabilities. *Behavior Modification, 31*(6), 749-771. https://doi.org/10.1177/0145445507300924

[27] Singh, N. N., Lancioni, E., Winton, A. S. W., Fisher, B. C., Wahler, R. G., Mcaleavey, K., Singh, J., & Sabaawi, M. (2006). Mindful parenting decreases aggression, noncompliance, and self-injury in children with autism. *Journal of Emotional and Behavioral Disorders, 14*(3), 169-177. https://doi.org/10.1177/10634266060140030401

[28] Bögels, S., Hoogstad, B., van Dun, L., de Schutter, S., & Restifo, K. (2008). Mindfulness training for adolescents with externalizing disorders and their parents. *Behavioral and Cognitive Psychotherapy, 36*, 193-209.

[29] This strategy was explained to me by Peggy DiVincenzo, LPC. She in turn said that she had adapted it from Christopher Germer, PhD. See Germer, C., & Neff, K. (2014). *Mindful self-compassion handouts.* UCSD Center for Mindfulness, Mindfulness-Based Professional Training Institute, 17.

[30] Rubak, S., Sandbaek, A., Lauritzen, T., & Christensen, B. (2005). Motivational interviewing: A systematic review and meta-analysis. *British Journal of General Practice, 55*(513), 305-312.

[31] Ryan, R. M., & Deci, E. L. (2000). Self-determination theory and the facilitation of intrinsic motivation, social development, and well-being. *American Psychologist, 55*, 68-78. https://dx.doi.org/10.1037/0003-066X.55.1.68

CHAPTER 3

Core Practices for Developing Compassion

What's in It for Me?

You might be wondering about what benefits come from developing compassion, which is defined here as the wish to alleviate the sufferings of others. Many people who are interested in mindfulness practice seem satisfied with just working on their own peace of mind. Thomas Joiner, a professor of psychology at Florida State University and author of *Mindlessness: The Corruption of Mindfulness in a Culture of Narcissism*, argues that the current Western trends of promoting mindfulness practice have become corrupted by themes of self-indulgence. He also says that its benefits are often overstated in the research community.[1] While I think that the research showing the mental health benefits of mindfulness is stronger than Joiner suggests,[2] I concur with his objection to the use of mindfulness practice in the service of narcissism.

Narcissism, which I refer to as our inner troll, has grown in our culture over the past few decades, especially among young people.[3] Most of us have at least some degree of narcissism, a deep tendency to focus on ourselves as primary. Western culture traditionally viewed it as a character flaw in need of remediation. However, in the last century, the author Ayn Rand (1905–1982) argued for "rational ethical egoism," saying that it is irrational and immoral to act against one's own self-interests, and she founded a philosophical school based on this stance called objectivism.[4] Rand encouraged her followers to follow selfishness and reject altruism,[5] suggesting that they follow their reasoning and face reality as it appears to their senses, disavowing any higher authority. Rand defines selfishness as "concern with one's own interests," saying that an action is rational only if it maximizes its own self-interests.[6]

The crucial question to consider here is whether selfishness promotes well-being individually and/or collectively. The Dalai Lama often jokes that a "wise selfish" person realizes that, for their own well-being, they should pursue compassionate care for others.[7] At first take, this might sound counterintuitive, but let us take a deeper look. If Rand is correct that our best interests are served by following self-interests, then it follows that people who are more inclined toward self-focus should find more contentment and well-being as they pursue their desires. But is this indeed the case?

Heightened self-focus is tied to prolonged dysphoric reactions to difficulties, a negative bias in interpreting them, and impaired problem-solving abilities.[8] There is a reciprocal relationship between self-focus and negative affect.[9] Self-focus is also tied to heightened social anxiety.[10] Furthermore, those who are focused on validating inflated views of self express heightened anger and aggression when feeling threatened or criticized.[11] Narcissists have difficulty maintaining long-term relationships and have a diminished sense of satisfaction and well-being.[12] In brief, self-focus is linked to increased internal discomfort and character traits that lead to social isolation.

Self-focus is also not good for your health. Narcissism has been tied to poor stress regulation.[13] Self-focus and maladaptive self-involvement have been linked to both anger and coronary artery disease.[14] So the more narcissism and self-involvement a person has, the more likelihood that she or he will become socially isolated, anxious, angry, and at risk for heart disease. Considering this research, it seems that Rand was mistaken. Increased selfishness seems to be a recipe for increased misery. So from a purely scientific point of view, one could respond to Rand, "Using your own philosophy, it is irrational and immoral to give up on developing your compassion and just follow your selfish impulses because doing so is destructive to your own self-interests."

Ask yourself about how you view people who act in a selfish way around you. Does their behavior produce affection or hostility? Logically, it follows that since everyone has self-interests, people whose level of self-focus leads them to behave in a manner to promote their own well-being to the detriment of others around them will be seen as a threat to the majority. This can be seen in the realm of politics when there is an outcry against politicians who make insensitive remarks or advocate for policies that benefit the few over the many. You can also observe adverse reactions to self-ishness within small communities and families.

Emerging neurological research indicates that we are hardwired for empathy. There is an overlap in how our nervous system reacts when we feel threatened and how it reacts when someone close to us is threatened.[15] Acts of kindness release endorphins, causing a sense of well-being, and help heart health through activating vagus nerve functioning.[16]

So let us consider the Dalai Lama's joke about the "wise selfish" person, who for their own well-being works to reduce selfishness, increase compassion, and begin to live a life of helping others. Researchers at Emory University have been studying a strategy for enhancing compassion called Cognitive Behavioral Compassion Training (CBCT), which like COMPASS was formulated from adapting Tibetan mind-training strategies. Participants introduced to these strategies were tested before and after a two-week training period and were found to exhibit enhanced empathic accuracy,[17] reduced stress-induced immune and behavioral responses,[18] and, based on frequency of use, increased hopefulness and decreased generalized anxiety.[19]

Another technique developed from Tibetan mind-training strategies, called Compassion Cultivation Training (CCT), was studied by researchers at Stanford University. They found that the practice of CCT resulted in significant improvements in compassion for others, receiving compassion from others, and self-compassion,[20] and in increased mindfulness and happiness as well as decreased worry and emotional suppression.[21]

The Benefits of Compassion in the Workplace

Supportive and compassionate work environments benefit workers as well as clients. They inspire inter-staff cooperation, productivity, and more competent service delivery. In contrast, when work environments are made toxic by short-sighted management strategies, infighting, and mistrust, workers and clients suffer. Negative working conditions contribute to professional burnout and substandard client care. Team building and supportive supervision strategies can turn around unproductive work environments.

In section 6 of the appendix, "A COMPASS Handbook for Helping Professionals," there is a discussion of ways to transform toxic school environments.

To put it simply, compassion helps strengthen our immune systems, calms and focuses us, makes us more in touch with others, increases our sense of hope and well-being, and helps open us to our emotions. Studies show that helping others contributes to subjective experiences of happiness.[22] There is a link between compassion and our brains' pleasure centers.[23] It is a positive emotion that makes us more humane and engaged, thus improving social connections, health, and quality of life. There is a burgeoning field of research emerging that is empirically showing a vast array of benefits that come from kindness and compassion.[24]

Sometimes, when my clients report feeling unsure of their direction in life, I suggest an exercise in which they imagine being at the end of their life, looking back at how they used it. It amazes me that almost everyone who tries this exercise reports a wish to have a positive effect on their loved ones, friends, community, and the world. Compassion and love are deep motivators of human change, commitment, and resilience.

Tibetans believe that there are several benefits that come from cultivating universal compassion with the intent to be of benefit. Universal compassion helps us find a higher purpose in life, bringing out the best in ourselves and those we meet. We become more courageous and therefore included in the ranks of heroes. Others tend to honor those who take on the task of compassionate activity. It promotes the development of internal virtues and new skills, helps us overcome negative habits and acquaintances, and leads us toward accomplishing our higher goals. We become a steady resource benefiting both ourselves and others. Therefore, cultivating compassion is indeed a way to be "wise selfish" as well as to be simultaneously altruistic.

Empathic children develop a sense of moral identity, imagination, and courage. Thinking inclusively, they have an easier time understanding how others feel and keep their cool when stressed. They grow up thinking of ways to make a difference in the lives of others.[25] Materialistic goals such as wishes for fame and wealth predict future mental health problems, whereas goals of helping others predict healthier long-term adjustment.[26] If future generations are going to be able to adapt and survive, compassion and insight may prove to be their most important assets.

Personally, I often think that our survival as a species depends on developing our compassion collectively. As networks of interdependency become more global, what happens in one place affects well-being in other places. A troubled leader in one nation causes ripple effects throughout the world. The world's interwoven ecosystem is already challenged and in disequilibrium. If we can summon the best in humanity, I believe we can find solutions to the complex survival issues that we all face in our communities, societies, and in the world.

Selecting a Focus

The path toward universal compassion is a gradual one because its scope is vast. As the Chinese philosopher Laozi said, "The journey of a thousand miles begins with a single step."[27] When embarking on a journey, you must take stock of where you are and where you're planning to go. So reflect for a moment on where you are now in your inner development. Is your mind calm and serene or troubled and tense? Do you feel empathic concern for others or are most of your concerns about yourself? Wherever you find yourself, it's a fine place to start.

Then, consider your long-term goals for yourself. What kind of person do you aspire to be? How wide would you like your compassion to extend? How deep would you like your insight to go? Whatever goals appeal to you, the first step in developing your inner capacities is to learn how to select your focus. Each moment presents us with a myriad of possible focal points. Most of us let our minds focus as they will on whatever most compels us in the moment. Since random impulses tend to steal away mental focus, we are often at their disposal. But it is also possible for us to be purposeful about where we focus our attention. While it is true that most of us can't control what thoughts and impulses enter our minds, most of us can control which thoughts and impulses we choose to follow.

I remember when I was in elementary school, my class went on a field trip to hear a symphony. The symphony hall was ornate and had a high, vaulted ceiling. As the conductor of the symphony was talking to us, my eyes wandered up to the ceiling and I found myself wondering how the ceiling was supported. What would happen if the supports weren't strong enough and the whole thing collapsed on us? As my mind pictured the destruction and mayhem that such a collapse would cause, my anxiety rocketed, and I completely tuned out from the beautiful music that had started to flow from the orchestra in front of me.

In that moment, there was a choice. I could continue to focus on the mental images of the ceiling collapsing, or I could focus on the symphonic music. The more I focused on the former, the more anxious I became. The more I focused on the music, the more relaxed and at ease I became. This power of selecting a focus was commented upon by the great psychologist William James, who said, "My experience is what I agree to attend to. Only those items which I notice shape my mind."[28]

So, in each moment, we are shaping our minds depending on which elements in our situations grab our focus. Our nervous systems have a survival bias, and therefore we have a predisposition to focus our attentions on possible dangers in our environments. These perceptions of danger can also include internally perceived dangers like fears of social rejection, job loss, stigma, becoming overwhelmed, and so forth. The process of having our attention hijacked by perceived threats can keep us in a state of guardedness and unease. We can temporarily suspend the trend of ruminating on dangers by various exercises like those described above on mindful awareness of breathing and by contemplating particular aspects of our experiences that can help us develop positive states of mind. We can also shape our internal dialogue by shifting our focus to specific topics of contemplation like those that will be described below.

Sarah Williams (1837–1868) commented on this process in her poem, "The Old Astronomer," in which an aging astronomer counsels his apprentice by saying, "I have loved the stars too fondly to be fearful of the night."[29] When we focus on the stars, the night becomes less scary. Our focal point and what we choose to ruminate upon determine the valence of our emotions. When we fully recognize this, we can begin to cultivate our internal gardens as we see fit. By shifting our focus away from thought patterns that cause us to develop afflictive emotions and focusing instead on modes of thought conducive to well-being, we can develop and strengthen positive mental states.

Tips for Helping Professionals

Focusing on Strengths and Solutions When Working with Addictions

Often, helping professionals interact with people going through tragic circumstances. When listening to client stories and experiences, it is important for professionals to selectively tune into the strengths their clients are exhibiting rather than exclusively paying attention to their weaknesses. Focusing only on client problems renders helpers and clients helpless, while focusing on client strengths is empowering and facilitates positive change. This is especially true when working with clients suffering from addictions, many of whom have traumatic histories. Connecting with a strengths approach helps to uplift such clients and provides support in helping them take progressive steps toward recovery.

In section 7 of the appendix, "A COMPASS Handbook for Helping Professionals," this subject is explored in more depth.

When I first describe this process to clients, I will ask them about whether they think that strengthening various emotions will be conducive to their mental health. Unanimously, everyone I have asked indicates that increased anger, jealousy, and anxiety will have adverse effects on their mental health. Most concur that contentment, kindness, and internal peace will enhance their well-being. As mentioned above, research supports their subjective experiences of these mental states.

Traditionally, Tibetan meditators employ three different types of meditation in their pursuit of positive mental states: scanning meditation, analytical meditation, and placement meditation. COMPASS utilizes each of these three approaches in order to allow the exercises to have a deeper impact on one's ability to generate and deepen compassionate insight.

Scanning meditation consists of a brief review of topics leading up to the main subject of contemplation. This is done to remind oneself of previous steps contemplated and to familiarize oneself with a particular line of reasoning. In the COMPASS approach, scanning meditation helps in generating emotional building blocks to compassion. There is a significance to the order in which the compassion exercises are sequenced with one contemplation providing access to a mental state that makes the next exercise more effective. By briefly scanning previous points, you can reboot your mental status, thus preparing yourself for the next point that you intend to contemplate.

Analytical meditation is a process of using logic and analysis to contemplate a particular subject. In the compassion exercises that follow, seven subjects are presented for your consideration. Each section will begin with an exploration of the subject, relevant research, and the logic supporting the exercise. A thorough consideration of each topic can lead to an emotional shift and/or to a resultant cognitive stance, which is then focused upon. By focusing your mind on the resultant mental state, you are practicing placement meditation. Placement meditation helps to create familiarity and habituation with the resultant positive mental state.

I hope you will savor each exercise and practice each one frequently. Repetition is the key. Researchers have found that frequent practice of compassion training exercises produces significant neurological change.[30] Such changes support the process of compassion becoming a normal part of one's personality. If you are already a compassionate person, these exercises will strengthen your compassion. If you tend toward narcissism, you can start to build habits that can produce compassionate traits, eventually changing your core. Such work takes time and perseverance, but it is definitely possible, especially when you have a road map of how to proceed.

Notes

[1] Joiner, T. (2017, August). Mindfulness would be good for you. If you weren't so selfish. *Washington Post.* https://www.washingtonpost.com/outlook/mindfulness-would-be-good-for-you-if-it-werent-all-just-hype/2017/08/24/b97d0220-76e2-11e7-9eac-d56bd5568db8_story.html

[2] For a sampling of some of the extensive research on the benefits of mindfulness, see mindfulnet.org: https://www.aheadforwork.com/mindfulnet

[3] Dingfelder, S. F. (2011, February). Reflecting on narcissism: Are young people more self-obsessed than ever before? *Monitor on Psychology, 42*(2), 64. https://www.apa.org/monitor/2011/02/narcissism

[4] Peikoff, L. (1993). *Objectivism: The philosophy of Ayn Rand*, xiv. Meridian.

[5] See Rand, A., & Branden, N. (1964). *The virtue of selfishness: A new concept of egoism.* New American Library.

[6] Ibid.

[7] An example of an entire quote on this subject by the Dalai Lama is: "It is important that when pursing our own self-interest we should be 'wise selfish' and not 'foolish selfish.' Being foolish selfish means pursuing our own interests in a narrow, shortsighted way. Being wise selfish means taking a broader view and recognizing that our own long-term individual interest lies in the welfare of everyone. Being wise selfish means being compassionate." Dalai Lama XIV. (2012). http://philosiblog.com/2012/01/29/it-is-important-that-when-pursing-our-own-self-interest-we-should-be-wise-selfish-and-not-foolish-selfish/

[8] Lyubomirsky, S., & Nolem-Hoeksema, S. (1995). Effects on self-focused rumination on negative thinking and interpersonal problem solving. *Journal of Personality and Social Psychology, 69*(1), 176-190. https://doi.org/10.1037//0022-3514.69.1.176

[9] Moberly, N. J., & Watkins, E. (2008). Ruminative self-focus and negative affect. *Journal of Abnormal Psychology, 117*(2), 314-323. https://doi.org/10.1037/0021-843X.117.2.314

[10] Vassilopoulos, S. P. (2008). Social anxiety and ruminative self-focus. *Journal of Anxiety Disorders, 22*(5), 860-867. https://doi.org/10.1016/j.janxdis.2007.08.012

[11] Bushman, B. J., & Baumeister, R. F. (1998). Threatened egotism, narcissism, self-esteem, and direct and displaced aggression: Does self-love or self-hate

lead to violence? *Journal of Personality and Social Psychology, 75*(1), 219–229. https://doi.org/10.1037/0022-3514.75.1.219

12 Konrath, S., & Bonadonna, J. P. (2014). Physiological and health-related correlates of the narcissistic personality. In A. Besser (Ed.), *Psychology of Narcissism*. Nova Science Publishers.

13 Ibid.

14 Scherwitz, L., Graham, L. E., Grandits, G., Buehler, J., & Billings, J. (1986). Self-involvement and coronary heart disease incidence in the multiple risk factor intervention trial. *Psychosomatic Medicine, 48*(3-4), 187-199.

15 Beckes, L., Conan, J. A., & Hasselmo, K. (2013). Familiarity promotes the blurring of self and other in the neural representation of threat. *Social Cognitive and Affective Neuroscience, 8*(6), 670-677. https://doi.org/10.1093/scan/nss046

16 Borreli, L. (2014). Human brain hardwired for acts of kindness, as vagus nerve activated during empathy. *Medical Daily.* https://www.medicaldaily.com/human-brain-hardwired-acts-kindness-vagus-nerve-activated-during-empathy-313020

17 Mascaro, J. S., Rilling, J. K., Negi, L., & Raison, C. L. (2013). Compassion meditation enhances empathic accuracy and related neural activity. *Social Cognitive and Affective Neuroscience, 8*(1), 48-55. https://doi.org/10.1093/scan/nss095

18 Pace, T. W., Negi, L. T., Sivilli, T. I., Issa, M. J., Cole, S. P., Adame, D. D., & Raison, C. L. (2010). Innate immune, neuroendocrine and behavioral responses to psychosocial stress do not predict subsequent compassion meditation practice time. *Psychoneuroendocrinology, 35*(2), 310-315. https://doi.org/10.1016/j.psyneuen.2009.06.008

19 Reddy, S. D., Negi, L., Dodson-Lavelle, B., Ozawa-de Silva, B., Pace, T. W., Cole, S. P., Raison, L. W., & Craighead, L. W. (2012). Cognitive-based compassion training: A promising prevention strategy for at-risk adolescents. *Journal of Child and Family Studies, 22*(2), 219-230. https://link.springer.com/article/10.1007/s10826-012-9571-7

20 Jazaieri, H., Jinpa, G., McGonigal, K., Rosenberg, E. L., Finkelstein, J., Simon-Thomas, E., & Goldin, P. R. (2013). Enhancing compassion: A randomized controlled trial of a compassion cultivation training program. *Journal of Happiness Studies, 14*(4), 1113-1126. https://doi.org/10.1007/s10902-012-9373-z

21 Jazaieri, H., McGonigal, K., Jinpa, T., Doty, J. R., Gross, J. J., & Goldin, P. R. (2014). A randomized controlled trial of compassion cultivation training: Effects on mindfulness, affect, and emotion regulation. *Motivation and Emotion, 38*(1), 23-35. https://doi.org/10.1007/s11031-013-9368-z

22 Aknin, L. B., Hamlin, J. K., & Dunn, E. W. (2012). Giving leads to happiness in young children. *PloS One, 7*(6), e39211. https://doi.org/10.1371/journal.pone.0039211

23 Esch, T., & Stefano, G. B. (2011). The neurobiological link between compassion and love. *Medical Science Monitor, 17*(3), RA65-RA75. https://doi.org/10.12659/MSM.881441

24 See https://www.kindnessevolution.org/kindness-curricula

25 Barbara, M. (2016). *UnSelfie: Why empathetic kids succeed in our all-about-me world.* Touchstone.

26 Kasser, T., Cohn, S., Kanner, A. D., & Ryan, R. M. (2007). Some costs of American corporate capitalism: A psychological exploration of value and goal conflicts. *Psychological Inquiry, 18*(1), 1-22. https://doi.org/10.1080/10478400701386579

27 Laozi, & Mitchell, S. (1988). *Tao te ching: A new English version*, chapter 64. Harper & Row.

28 James, W. (1890). *The principles of psychology* (Vol. 1). Henry Holt and Company.

29 Williams, S. (1868). The old astronomer. In *Twilight hours* (p. 69). Strahan & Co.

30 Calderon, A., Ahern, T. H., & Pruzinsky, T. (2018). Can we change our mind about caring for others? The neuroscience of systematic compassion training. In L. Stevens & C. C. Woodruff (Eds.), *The neuroscience of empathy, compassion and self-compassion* (pp. 213-234). Academic Press.

CHAPTER 4

Equanimity

We are living in a time where competition for resources and cultural differences often become a source of conflict. Many of us seem to have the capacity to care for our immediate family and friends but hold distrust for whoever seems different or outside of our select group. Racism, sexism, religious intolerance, and other forms of "us and them" polarization are signs of an internal problem in which people are driven by emotional reasoning. The emotions say, "People like me are safe; people who are different from me are threatening." This tendency to see sameness as safe and differences as a threat is a major factor in racial bias.[1] Stress can exacerbate this trend by causing the brain to tune out from the prefrontal cortex and higher reasoning faculties, and base judgments on fear-induced habitual emotional impulse.[2]

Compassion can become biased and limited when under the sway of our reactions to those whom we perceive as safe versus those whom we perceive as not to be trusted. Based on the ensuing emotions, we tend to objectify people as friends, enemies, and strangers. These three categories are related to core impulses to pursue that which brings pleasure, avoid potential sources of discomfort, and ignore the rest. We tend to develop care and consideration for those considered friends in order to keep them near, fear and hatred for those considered enemies in order keep them away, and indifference or distrust for those considered strangers because they do not hold emotional significance to us. Therefore, some people can display selfless compassion for one group of people and animosity or indifference toward another.

Consider a terrorist who wants vengeance for atrocities perpetrated on his loved ones. He might have deep compassion for people he perceives to be like him, but a ruthless disregard for the lives of people he perceives as dissimilar or hostile to his kind. At a milder but still dysfunctional level, consider how teachers and parents sometimes display favoritism for one child over another and the distress this causes the children who are disfavored. Bias leads to partisanship, social exclusion, and marginalizing of various individuals and groups of people.

Researchers are beginning to study the relationship between population trends and war.[3] It has been postulated that overpopulation leads to increased stress and conflict.[4] This is particularly dangerous in areas where population increase is brisk and resources are scarce.[5] The relationship between crowding, stress, and hostility has been shown to be moderated by how people interact with each other.[6] Therefore, as the world population increases, unless we as a species learn how to live harmoniously with each other, we can expect an increase in conflict, bias, and warfare.

Currently, we can see that there is a debate between globalists and nationalists around the world. Nationalists advocate strengthening boundaries between countries and cultures to preserve cultural identity, whereas globalists advocate for diversity, tolerance, and acceptance. Hate crimes in the United States have risen as this debate has intensified, mostly enacted by those advocating for a White nationalist perspective.[7] The crimes against humanity brought on by the ensuing violence are devastating, horrifying, and polarizing. As people discuss how this trend can be reduced, it is hoped that the psychological causes will be considered. After all, if bias, hate, and fear are reduced, the fuel for the problem will diminish. Equanimity practice can bring balance into our hearts, giving us a method for removing such bias and the turmoil it causes.

I remember my first experience of witnessing bias as a child. A White peer on the playground at my elementary school used a racial slur against another peer, who was African American. No one had to tell me that it was wrong; I just knew it. As humans, it is very difficult not to have bias. It seems built into our hardwiring. We all have unique histories and memories that inform us about who is safe and who is not to be trusted. However, if our goal is to develop a universal form of compassion, we need to find some way to step out of this process and to invoke our higher capacities for tolerance and equanimity.

Thomas Pruzinsky, who helped develop the COMPASS approach, defined equanimity as "an unbiased mind focused on our shared humanity and everyone's equal wish to find happiness and avoid suffering."[8] If we look deeply into human conflict, often we'll find that this perspective is missing. The more that individuals focus on self-interest and forget to consider the interests of people around them, the more "us versus them" thinking takes over. The thought that "in order for my interests to prevail, my enemies must be disempowered and destroyed" has plagued humanity since its inception and grows even more treacherous as our numbers increase and resources become harder to procure.

Equanimity reverses this pernicious process by helping us consider the similarities between ourselves and others. I often begin to instruct social work students in the equanimity exercise by asking them if everyone in the classroom is the same or different. My classes tend to be diverse, with students from different nationalities, races, religions, and genders. So usually their first response is "we're all different." I then ask them, "Who here wants to suffer, be disrespected, or excluded?" No one ever raises their hand. Then I ask, "Who here wants to be happy, respected, and included?" Everyone raises their hand.

This is because, at a fundamental level, we are all equal in wanting well-being, acceptance, love, and consideration. Likewise, we are all equal in wanting to avoid suffering, condemnation, disrespect, and exclusion. In our cores, we strive continually to find happiness and to avoid suffering. This trait makes us a part of humanity. Humans, in all our diversity, share this goal. In fact, all forms of life strive for equilibrium and well-being. This is our common condition. When we focus on this shared trait, it is easier to find tolerance and acceptance of diversity and difference. It becomes clear that we ourselves are like all sentient life in all its manifestations. Such a perspective helps widen our view and open our hearts.

Some grow fearful of such a perspective and think, "If I open myself to all of humanity in this way, I'll be taken advantage of,

I'll be played for a sucker. Others are out to get you and will walk right over you if you let them." If such misgivings arise, it is helpful to consider the sections above on self-care, setting boundaries, and the benefits of compassion over selfishness. Opening one's heart to others does not mean neglecting your wisdom, discernment, and self-care. As mentioned above, compassion builds resilience emotionally and helps overcome afflictive mental states that cause us emotional and physical harm. It is the inner enemies of hate and fear that do us the most damage.

It can be argued that someone with equanimity gains a more realistic perspective of others, which is helpful when considering how to respond to complex situations. If one acts impulsively from a place of fear and distrust, it is likely that one's actions will escalate difficult circumstances into conflicts that are harmful to oneself and others, whereas people operating from a perspective of equanimity and tolerance are more likely to find win-win solutions to complex problems that increase mutual well-being. When we encounter people with malevolent intent, by understanding what motivates them, we can be more skillful in how we work to keep ourselves and others safe from potential harm.

In Buddhist traditions, equanimity is defined in different ways. One definition is that it is a neither pleasant nor unpleasant feeling.[9] At a deeper, more refined level, it is "the state of mind which cannot be swayed by biases and preferences."[10] Another definition of equanimity is a "mind which prevents dimness and agitation from impairing those consciousnesses and mental functions which are associated with it."[11] An even more detailed definition of equanimity can be found in Asanga's *Compendium of Higher Knowledge*, which states that it is "a mind effortlessly abiding in a state of non-attachment, non-hatred, and non-ignorance that is incompatible with any afflicted states of mind. It is an even-mindedness, a natural abiding in ease, and a state of spontaneity, which has the function of not allowing any occasion for the mental afflictions to arise."[12]

Researchers have begun to suggest ways to measure equanimity, endorsing it as an aid to mental health and well-being.[13] It supports emotional regulation,[14] helps us disengage from emotional pushes and pulls,[15] and enhances compassion development.[16] Mindfulness practice has been shown to increase equanimity by reducing reactivity to unpleasant experience.[17] This reduction in reactivity to unpleasant experience aids well-being by increasing our tolerance of uncertainty and ambiguity, thus enhancing emotional stability and mental ease in the midst of an unpredictable world. When applied to relationships, equanimity can help us to tolerate, accept, and even relish a wide range of people from diverse backgrounds. It is this latter aspect of equanimity that is being emphasized here in the service of developing compassion.

In the Buddhist traditions of mental training, equanimity is sometimes practiced in the beginning, before training in compassion techniques, as a way to level the playing field before starting the main practices. At other times, it is practiced midway into the training as a way to expand the focus of the compassion that one has already developed. There are various contemplations that are used to cultivate equanimity including strategies for considering how you are the same as others, ways to help you see others as precious, and ways to see others as having kinship to you.[18]

For example, in one technique, you imagine a person toward whom you feel indifferent in front of you and consider how he or she is the same as you in not wanting to suffer and in only wanting happiness. The exercise begins with a stranger because usually it is easier to maintain a neutral feeling for someone who is not well known. Once you develop a sense of equanimity with them, free from attachment or aversion, you then change the object of your contemplation to someone with whom you have a close relationship. Consider how your attachment for your friend makes them appear in an appealing way to you. This may not seem problematic at first, but consider how attachment distorts perception, exaggerating the positive qualities of what it focuses upon.

Buddhists consider attachment problematic because they believe that we all have past and future lives, postulating that attachment is what binds us in a cycle of suffering.[19] For those without this belief, we can still see problems that attachment can bring. For example, in addictions, an initial desire for something eventually leads to a psychological dependence as we repeatedly enjoy it. The positive initial feelings associated with it can turn into more tormenting ones when we are separated from the desired person or object. We can also see how attachment for some people over others increases our bias, thus making it more difficult to maintain equanimity. By recalling some of the defects of attachment, as we picture a close person or friend in front of us, we can try to let go of clinging, and instead, try to enhance our appreciation of how our friend is equal to us in wanting to be happy and in not wanting to suffer.

Once a sense of equanimity is established with the friend and with the stranger, you then bring an enemy to mind. The enemy exercise is saved for last because it can sometimes be the most difficult depending on how deep one's anger, fear, and hurt toward the person go. Consider how the feeling of aversion you feel toward the enemy keeps you in bias and disequilibrium, blocking your capacity for compassion development. By recalling that this person is also equal to you in wanting to be happy and not wanting to suffer, and by recollecting some of the problems that anger and fear bring to your mind, it is possible to eventually start to feel equanimity toward them.[20]

Working to reduce anger and fear toward enemies can be very challenging. It is a subject that will continue to be discussed from different vantage points in the exercises that will be described in later sections. One point that is often brought up in the context of developing equanimity is that we can see from our own experience how friends can become enemies, enemies can become friends, and strangers can become people of significance in our lives. There is no fixed category in which an enemy always must be an enemy, a stranger always has to remain a stranger, or a friend always has to be a friend. Our reactions to people and ensuing judgments about them give rise to these categories. Whether we adhere to and reinforce them is really our choice. While it makes sense to protect ourselves from people who would do us harm, we don't need to perpetuate our internal mental states of hate and fear, which by their very nature do us harm.

So equanimity can be seen as mental factor that helps us maintain openness to everyone, and it can also be seen as a mental factor that helps in reducing bias. This latter aspect of equanimity can allow us to identify when we've been emotionally hijacked by attraction or aversion. Identifying impulses of attraction and aversion is the first step to going beyond them. Rather than objectifying people into the rigid categories of friends, enemies, and strangers, wouldn't it be refreshing to simply see people as they really are, in all their complexity? Stepping outside of bias allows us to gain a more realistic view of people and helps us to accept the humanity of ourselves and others.

In a presentation of COMPASS on January 3, 2015, after trying an equanimity exercise, participants reported many positive feelings they took away from it including calmness, happiness, joy, hopefulness, connectedness, letting go of anger, peacefulness, gratitude, reflectiveness, relaxation, and equanimity. When asked about negative feelings they experienced during the exercise, they reported feelings of sadness, mental wandering, anxiety, hatred, fear, dislike, and concerns about losing the positive feelings induced by the exercise. It is not unusual to have a mixed experience when trying these techniques.

Tips for Helping Professionals

Equanimity and Honoring Diversity

Helping professionals embrace diversity and strive to reduce or eliminate bias in order to be available to all clients. The equanimity exercise is designed to help with this by increasing evenness of mind, our ability to stay open to a wide variety of people from various backgrounds and cultures, and our scope of compassion, making it more inclusive. Research has shown that equanimity supports emotional regulation, helps us disengage from emotional pushes and pulls, and provides a support for developing compassion. When working with clients who are different from us, one way to use equanimity to help us stay out of bias and judgment is to remember that, just like us, our clients only want well-being and happiness. Just like us, our clients do not want to feel judged, mistreated, or disregarded. We all are equal that way.

Section 8 of the appendix, "A COMPASS Handbook for Helping Professionals," discusses the professional use of equanimity in more detail.

In a pilot study of COMPASS on January 25, 2015, at George Mason University, participants reported positive experiences from this exercise that included feelings of peace, contentment, joy, calm, tranquility, softening, "an opening to people in my life," "glad to be pursuing this path," caring, happiness, gratitude, warmth toward close ones, hope, connectedness, "care for people I didn't even know," and "a sense that . . . I can live outside of internal conflict brought on by external triggers." The negative experiences that were reported included feelings of "regret that I couldn't cultivate positive feelings toward some people in my life," shame over previous lack of awareness and possible harm/disrespect of others, thoughts about people who are intolerant/inflicting harm, brief sadness that people don't care about each other like they could, and thoughts of conflicts with others.

This feedback sheds light on the internal dynamics that are set into motion when trying to introduce new patterns of thought and feeling. Each of us has a current mindset that has grown over time based on our unique experiences and how we have reacted to them. This is our filter through which we perceive the world. Within that mindset, we all have a side of ourselves that is self-protective and based on self-interests. We also have a side that is aware of others and capable of empathy and compassion. When we stretch the bounds of one side of the mind, we can expect a reaction and holding on from the other. Thus, stretching the boundaries of our mindset can feel both liberating and uncomfortable at the same time.

Participant reports of disturbing feelings like sadness, anxiety, hatred, fear, and dislike might be due to increased awareness of feelings that were already present but previously unnoticed, or they might have arisen in reaction to trying the exercise. That aspect of participant feedback is unclear. If such reactions occurred in response to the exercise, it might be due to either contemplating the negative outcomes of bias and intolerance, or to misgivings about becoming vulnerable. It is hoped that the positive feelings of equanimity will eventually calm distress brought on by contemplating the negative effects of bias and intolerance. Misgivings about becoming vulnerable are a deeper issue.

The dilemma of deciding whether to allow ourselves to become vulnerable by opening ourselves to others is something that we all face. If we let ourselves start to care about others, it might increase a sense of vulnerability. By closing ourselves off to others, we might temporarily feel more invulnerable. However, closing ourselves off comes with many liabilities and limitations. When we open ourselves to others, the paradox is that our initial feelings of vulnerability are a portent of a new, emerging emotional fortitude and well-being. Participants hint at this paradox in their reported fears of losing the positive feelings induced by the exercise, and their regret and shame tied to difficulties in extending equanimity to everyone and their previous acts of harm or disrespect. Underlying these concerns is an unstated acknowledgment that a more compassionate stance would feel better and bring with it a better way of relating to people. It is normal that internal struggles will arise as we attempt to extend our mindsets beyond self-preoccupation and expand our focus toward concern for others.

As mentioned above, practice can be compared to flexing a muscle group repeatedly. It might cause some temporary discomfort but leads to enhanced strength over time. It's up to us to choose which mental muscles to strengthen. Repeated practice over time can develop our courage to overcome our hesitations and help us to stabilize and develop the more positive experiences equanimity can produce until they become natural and steady. A simple exercise on equanimity can be practiced as follows:

A. Contemplate some of the benefits of equanimity mentioned above and begin with a brief practice of mindfulness.
B. Once settled, consider the following points:

- We are all equal in wanting to be happy and in wanting to avoid suffering.
- Just as I want to be loved, valued, and respected, everyone wants to be loved, valued, and respected.
- If people treated each other with equal friendship and respect, it would reduce conflict and strife. The world would be a happier and more peaceful place.

- Think "how wonderful it would be if everyone abided in equanimity. In order to make my own mind more peaceful, and in order to help reduce conflicts, I will try to develop an equal sense of friendliness for everyone." Hold this thought for a while.

Notes

[1] Louis, B. (2005). *The difference sameness makes: Racial recognition and the "narcissism of minor differences."* Sage Publications. http://journals.sagepub.com/doi/abs/10.1177/1468796805054960

[2] Yu, R. (2006). Stress potentiates decision biases: A stress induced deliberation-to-intuition (SIDI) model. *Neurobiology of Stress, 3,* 83-95. https://doi.org/10.1016/j.ynstr.2015.12.006

[3] Thayer, B. A. *Considering population and war: A critical and neglected aspect of conflict studies.* https://www.ncbi.nlm.nih.gov/pmc/articles/PMC2781832/

[4] See https://www.voanews.com/a/a-13-2007-07-01-voa12/343044.html

[5] See https://www.populationinstitute.org/resources/why-population-matters/

[6] Epstein, Y. M. (1981). Crowding stress and human behavior. *Journal of Social Issues, 37*(1), 137. https://spssi.onlinelibrary.wiley.com/doi/abs/10.1111/j.1540-4560.1981.tb01060.x

[7] Bjork-James, S. (2017, November 27). What the latest FBI data do and do not tell us about hate crimes in the US. *The Conversation.* http://theconversation.com/what-the-latest-fbi-data-do-and-do-not-tell-us-about-hate-crimes-in-the-us-87561

[8] Pruzinsky, T., & Hurley, W. (2013, September 22). *COMPASS* [PowerPoint slides].

[9] Bodhi, B. (2000). *A comprehensive manual of Abhidhamma: The philosophical psychology of Buddhism,* 34. Buddhist Publication Society Pariyatti Editions.

[10] Ibid.

[11] Tharchin, Geshe Lobsang. (1979). *The logic and debate tradition of India, Tibet, and Mongolia,* 167. Rashi Gempil Ling.

[12] Asanga, *Compendium of knowledge.* 2010. Quoted in Yongdzin Yeshe Gyentsen, *A necklace for the lucid: A clarification of the workings of the mind and mental factors* (Vincent Montenegro, Trans.). Ganden Mountain Press.

[13] Desbordes, G., Gard, T., Hoge, E. A., Hölzel, B. K., Kerr, C., Lazar, S. W., Olendzki, A., & Vago, D. R. (2014). Moving beyond mindfulness: Defining equanimity as an outcome measure in meditation and contemplative research. *Mindfulness, 6,* 356-372. https://doi.org/10.1007/s12671-013-0269-8

[14] Ibid.

[15] Shoham, A., Hadash, Y., & Bernstein, A. (2018). Examining the decoupling model of equanimity in mindfulness training: An intensive experience

sampling study. *Clinical Psychological Science, 6*(5), 704-720. https://doi .org/10.1177/2167702618770446

[16] Weber, J. (2017). Mindfulness is not enough: Why equanimity holds the key to compassion. *Mindfulness & Compassion, 2*(2), 149-158. https://doi .org/10.1016/j.mincom.2017.09.004

[17] Hadash, Y., Segev, N., Tanay, G., Goldstein, P., & Bernstein, A. (2016). The decoupling model of equanimity: Theory, measurement, and test in a mind-fulness intervention. *Mindfulness, 7*(5), 1214-1226. https://doi.org/10.1007/ s12671-016-0564-2

[18] Jampa, Gyumed Khensur Lobsang. (2013). *The easy path, Illuminating the First Panchen Lama's secret instructions* (L. Ladner, Ed.), 155-156. Wisdom Publications.

[19] For a detailed explanation of this viewpoint together with references and supporting research, see pages 13-60 of the translators' introduction to Gungthang Rinpoche the Third, Venerable Konchok Tenpai Dronme. (2012). *The water and wood shastras* (Y. Khedrup and W. Hurley, Trans. from the Tibetan). Karuna Publications.

[20] Ibid., 156-159.

CHAPTER 5

Gratitude

Having begun to try to even the playing field of our minds with equanimity, we are now ready for the next step in our journey toward compassion. In the Tibetan mental training traditions, there are two main approaches for developing compassionate insight. One system is called the sevenfold instruction of cause and effect. The other is called exchanging and equalizing self and others. They were preserved in Tibet as two distinct lineages of instruction until combined into a single system of 11 contemplations by a great Buddhist scholar and practitioner named Je Tsongkapa (1357–1419). This combined approach was used in designing the content and sequence of the COMPASS exercises.[1]

The reason that gratitude comes next in the series of contemplations leading to compassion is that it serves to bolster a positive feeling based on a sense of being cared for by others and therefore helps one to become willing to consider caring for others. People begin the journey to compassion from different places based on different life experiences. Many people may feel that life has offered nothing but hardship and loss, while others might have experienced consistent support and love. These differences in life experiences often lead to quite different emotional stances.

For instance, sometimes a child who experiences constant neglect and criticism during the early years of development grows up with a sense of worthlessness, need, anger, and distrust. It can be difficult in such a position to feel much compassion for the needs of others. Instead, thoughts might arise such as, "What has anyone ever done for me? Why should I care for them? No one cares about me." This kind of self-talk tends to stunt the development of compassion. Therefore, it is important to first make changes in the internal dialogue and emotional stance before considering the well-being of others. Gratitude can be a support in making such a shift.

Fostering a sense of gratitude can be a challenge when life has been harsh. But it is not impossible. According to the famous meditation instructor, Thich Nhat Hanh, "When we have a toothache, we know that not having a toothache is a wonderful thing."[2] Suffering can remind us to be grateful for its absence. So it is possible to feel gratitude by thinking how lucky we are not to be experiencing a toothache in this moment. It is also possible to see positive aspects of negative events. An example of this can be found in a beautiful poem by Mizuta Masahide (1657–1723) that says, "Barn's burnt down, now I can see the moon."[3] Appreciating aspects of our reality that are bearable or even uplifting can sometimes engender a sense of gratitude. This is sometimes referred to as counting one's blessings.

Over recent years, many studies have shown that counting your blessings leads to more happiness and less depression.[4] In one study, depressed and anxious students who wrote weekly letters of gratitude had better mental health outcomes than students who wrote about their negative feelings or who did nothing. They also showed greater activation in their medial prefrontal cortex, a part of the brain that helps us decide on emotional and active responses to specific events, even three months after writing the letters.[5] Indeed, writing about things one is grateful for can improve optimism and self-care.[6] Couples who express gratitude for their partner show more positive regard for each other, and a higher capacity for discussing relationship issues.[7] Expressing gratitude directly has been shown to increase happiness.[8] Workers who are shown gratitude by their bosses may work harder than those who do not receive expressions of gratitude.[9] People who display a capacity for gratitude are more sensitive and empathic, and tend to be less likely to retaliate when treated harshly.[10]

Other important benefits of gratitude include enhancing self-esteem, reducing suicidal ideation, increasing personal appeal and social support, and developing optimism.[11] People who practice gratitude tend to have an easier time being generous, spiritual, less focused on acquiring, and more satisfied.[12] In the workplace, grateful people make better managers, are more patient, have an easier time making decisions, find more meaning in their work, reduce turnover, and experience less stress and depression.[13] Gratitude is also good for our health.[14] The positive states of mind that can be generated by merely counting your blessings make the simple exercises involved well worth the effort.

Some researchers argue that, for compassion training to be effective, it is crucial to start by tapping into positive relational memories.[15] One exercise that I have used successfully with adult clients who felt uncared for as children is to have them think of someone in their life whom they admire, or who has been supportive of them. Having the client imagine that person in front of them, smiling with total acceptance and positive regard, can uplift a sullen heart. To strengthen this contemplation, you can imagine that the supportive person's unconditional love takes the form of healing light, pouring from their heart into your heart, healing past wounds, nurturing your own sense of worth and well-being. It can also be strengthened by considering each kindness the person has shown you.

Research has shown that our emotions, particularly negative emotions, play a vital role in what we remember of our past experiences and how we recall those memories.[16] There is a link between emotional valence and memory retrieval.[17] When we engage in purposeful attempts to regulate our emotions, it is possible to influence both what is remembered and what feelings are engendered. For instance, when we savor positive memories from the past, we can retrieve some of the positive feelings associated with those memories.[18] The Tibetans use this mechanism to build feelings of gratitude by beginning with contemplating the kindness of one's mother. They suggest contemplating each step of what a mother provides, from carrying her child in her womb, restricting her diet due to care for her unborn child, through bearing the discomfort of pregnancy and the agony of childbirth.

Think for a moment about your own mother. Whether you were raised by your biological mother or by a surrogate, someone carried you in her womb. She had to bear the suffering and risk of childbirth in order for you to be alive. Someone had to feed you, comfort you, nurture you, protect you from harm, or you never would have survived your infancy. Who taught you how to walk, talk, and clean yourself? Who made sure that you received an education? We all needed someone to help us through each step of our development in order to make it into adulthood.

Tibetans call this process of recollecting each instance of care we received from our mothers "remembering kindness." By remembering the details of kindness that we have received in the past, a sense of gratitude can begin to develop. The Tibetans expand this process by considering their belief in past lives, asserting that in our infinite previous lives we have been the child of every being in existence many times. This may be hard to imagine for most of us, but the process of considering such a possibility can have a profound effect on how others are perceived. For those of us who believe we only have one life, there are ways to approximate this experience by considering how others benefit us both directly and indirectly in our daily lives.

For instance, as I sit down to write this on my iPad, I can take a moment to marvel at the technology beneath my fingertips and the countless people who helped to bring this to me. From Steve Jobs, who released the first iPad in 2010, to all the people at Apple who contributed to developing the technology, manufacturing, and distribution, hundreds of thousands of people were directly or indirectly involved in producing this product. But each of them depended on countless people to educate them, sustain them, and develop their potentials. Each component of the iPad, from its screen and audio components to its battery, processing, storage, Wi-Fi connectivity, and myriad app capacities have long legacies of research, discovery, innovation, and technological development that were contributed to by millions of people both directly and indirectly. The materials used to build it were collected from many sources, transported by vehicles made by countless people along roadways constructed by untold numbers of workers. Someone built the trucks that transported the materials, etc., etc., etc.

So in a single moment of reflecting on something I am making use of, I can generate a sense of awe and gratitude to many people whom I have never met, but who nonetheless have had and are continuing to have a positive impact on my life. This same type of reflection can be done when I consider the people who directly or indirectly have contributed to the food I've eaten today, the clothes

I'm wearing, the house where I live, the water I drink, the education I've received, the medical care that sustains me, the protection from calamities and violence that I receive from first responders, the financial benefits from employment, and so forth. Each moment of our lives is sustained by our interdependence with a network, a community, a civilization. By appreciating this, it is possible to generate tremendous gratitude.

If you have time, it is also helpful to remember specific events in your life when someone helped you at a vulnerable time. For instance, I can remember incidents when complete strangers went out of their way to help me. Once, when I was 16 and lost in a rough section of town at night, a stranger walked up to me and helped me find my bearings so that I could get home safely. Another time, when I was in college, I got off at the wrong bus stop when traveling to meet up with some friends. As I was standing for hours, alone on a winter night waiting for my friends to find me, I began to wonder what it would be like to freeze to death. Fortunately, a man walking his dog approached me and said he had noticed me there hours earlier. He took me into his home, gave me something to eat, and let me use his phone and phone book to track down my friends.

Another time, when I was traveling alone to Nepal to take a course on Buddhist meditation in Kathmandu, I got waylaid in the airport in Delhi for half a day. Officials in the airport were hassling me about my passport, I think because I was young, and they were hoping that I would give them money to let me be. I was feeling alone and vulnerable in a foreign land. A young Tibetan man who was waiting for the same flight struck up a conversation and helped me navigate the journey into Nepal, through the city of Kathmandu, and find my way to the monastery where I was to take the course. Later, he took me to meet his family, who fed me dinner and introduced me to their culture. He never asked anything from me, but his kindness had a deep impact. It challenged me to think beyond my own needs and to consider ways I can reach out to others when I see them in need. To this day, I feel deep gratitude to such people who have helped me along the way.

Thomas Pruzinsky defines gratitude as "a recognition and appreciation of the help we have received that engenders thankfulness and a wish to repay kindness."[19] The Tibetans break this into two separate actions: remembering kindness and repaying kindness. In modern parlance, we call the second part of this paying it forward. Children who have been kept safe and well-nurtured often have a natural predisposition to help others. Nurturing environments have been shown to contribute to well-being and prosocial behaviors in children.[20]

A fundamental building block of human behavior is a defense mechanism called "turning passive into active." We tend to turn the things that we experience passively into active, outward expressions of what we have internalized from our experiences. Therefore, when treated with aggression and criticism, many people externalize that internalized experience into an outward behavior of being critical and aggressive to others. Conversely, when treated respectfully and with care, we all have the capacity to internalize a positive sense of self and of human behavior. This can help us to become more outwardly friendly and helpful. By reflecting repeatedly on people to whom we feel grateful, we can enhance our internal sense of well-being, which in turn allows us to become more outwardly positive in relationships. In this way, a feedback loop of positive relationships can begin to grow.

Participants in a January 3, 2015, presentation of COMPASS, after trying the gratitude exercise, reported positive experiences that included feelings of intense happiness, joy, warmth, comfort, gratitude, calmness, being humbled, mindfully in the moment, a desire to give more, being part of a group, peace, respectful, overwhelmed with interconnectedness, pleasantness, and being aware of the important and good things in life. Negative experiences that were reported included feelings of being small and ungiving, distraction, unhappiness at thoughts of being a doormat, and anger and irritation reported by one participant with concerns about being a narcissist.

Participants in the January 25, 2015, pilot study of COMPASS at George Mason University reported some of the following experiences after trying the gratitude exercise. Positives included being thankful "for all I have and who I am," gratitude, joy, "a greater feeling and understanding of interdependence," warmth, appreciation, "tearfulness . . . sense of being overwhelmed by the gift of being helped," happiness, "love—being loved," blessed, lucky, valued, cared for, positive memories, forgiveness, calm/relaxation, awe, connectedness, and overcoming of resistance for/critiquing of the practice of gratitude. Negative experiences that were reported included feelings of a "shadow of guilt," some discontent over lack of control in life circumstances/acknowledging privilege, sadness about those who should have provided support/nurturance but did not, some resistance based on previous negative experiences with gratitude practices, and a wish that people were more grateful.

Tips for Helping Professionals

Filling Your Cup with Gratitude When Taking Care of Others

When caregivers become emotionally depleted from constantly caring for others, a moment of gratitude can have an uplifting effect, replenishing a sense of well-being. It can increase happiness, confidence, and other positive emotions, making us more optimistic and less anxious and depressed. Gratitude also improves sleep, reduces blood pressure, and enhances overall health. It is as easy to cultivate as counting your blessings, thinking of positive things in your life, and considering the people in your life who support you both directly and indirectly. Practicing gratitude each day renews our sense of having been cared for by many others, enhancing our willingness to continue to care. It also improves relationships and social support.

In section 9 of the appendix, "A COMPASS Handbook for Helping Professionals," there is a discussion about ways to use gratitude to prevent and recover from emotional depletion.

It is interesting to see the same dynamic of internal conflict that seemed apparent in self-reports after the equanimity exercise. The challenge when practicing this exercise is to step into the new emotional territory of allowing yourself to feel gratitude, and the obstacles to doing so seem to hover around old patterns of self-clinging, fear, and guilt. For instance, one participant noted unhappiness at the thought of becoming a doormat. As mentioned previously, this internal fear of becoming vulnerable is present at all levels when moving toward greater compassion. The Tibetans call the process of stepping beyond self-centered fear "compassionate courage,"[21] seeing it as a heroic enterprise to step beyond the confines of self-interests.

Our experiential reactions at an emotional level might be to retreat into self-preservation, and to withdraw from the experience of opening our hearts and letting ourselves feel vulnerable, even though there is a positive feeling engendered by doing so. Therefore, it takes courage to allow ourselves to be vulnerable and open. The emotional rewards will start to outweigh the fears as we become accustomed to doing this, and our previous training in self-care and setting boundaries can offer us some reassurance that we are still able to protect ourselves from harm while we step outside of self-clinging fear. Then we can more fully experience some of the positive emotions described above by the participants in the pilot studies.

The reservations reported by one participant who feared being a narcissist open an even deeper conundrum. If we have become hardened by experience to the point that we are fully committed to our narcissism as a self-preservation strategy, it might be difficult at first to feel immediate benefits from these exercises. But that does not mean that we should give up. Even a repetitive thought, over time, can eventually produce an associated feeling.[22] This is analogous to planting a new garden in hard soil. We might have to break apart the ground a bit, nurture it with repeated contemplation, and strengthen it with patience. Every time we come back to consider our gratitude for things and people in our lives, we are planting new seeds in the gardens of our minds.

The participants who reported feeling small and ungiving have a second obstacle to work on in addition to self-focus: the self-critical mind. Again, we all start wherever we are, and we all have histories that helped to shape us into what we have become. We are imperfect and yet filled with potential for growth and change. Remembering self-acceptance and self-compassion is a constant asset in self-transformation.

Finally, the participant who mentioned sadness about those who should have provided support but did not touches on an issue that we will delve into in the next section. We all have had people in our lives who have disappointed or hurt us. Their harm can leave long-lasting scars on our hearts and minds. Often, the more we trusted and opened our hearts to the person who hurt us, the deeper the psychological wound. Healing such wounds is a slow process, but a crucial one for compassion development. It is even possible over time to feel gratitude toward those who have harmed us for the lessons we have learned due to their mistreatment of us. However, this is a very challenging perspective that will be discussed later. A simple exercise for practicing gratitude follows:

A. Contemplate the benefit of gratitude and begin with brief practice of mindfulness and equanimity.
B. When settled, bring to mind someone for whom you feel grateful and imagine him or her in front of you. Think of ways that this person has helped you.

- Surrounding you, imagine others in your life who have been helpful to you. For example, consider the following:

  ◦ How many people helped construct the building you are now using?
  ◦ How many people help directly or indirectly to sustain your daily life?

- Now ask yourself the same questions about how many people have contributed to:

  ◦ The food you've eaten?
  ◦ The clothing you've worn?
  ◦ Your health care?
  ◦ Your education?
  ◦ The technology you've used?
  ◦ How many have been a friend, a parent, an ally, a protector?

- If you feel a sense of gratitude, focus on it for a while and sustain it. Then, think of ways you might be able to repay some of the kindness you have been shown.

Notes

1. For a detailed explanation of this combined tradition, see Tharchin, Sermey Khensur Lobsang. (1999). *Achieving Bodhicitta: Instructions of two great lineages combined into a unique system of eleven categories.* Mahayana Sutra and Tantra Press.
2. See http://famousquotefrom.com/thich-nhat-hanh/
3. Ueda, M. (1995). *Basho and his interpreters.* Stanford University Press.
4. Wong J., & Brown J. (2017, June 6). How gratitude changes your brain. *Greater Good Magazine.* https://greatergood.berkeley.edu/article/item/how _gratitude_changes_you_and_your_brain
5. Ibid.
6. Emmons, R. A., & McCullough, M. E. (2003). Counting blessings versus burdens: An experimental investigation of gratitude and subjective well-being in daily life. *Journal of Personality and Social Psychology, 84*(2), 377-89. https:// doi.apa.org/doiLanding?doi=10.1037%2F0022-3514.84.2.377
7. Lambert, N. M., & Fincham, F. D. (2011). Expressing gratitude to a partner leads to more relationship maintenance behavior. *Emotion, 11*(1), 52-60. https://doi.org/10.1037/a0021557
8. Grant, A. M., & Gino, F. (2010). A little thanks goes a long way: Explaining why gratitude expressions motivate prosocial behavior. *Journal of Personality and Social Psychology, 98*(6), 946–955. https://doi.org/10.1037/a0017935
9. Sansone, R. A., & Sansone, L. A. (2010). Gratitude and well being: The benefits of appreciation. *Psychiatry, 7*(11), 18-22.
10. Ziegler, E. H. (2011, October 20). Gratitude as an antidote to aggression. University of Kentucky College of Arts and Sciences: *Psychology.* https://psychology .as.uky.edu/gratitude-antidote-aggression
11. Positive Psychology Program. *The benefits of gratitude: 28 questions answered thanks to gratitude research.* https://positivepsychologyprogram.com/benefits -gratitude-research-questions/#benefits
12. Ibid.
13. Ibid.
14. Ackerman, C. E. (2019). 28 benefits of gratitude & most significant research findings. *PositivePsychology.com.* https://positivepsychology.com/benefits-gratitude -research-questions/
15. Condon, P., & Makransky, J. (2019, November 20). Recovering the relational starting point of compassion training: A foundation for sustainable and inclusive care. *Perspectives on Psychological Science.* https://doi.org/10.31231/osf .io/dmxj7
16. Kensinger, Elizabeth A. (2009). Remembering the details: Effects of emotion. *Emotion Review, 1*(2), 99-113. https://doi.org/10.1177/1754073908100432
17. Buchanan, T. W. (2007). Retrieval of emotional memories. *Psychological Bulletin, 133*(5), 761-779. https://www.ncbi.nlm.nih.gov/pmc/articles/PMC 2265099/#!po=6.00000

[18] Speer, M. E., Bhanji, J. P., & Delgado, M. R. (2014). Savoring the past: Positive memories evoke value representations in the striatum. *Neuron, 84*(4), 847-856. https://doi.org/10.1016/j.neuron.2014.09.028

[19] Pruzinsky, T., & Hurley, W. (2013, September 22). *COMPASS* [PowerPoint slides].

[20] Biglan, A., Flay, B. R., Embry, D. D., & Sandler, I. N. (2012). The critical role of nurturing environments for promoting human well-being. *American Psychologist, 67*(4): 257-271. https://www.ncbi.nlm.nih.gov/pmc/articles/PMC3621015/#!po=71.2766

[21] Tibetan transliteration: *snying stobs* (pronounced nyingtob).

[22] Reynolds, S. (2011, August 2). Happy brain, happy life. *Psychology Today.* https://www.psychologytoday.com/us/blog/prime-your-gray-cells/201108/happy-brain-happy-life

CHAPTER 6

Kindness

Kindness practice lays the final building block for the foundation of emotional states leading to compassion. Equanimity evens and widens the emotional focus. Gratitude replenishes and opens the heart in appreciation of others, orienting our minds to help them. Kindness then engenders a wish for us and others to experience well-being. This next step is crucial because, without it, there is a danger of developing sadism instead of compassion when considering the hardships of others. For example, if a negative event befalls an enemy, one might become gladdened by its poetic justice and think "they got what they deserved." Such thoughts and feelings bolster revenge mentality, not compassion. In order to fully understand how important it is to develop kindness as a precursor to compassion, it is useful to consider the destructive nature of the opposites of kindness: fear, anger, and thoughts of revenge.

Revenge is one of the strongest and most tragic motivations that we humans engender when faced with harm. You can see the lure of revenge in the themes of many action movies, where the happy ending constitutes the villain encountering a violent end to his treachery. While temporarily satisfying at some level, revenge is responsible for many tragedies in history. For example, in the 13th century Genghis Khan (1162–1227) united the Mongol tribes and defeated Western Xia and Kara-Khitan. Shortly after this, a neighboring king of the Khwarezmid Empire killed his emissaries who had been sent by Genghis Khan in an act of friendship to negotiate a trade relationship. In retaliation, Genghis Khan wiped out the entire kingdom of Khwarezmid, taking countless innocent lives with his rage.[1]

In the history of civilization, how many atrocities have been propelled by thoughts of revenge, fear, and hate? We can see modern-day atrocities as we watch the news each night, and we can notice our own reactions when feeling subject to injustice or harm. Revenge and thoughts of retaliation seem to be an automatic response to perceived harm. Some theorists suggest that it benefits us by deterring potential transgressors, punishing wrongdoing, and discouraging freeloaders. However, researchers also point out that it leads to counter-revenge, cycles of revenge, depression, life dissatisfaction, and health problems.[2] Acting on thoughts of revenge might produce some immediate satisfaction, but it is followed by sadness and dissatisfaction.[3] Buddhists call this the second arrow. The first arrow is whatever original harm we suffer. The second arrow consists of the afflicted states of mind and actions they propel that continue to harm us and others long after the original injury has healed.

If we are going to be able to generate compassion, we need a way to overcome grudges, fears, anger, and thoughts of revenge that have become encrusted around past injuries. As Carl Jung once said, "Nobody, as long as he moves among the chaotic currents of life, is without trouble."[4] In one worldwide study on exposure to traumatic events, more than 70% of respondents reported being subject to or witnessing a close loved one being impacted by a traumatic event; 30.5% reported being exposed to four or more traumatic events.[5] Severe trauma can result in post-traumatic stress disorder, which in cases of trauma due to aggressive acts of others can lead to strong wishes for revenge and a propensity to act on such wishes.[6] Even if we have been lucky enough to have avoided traumatic events in our lives, none of us get through without facing difficult encounters in one form or another.

In dangerous situations, checking our impulse for revenge can be lifesaving. Personally, I can remember times in my early adulthood when I was protected by not reacting or escalating when encountering a threatening situation. In one instance when I was working during the summer before starting college, I was sitting with a group of fellow construction workers on a lunch break when a young man across from me pulled out a shotgun he had brought to lunch and pointed it at me. I did not know him or understand why he would threaten me like this, but I imagine that it was an attempt to impress the other workers. My first reactions were fear and anger along with an impulse to charge him and try to take the shotgun away, but my deeper instincts told me to remain calm and eat my sandwich. After a few tense moments, he grew bored of his dark amusement and put down the shotgun. If I had charged him, it might have provoked a fatal reaction.

On another occasion, I had stepped out of an ice cream shop on a street in New York City to enjoy my ice cream while waiting for my friends, who were still inside the shop. A homeless man passed me by and then doubled back. He held a clenched fist up to my face and told me he had killed men with his fist. Rather than escalate, I offered him my ice cream. He seemed baffled for a moment, and then said, "no thanks" and went along his way. In contrast, I can think of many times when faced with threatening behaviors from others where I tried to escalate and intimidate them, but those outcomes did not go so well. Obviously, situations of extreme danger, like mass shootings, require that one take immediate and swift action to attempt to secure the safety of oneself and others. However, in situations that are less life threatening, it is usually wise to take some time to de-escalate, regain equilibrium, and ponder options before responding to harm.

Studies show that reducing thoughts of revenge and working on forgiveness reduces stress, improves life satisfaction, and enhances health outcomes.[7] People who have been subject to severe trauma may need to pursue psychotherapeutic supports in order to heal, but there are also exercises that will be explained in this section that can be an aid in the process of reducing anger and letting go of grudges. Healing anger, reducing fear, and replacing revenge thinking with forgiveness are all important skills for finding equilibrium and bringing our hearts back to kindness. My father used to tell me that the best revenge is just to move forward and have a good life.

Many cultural sayings through the ages have weighed in on the problems with choosing the path of revenge. "An eye for an eye leaves the whole world blind." "He who sets out on a journey of revenge should first dig two graves. One for his enemy and another for himself." "Holding onto a grudge is like drinking poison wishing that your enemy would die." These and other sayings point to an undeniable truth: thoughts of revenge harm us more than the ones toward whom they are directed. However, when contemplating the choice between feeding thoughts of revenge or working toward forgiveness, some people may feel that letting go of their anger would allow the person who harmed them to continue their treachery unchecked.

We can argue that without revenge, there is neither justice nor deterrent, but seeking justice and deterring wrongdoers can also be done with a motive of compassion rather than one of vengeance. Buddhists believe that karma will punish offenders in future lives. Other religions leave justice in God's hands. These beliefs may allow some people to let go of seeking vengeance. If you believe that it is better for the well-being of others to hold an offender accountable, you can always consider your options. For example, it is often best to involve law enforcement. However, it is good to remember that our justice system is built on the principles of innocence until proof of guilt, equality under the law, and due process with the burden of proof on the shoulders of the person seeking justice, so one must document a solid case in order to be successful with this approach. Many victims, especially of sexual assault, find the court process demeaning and re-injuring.[8] It is also possible that offenders may try to retaliate against attempts to hold them accountable. Therefore, caution is advised.

Another approach some people take toward holding offenders accountable is through advocating for social reform, policy change, and social justice. This is a broader approach but has several advantages. It brings people who have been harmed together with others who have experienced similar hardships, which can help in the healing process. Often victims may inadvertently internalize a negative self-image in response to how they have been treated. Sharing their experience with others can validate them and allow the harm to be seen in its true light, as something wrong in the perpetrator rather than within the victim. Social action helps victims move from a passive into an active stance toward righting how they've been wronged, therefore helping to empower them. Before starting and while engaged in seeking justice, I think it is wise to work inwardly to regain equilibrium and compassion, which will help as you try to discern the best courses of action to take. This will help you feel better and make your next steps more effective. Better judgment and planning allow for better outcomes.

One strategy that can help in regaining equilibrium after being hurt is to contemplate forgiveness. Jack Kornfield once described how he was in a refugee camp with one of his teachers in Cambodia after its great holocaust in 1979.[9] His teacher, in defiance of a warning from the Khmer Rouge, had set up a temple in the refugee camp where 25,000 people gathered despite the possible threat to their lives. As they sat down, they began to weep, and his teacher had them recite a saying from the time of the Buddha, "Hatred never ceases by hatred, but by love alone is healed. This is the ancient and eternal law." Jack noted that "as they chanted, you could feel that the truth of their words was even greater than their sorrow."[10]

Jack developed a three-part meditation that can be used as an aid to forgiveness. In the first part, after settling yourself with mindfulness of breathing, you contemplate the following: "There are many ways that I have hurt and harmed others knowingly and unknowingly in this life. Many times, I have caused sorrow, betrayed, or abandoned others. I remember these now, I feel these. In the many ways that I have hurt others out of my fear, out of my pain or confusion, I ask their forgiveness. May I be forgiven."

Since many of us are hard on ourselves, in the second part of this contemplation, one's focus is on forgiving oneself. Therefore, with self-compassion, the next step is to contemplate, "There are so many ways I harm myself, knowingly and unknowingly, I abandon or betray myself, cause myself pain. I remember these now. I picture and feel the sorrows I have caused to myself. And in the many ways I have hurt or harmed myself out of confusion, out of fear, pain, I offer myself forgiveness and mercy. I forgive myself. I hold myself with kindness, mercy, and forgiveness. May I be forgiven."

The final step is to begin to forgive others who have harmed you in the past by contemplating, "In the many ways others have hurt me, abandoned or betrayed me, knowingly or unknowingly, out of their confusion, out of their anger and pain, out of their fear and ignorance, I see these now and feel what I have carried. And to the extent that I am ready, I offer forgiveness. I release you. I release my hatred or anger if I am ready. I will not put you out of my heart."[11] You might feel strong emotions well up during this practice, and it is good to return to your breathing and sense of well-being after each contemplation. Forgiveness lightens our emotional load and returns our capacities as humans to live a life filled with kindness instead of bitterness.

Many people might find it difficult to forgive, especially if they have been repeatedly hurt by someone in an inhumane way. For instance, I have worked with people who were physically and/or sexually abused repeatedly by a parent, who harbor murderous rage toward the perpetrator. Over time, with support, it is possible to reduce the intensity of the rage and begin to heal some of the wounds. At some point, it might be possible for a survivor of abuse to consider moving beyond anger in order to regain peace of mind. However, sometimes there is a fear that if one lets go of the anger, one will become vulnerable to being re-victimized. I find that it helps people in this process to discuss the difference between forgiveness and trust. Forgiveness is done for oneself, so that the burden of anger and hate can be released. Trust is another matter; trust needs to be earned. Forgiving does not mean that the perpetrator of past harm is free to reenter one's life.

In the feedback from one of the COMPASS pilot studies that is mentioned below, a participant mentioned having problems generating thoughts of kindness toward a particular person who had harmed his or her family. This is not uncommon, and it is the reason that practicing forgiveness is suggested before practicing the contemplations on kindness. Kindness itself can help to heal anger because anger and kindness do not coexist easily with each other. One tends to override the other, just like water puts out fire or fire boils away water. When you imbue your mind with kindness, you can feel anger collapse and evaporate. But if the anger is deeply rooted, it might first need to be released through attempts at forgiveness.

Much of the healing process in recovering from harm seems to depend on how one relates to adverse experiences. There is a danger that, when someone is repeatedly subjected to abuse and maltreatment, they might identify with their aggressors and become aggressors themselves.[12] However, this does not need to be the case. Many people show a deepening of empathy and compassion in response to adversity.[13] Even people who have been subjected to severe mistreatment, depending on how they internalize and react to what has happened to them, can go on to become compassionate, strong, and resilient.

Take the Tibetans for example. The culture of old Tibet was steeped in the pursuit of kindness and compassionate insight. When their country was devastated by China's invasion (1950 to present) and their people were murdered and tortured in concentration camps, countless stories began to emerge of resilience in the face of hardship. For instance, I once heard an account of a Tibetan, who after years of being tortured in a prison, was released from captivity and made his way to India, where he had an audience with His Holiness the Dalai Lama. When His Holiness asked him what his most frightening experience was while he was in prison, the man said that at one point he became frightened that he was going to lose compassion for a guard who was torturing him. Such compassion is not uncommon in older Tibetans, who were raised in Tibet's rich, spiritual culture. I have met personally with Tibetans who were subjected to unimaginable suffering at the hands of their captors, whose gentleness, sanity, and good nature seem intact and even strengthened by their experiences.[14]

After the holocaust occurred in Tibet, some Tibetans faulted their tradition of kindness and compassion, seeing it as responsible for their vulnerability to China's takeover. But even if the Tibetans had tried to fight back more forcefully, the size of China's population, army, and economic power would have made it impossible for Tibet to prevail. What has been interesting to notice is that the efforts of Tibetan refugees to resettle and rebuild their lives in countries around the world has been highly successful. Their adaptability, compassion, and fortitude have made them welcome by diverse cultures and nations. So it seems that their kindness and compassion have continued to contribute to their well-being and survival.

Tibetans see anger as an unhealthy emotion that causes spiritual, mental, and physical harm. It is interesting that their perspective coincides with research showing the harmful effects anger has on our health, well-being, and relationships.[15] In contrast, the typically held Western assertion is that anger is a healthy emotion.[16]

Where Tibetans and Western traditions of mental health concur is that it is better to be aware of anger and express it in appropriate verbal ways than it is to deny, suppress, or enact it. Anger often holds a protective message, and if we can decipher the message without acting out the anger, it can inform us about injustice, the need to set boundaries, and the ways we need to grow or adapt. As Ron Potter-Efron, an anger management specialist, says, "Anger is a good messenger, but a lousy manager."[17] If we can calm our immediate reactions and regain a state of kindness and self-compassion, we can consider the messages our anger is sending us:

- Is this anger about an injustice? If so, what is the best way to advocate for change?
- Is my anger about a wound to self-esteem? If so, how can I heal it and move forward?
- Am I reacting because I'm drained, tired, or hungry? If so, how can I take care of myself?
- Has something blocked me from my goals? If so, how might I fix the problem, or must I learn to accept it?

Once we have figured out the message our anger is sending us, it no longer serves a purpose, and it can get in the way of effective problem solving. The main thing is not to get stuck in anger. If our objective is to cultivate patience, we can learn how to reduce anger's intensity and even uproot it over time. Research is emerging showing that patience benefits our overall mental well-being, relationships, and health.[18]

Tibetans often quote verses from an Indian sage, Santideva (c. 685–763), when talking about the logic for patience and forgiveness:

My mind will not experience peace
If it fosters painful thoughts of hatred.
I shall find no joy or happiness;
Unable to sleep, I shall feel unsettled.
Hence the enemy, anger,
Creates sufferings such as these,
But whoever assiduously overcomes it
Finds happiness now and hereafter.

Having found its fuel of mental unhappiness
In the prevention of what I wish for,
And in doing what I do not want,
Hatred increases and then destroys me.

Therefore, I should totally eradicate
The fuel of this enemy;
For this enemy has no other function
Than that of causing me harm.

Whatever befalls me,
I shall not disturb my mental joy;
For having been made unhappy, I shall not accomplish what
    I wish,
And my virtues will decline.

Why be unhappy about something
If it can be remedied?
And what is the use of being unhappy about something
If it cannot be remedied?[19]

These and other modes of logic can be helpful in thwarting anger's tendency to fuel itself and overtake our thoughts and feelings. Ruminating on reasons to stay angry tends to build further resentment. Left unchecked, this process can lead us to become bitter and hostile. People with high levels of anger tend to externalize blame and hold others responsible for their dissatisfaction, thus ruining relationships, increasing negative responses from others, and causing more isolation. Only the one experiencing the anger can stop this process because its causes repeated thoughts of anger and the reasoning sustaining it are generated internally. Corrective thoughts and lines of reasoning leading to self-calming, regaining equilibrium, and bringing the mind back to kindness are therefore essential to emotional well-being.

Another reason for working on identifying, reducing, and eventually uprooting pockets of anger is that anger tends to distort our perceptions of others. Often it leads to holding others in judgment and seeing only their worst characteristics. This makes it difficult to see the world through the other person's eyes, thus blocking compassion. Anger leads us to objectify the person as someone to be avoided or subdued rather than allowing us to appreciate them for who they are and having curiosity about what factors in their lives are driving them to their choices and behaviors. We might misattribute hostile intent to a person's behaviors, only to discover later that their behaviors were driven by something other than anger, like fear or misunderstanding.

If we can step outside of anger and judgment for a moment, we will become more able to understand people more clearly and thoroughly. We can develop a true appreciation of their complexity. John Koenig, author of *The Dictionary of Obscure Sorrows*,[20] called this experience "sonder," which is a moment of realizing that others who appear as a passerby in your life have their own feelings, stories, thoughts, ambitions, networks of relationships and so on; and that from their perspective, you are the passerby. Such moments can be profoundly humbling and can expand our appreciation and understanding of people around us.

It has often become apparent to me as I work with my own anger and with my clients who are struggling with anger, how a moment of appreciation for someone can disrupt anger's hold over the emotions. For instance, when angered by a family member, a moment of reflection on the positive things the family member has done for you and the history you've shared can immediately cut through animosity and soften your response. This is the power of selective focus. We can make our minds angrier or gentler by choosing what we focus on.

Tibetans have many meditational practices, based on using visualization, mantra recitation, and other techniques, to bring their minds into calmness and begin purifying internal obstacles like anger, sadness, and fear. These practices constitute a form of internal housecleaning. One practice that can help when trying to heal wounds from past harms, and the anger and fear associated with them, is to imagine a completely compassionate and wise mentor in front of you. It can be someone you have met, someone you admire, a spiritual figure, or even someone created from your imagination. The important point is to see the figure as embodying a complete form of compassionate insight. Imagine opening your heart to them, revealing all your hurt, anger, and fear. Request their help in letting go and purifying. Then imagine light radiating from the figure's heart into yours, dissolving your anger, hurt, and fear, and replacing it with a sense of calm, loving serenity.

Barbara Fredrickson, a Kenan distinguished professor of psychology at the University of North Carolina, talks about the benefits of "micro-moments" of loving-kindness, cultivated by deliberate direction of one's thoughts to contemplate positive wishes for oneself and others. In one study, she and her research team found that there was a slight positive shift in measures of cognitive, social, and psychological functioning and self-reported health in participants who tried to cultivate micro-moments of kindness.[21]

When we witness an act of kindness, our bodies produce oxytocin, which helps reduce blood pressure, improves heart health, and enhances self-esteem and optimism. Kindness also causes the release of endorphins thus mitigating pain, and it enhances levels of the neurotransmitter serotonin, which helps us to stay calm and happy. In addition, it reduces levels of the stress-hormone cortisol. When a group of anxious individuals was asked to practice at least six acts of kindness each week, after a month they reported a decrease in social avoidance and an increase in positive moods and relationship satisfaction. Practicing acts of kindness has also been linked to increased lifespan, pleasure, happiness, energy, calmness, feelings of self-worth, and well-being, as well as to decreased depression. Kindness is contagious in that it inspires people who witness it to act in a similar way.[22]

Kindness can be extended without limit and its benefits are immeasurable. So how do we start? From a self-compassion point of view, it is best to start with yourself. This is as simple as sitting mindfully for a few moments and inwardly wishing yourself good things: "May I be happy, peaceful, and comfortable. May no problems come to me. May no difficulties come to me. May I be free from danger and fear. May I dwell in contentment and joy. May I have strength, determination, and success in facing the challenges we all encounter in life." After basking in these thoughts for a while, then extend them to friends and loved ones. "May my loved ones and friends be happy, peaceful, and comfortable. May no problems come to them. May no difficulties come to them. May they be free from danger and fear. May they dwell in contentment and joy. May they have strength, determination, and success in facing the challenges we all encounter in life." This step is usually easy, in that we usually see wishing well for friends and family as a natural extension of wishing well for ourselves. These kind thoughts constitute micro-moments of loving-kindness. Sometimes they can produce a feeling of kindness, which is a very pleasant emotion.

The challenge comes when we extend the wishes beyond our circle of friends and family. To do so, consider neutral people, whom you know less well. "May acquaintances and people who I don't know be happy, peaceful, and comfortable. May no problems come to them. May no difficulties come to them. May they be free from danger and fear. May they dwell in contentment and joy. May they have strength, determination, and success in facing the challenges we all encounter in life." The circle of our focus grows larger with this contemplation, which often can be experienced as an opening of the heart and expanding of the feelings of kindness. Sometimes, however, it might also give rise to ambivalence if we start to think of people we don't like or who have harmed or threatened us.

If you start to feel hesitation about expanding your circle of those to whom you make kind wishes, it might be a sign that more forgiveness work is needed, or it might help to consider that people who are happy and secure rarely pose a threat. So, wishing peace of mind, security, and well-being for strangers and former enemies poses no danger to ourselves. If anything, were our kind wishes ever to become true, such people would likely become sources of support rather than threats. I personally find that when I wish well-being toward someone who has harmed me, I feel a sense of relief. It frees me from holding on to thoughts of fear or malice, and I feel unburdened. I regain my own peace of mind and the well-being that comes with thoughts of kindness.

As a final step, we can extend our kind wishes to everyone. "May everyone, everywhere be happy, peaceful, and comfortable. May no problems come to them. May no difficulties come to them. May they be free from danger and fear. May they dwell in contentment and joy. May they have strength, determination, and success in facing the challenges we all encounter in life." Hold this thought for a while and imagine for a moment that people everywhere are experiencing well-being, enjoying the feeling of universal kindness. This sets an imprint in your mind associating the well-being of others with a happy feeling in yourself.

A nice meditation that can sustain this thought and feeling is to imagine that, as you breathe in, a soft light travels in with your breath, bringing in kind wishes and well-being to yourself. As you breathe out, the soft light travels out, bringing kind wishes and well-being to others.[23] In this way, thoughts and feelings of kindness are linked with your imagination and breathing. Meditate this way for however long it feels comfortable.

Tips for Helping Professionals

Maintaining Patience and Kindness When Confronted by Workplace Bullying

Worker frustration can contribute to professional burnout and can be provoked by a sense of worker isolation, powerlessness, and bureaucratic obstacles to serving client needs. Bullying behaviors between coworkers or by leadership exacerbate hostile work environments, resulting in staff distress, anger, fear, anxiety, depression, health problems, and absenteeism. It is therefore crucial that helping professionals who work in such conditions take external steps to set boundaries with bullies and internal steps to regain a sense of well-being. Kindness practice can support this process.

Section 10 of the appendix, "A COMPASS Handbook for Helping Professionals," explores this issue in more depth and offers a practical guide for external and internal remedies to the problem.

Thomas Pruzinsky defines loving-kindness as "the wish for all beings, including ourselves, to have happiness in all its many forms."[24] At first, we might not be able to generate the actual feeling of loving-kindness depending on how accustomed or unaccustomed we are with it, but by generating micro-moments of kind thoughts, eventually the feeling of kindness will start to grow. Micro-moments of kind thoughts are like seeds we are planting in the ground of our minds. With practice and time, they will begin to take root and flourish. As kindness begins to define our inner garden, the roots of hate and fear will have less room to take hold. Eventually, with consistent effort, weeds of past grudges can be uprooted completely.

Participants in a January 3, 2015, presentation of COMPASS were asked about their positive and negative experiences of trying out the kindness exercise. Positive experiences that were reported included feelings of calm, peace, compassion, sympathy, a softening sensation in the heart, well-being, self-love, contentment, warmth, rejoicing at receiving kindness, positivity, goodness, relief, gratitude toward helpers, and a wish to be kind to everyone. Negative experiences that were reported included feelings of sadness, melancholy, agitation and holding back, unresponsiveness to the kindness of others, self-anger at selfishness, and a sense that kindness is easier said than done.

Participants in the pilot study conducted at George Mason University on January 25, 2015, also gave feedback after practicing the kindness exercise. Positive experiences that were reported included feelings of a lessening in agitation, calm, care, hopefulness, sincerity, appreciation, tolerance, less physical tension, acceptance, a wish for well-being of family, "warmth in my heart," overall well-being, self-compassion, and kindness. Negative experiences that were reported included feelings of "skepticism that I can maintain these feelings," "I wish I could have kept my mind on cultivating kindness," resisting the thought of including someone who harmed one's family, and resistance for "people I'm feeling negative about."

As was found in previous sections, the internal conflicts between the parts of the mind that want to experience more positive states versus the parts of the mind that are holding onto past patterns of self-protection can be seen in the responses of these participants. Sadness, melancholy, and holding back are often the costs that come with attempts to protect ourselves from emotional pain by resisting connection to others. Anger at selfishness can be a sort of recognition that the process of self-protection can cause more limitations than benefits. It is also an invitation to try to move beyond such cocooning and take the risk of opening our hearts to real connections with others. If frustration at one's own selfishness turns into self-anger, it is important to return for awhile to the foundation practices of self-acceptance and self-compassion.

Indeed, cultivating and maintaining kindness is easier said than done, but it is fairly simple to practice it. Therefore, the skepticism about being able to maintain it can be replaced by the reassuring thought that "I can practice it wherever I want to." Resistance to the thought of extending kindness to negative people or to those who have harmed us or our loved ones is a natural response to harm. As mentioned before, it does limit us by creating an internal obstacle to the full experience of kindness and to the development of compassion, so I encourage you to put effort into contemplating forgiveness as a support for the practice of kindness. A simple format for practicing kindness is as follows:

A. Contemplate the benefit of kindness and do a brief practice of mindfulness followed by a short review of equanimity and gratitude.
B. When settled, contemplate the following:

- May I be happy, healthy, and peaceful; may I have joy, contentment, and security; may I have strength, determination, and success in overcoming the difficulties in my life.
- Make the same wishes for loved ones.
- Make the same wishes for friends.
- Make the same wishes for those who upset you (if they were calmer, happier people, they might be better company).
- Make the same wishes for everyone, everywhere.
- As you contemplate these kind thoughts, imagine a soft light of kindness travels in with your breath, bringing well-being to yourself and then travels out with your out-breath, bringing well-being to others. Meditate this way for however longs feels comfortable.
- If you feel a sense of loving-kindness, focus on it for a while, thinking how wonderful it would be if everyone could have happiness and its causes.

Notes

1 Saunders, J. J. (2001). *History of the Mongol conquests*. University of Pennsylvania Press. (Original work published 1972.)

2 Schumann, K., & Ross, M. (2010). The benefits, costs, and paradox of revenge. *Social and Personality Psychology Compass 4*(12), 1193-1205. https://onlinelibrary.wiley.com/doi/abs/10.1111/j.1751-9004.2010.00322.x

3 Jaffe, E. (2011). The complicated psychology of revenge. *Association for Psychological Science*. https://www.psychologicalscience.org/observer/the-complicated-psychology-of-revenge

4 Jung, C. G. (1964). *Civilization in transition* (R. F. C. Hull, Trans.). Routledge & Kegan Paul.

5 Benjet, C., Bromet, E., Karam, E. G., Kessler, R. C., McLaughlin, K. A., Ruscio, A. M., Shahly, V., Stein, D. J., Petukhova, M., Hill, E., Alonso, J., Atwoli, L., Bunting, B., Bruffaerts, R., Caldas-de-Almeida, J. M., de Girolamo, G., Florescu, S., Gureje, O., Huang, Y., ... K. C. Koenen. (2015). The epidemiology of traumatic event exposure worldwide: Results from the World Mental Health Survey Consortium. *Psychological Medicine, 46*(2): 327-343. https://www.ncbi.nlm.nih.gov/pmc/articles/PMC4869975/

6 Cardozo, B. L., Kaiser, R., Gotway, C. A., & Agani, F. (2003). Mental health, social functioning, and feelings of hatred and revenge of Kosovar Albanians one year after the war in Kosovo. *Journal of Traumatic Stress, 16*, 351-360.

7 Bono, G., McCullough, M. E., & Root, L. M. (2008). Forgiveness, feeling connected to others, and well-being: Two longitudinal studies. *Personality and Social Psychology Bulletin, 34*, 182-195.

8 Herman, J. L. (2005). Justice from the victim's perspective. *Violence against Women, 11*(5), 571-602. https://doi.org/10.1177/1077801205274450

9 Kornfield, J. (2000, February). The practice of forgiveness. *Spirit Rock Meditation Center Newsletter, 5*.

10 Ibid.

11 Ibid.

12 Howell, E. F. (2014). Ferenczi's concept of identification with the aggressor: Understanding dissociative structure with interacting victim and abuser self-states. *American Journal of Psychoanalysis, 74*(1), 48-59. https://doi.org/10.1057/ajp.2013.40

13 Suttie, J. (2016, January 25). What doesn't kill you makes you kinder. *Greater Good Magazine*. https://greatergood.berkeley.edu/article/item/what_doesnt_kill_you_makes_you_kinder

14 For examples of what Tibetans endured, see Gyatso, P. (1997). *The autobiography of a Tibetan monk*. Harvill Press. And also, a dear friend wrote a grueling account of what he went through in the concentration camps with a vivid historical overview of what happened: Khedrup, Thubten. (2008). *Memories of life in Lhasa under Chinese rule* (Matthew Akester, Trans.). Columbia University Press.

[15] Staicu, M. L., & Cuţov, M. (2010). Anger and health risk behaviors. *Journal of Medicine and Life, 3*(4), 372-375.

[16] For example, see Brandt, A. (2016, July 1). 4 reasons why you should embrace your anger. *Psychology Today.* https://www.psychologytoday.com/us/blog/mindful-anger/201606/4-reasons-why-you-should-embrace-your-anger

[17] Potter-Efron, R. T. (1994). *Angry all the time: An emergency guide to anger control.* New Harbinger Press.

[18] Mindfulness Academy. *The benefits of patience.* http://mindfulnessacademyuk.org/the-benefits-of-patience/

[19] Santideva, A. (1979). *A guide to the Bodhisattva's way of life* (Stephen Batchelor, Trans.), 53-54. Library of Tibetan Works and Archives.

[20] Koenig, J. (2012). *The dictionary of obscure sorrows.* YouTube. https://youtu.be/AkoML0_FiV4. Gratitude to Adam DeWald for bringing this term to my awareness.

[21] Fredrickson, B. L. (2013). *Love 2.0: Creating happiness and health in moments of connection.* Hudson Street Press; O'Donnell, E. (2013, May 10). Micro-utopia, anyone? Fredrickson describes nourishing power of small, positive moments. *NIH Record.* https://nihrecord.nih.gov/newsletters/2013/05_10_2013/story3.htm

[22] See Random Acts of Kindness Foundation. Did you know there are scientifically proven benefits of being kind? https://www.randomactsofkindness.org/the-science-of-kindness); Mautz, S. Science says "Random Acts of Kindness" week has astonishing health benefits. *Inc.* https://www.inc.com/scott-mautz/science-says-random-acts-of-kindness-week-has-astonishing-health-benefits.html; Random Acts of Kindness. Kindness health facts. https://www.dartmouth.edu/wellness/emotional/rakhealthfacts.pdf; and Hamilton, D. R. (2011). 5 Beneficial Side Effects of Kindness. *Huffington Post.* https://www.huffingtonpost.com/david-r-hamilton-phd/kindness-benefits_b_869537.html

[23] This combination of contemplating kindness together with awareness of breathing and visualization is an amalgam of techniques that can be found in Theravadin Buddhism, Tibetan Buddhist practices, and a similar strategy that was shared with me by a friend and colleague, Peggy DiVincenzo, LPC, based on a guided meditation she received from Christopher Germer, PhD. For Germer's approach to this strategy, see Germer, C., & Neff, K. (2014). *Mindful self-compassion handouts,* p. 17. UCSD Center for Mindfulness, Mindfulness-Based Professional Training Institute.

[24] Pruzinsky, T., & Hurley, W. (2013, September 22). *COMPASS* [PowerPoint slides].

CHAPTER 7

Compassion

All the exercises leading to this point prepare the mind for the experience of compassion. Compassion is often a natural part of being human, but it also can be a produced thing. Thoughts and feelings of kindness set the emotional ground upon which the home of compassion can be built. When we sincerely start to wish that others could find happiness and its causes, it is a natural response to feel compassion for these people when they do not find them. When seeing someone for whom we feel kindness encounter suffering, our kindness toward them easily turns into compassion. Tom Pruzinsky defines compassion as "the wish that others be free from suffering and its causes."[1] The Sanskrit term karuna is usually translated as compassion, and in Buddhism it is defined as the wish to remove the pain and suffering of others.[2]

Compassion, while a beautiful emotion, is not always associated with a pleasant feeling. This is because it is linked with empathy. Empathy allows us to understand the experiences of others both cognitively and emotionally. In cognitive empathy, we can understand what it is like to be in someone else's shoes. In emotional or resonant empathy, we can imagine and feel an approximation of what the other person is going through. With compassion, in addition to empathy, there is a strong wish that the person be freed from painful emotion and experience.

Empathy is not necessarily accompanied by compassion. This is an important point because even some sociopaths are capable of empathy by itself. An empathic sociopath can understand what others are going through, but they just do not care. Instead, they use their empathy as another tool to better manipulate people to satisfy their own needs. In contrast, a compassionate person feels compelled to help if they are able. Compassion may not always feel good, but as mentioned before, it helps us in many crucial ways by connecting us to others, buffering against stress, giving our lives purpose, and promoting health and well-being in ourselves and others.[3]

Compassionate people tend to be less judgmental, more appreciative, helpful, calm, and harmonious.[4] Compassion helps us develop our strength and fortitude by helping us face the harder side of life. It increases our courage to do the right thing rather than shrink away from doing what is needed. It makes us resilient in life's ups and downs, helping us weather and bounce back from adversity. This makes us attractive to others and helps us to uplift ourselves and others. It is contagious, which means that others may want to model after the compassion they see in us. Studies have shown that compassionate acts stimulate the pleasure centers of the brain, producing a special form of happiness, and that compassionate activities are an aid in overcoming depression.[5]

It takes some courage to allow yourself to feel compassion, because in order to be able to do so you must recognize and accept that someone around you is unhappy and suffering. I remember as a child that adults on fishing excursions used to tell me that animals like fish don't have feelings. I suppose they told me that untruth in the hopes that I would find more enjoyment in the experience of fishing and not be bothered by the obvious suffering being experienced by the hapless fish. I've seen similar rationalizations expressed by people about the poor and homeless. "They want to live that way. They're just lazy." Again, such rationalizations seem to be voiced by people who do not want to feel bothered by contemplating the misfortunes of others.

Compassion starts when we allow ourselves to connect with the suffering we see in others and stay with it for a while, asking ourselves "What is this like for them?" If we have done a good job cultivating a natural feeling of kindness, compassion will rise spontaneously as we connect with the suffering of others. This, of course, might feel overwhelming at times, but with practice we can become used to it and even relish it. Tuning in to the cognitive and emotional states of others does not come naturally to all of us, but it can be learned with time and practice.

Social workers train in empathy by considering the age, gender, ethnicity, beliefs, history, and current situation of the client with whom they are working, trying to imagine what life might be like for them. We listen closely to their description of what they are going through, paying attention to tone of voice and delivery, what is said and what is implied, as we try to understand their experience from their point of view. To increase the accuracy of our attempts at empathy, we need to stand ready to discard inaccurate assessments as new information comes to light through client self-disclosures. All of this, of course, takes effort.

In addition to the effort it takes to understand someone else's experiences, caring about how they feel is also important. This holds true for practitioners of other helping professions, including doctors, nurses, psychologists, counselors, etc.[6] Not all helping professionals have an easy time developing and maintaining high levels of empathy and care. Even those professionals who begin their careers filled with care and compassion can face challenges with burnout, compassion fatigue, or vicarious trauma as they come face to face with the hard realities that their clients bring to them. There are subtle differences between these three types of discouragement.

Burnout is associated with stress and being overworked. Compassion fatigue, which is referred to clinically as secondary traumatic stress, is emotional depletion associated with being exposed repeatedly to trauma in the lives of others. Vicarious trauma occurs when repeated exposure to trauma in the lives of others begins to change our view of the world and of ourselves.[7] When affected by one or a combination of these, workers often report feeling exhausted, stressed out, and depressed. Sometimes they withdraw from caring, or even quit their profession. In order to prevent these problems, self-care is extremely important. We must find the right balance between caring for others and caring for ourselves.

For instance, if we are starting to burn out, it is important to set boundaries on how much we take on, and to get enough sleep, eat healthy foods, and engage in stress reduction strategies like exercise, yoga, and meditation. If we find ourselves starting to detach in order to protect ourselves from exposure to the suffering and trauma in our clients, it's important to seek supervision, talk with colleagues, and shift our focus for a while to things that renew us.

If vicarious trauma starts to change our views about the world and ourselves, it is important to analyze our new perspective once we have renewed ourselves in order to weed out cognitive distortions. This latter approach will be described in detail in the section of this book on analytical skills. The COMPASS exercises can all be used as preventative strategies to ward off these problems, but also as ways to reboot emotional well-being when we are thrown off course. The appendix, "A COMPASS Handbook for Helping Professionals," offers many strategies for preventing and overcoming compassion fatigue.

It is normal for people in everyday life to avoid exposure to the suffering of others. Once, while attending a funeral for my uncle, I asked an elderly friend how he and his wife were doing. He smiled and said, "Wilson, when you get to be my age, you don't ask people that question." His humorous response went to the deeper truth that we all know: Aging is no fun. Our bodies start to break down, our friends start to fall ill and die, and our ability to enjoy the amusements of our youth wanes. This is one reason that elderly people often feel isolated and neglected. Youthful people do not find it fun to be around them and they know it.

However, if we choose to continually distance ourselves from people experiencing various forms of suffering, we are choosing to follow only our instincts for self-protection and our desire for pleasurable encounters, which can become a support for narcissism. If we repeatedly seek only our own sense of comfort and well-being, we are being guided by our inner troll into increasing self-absorption in our yearning for immediate gratification. This poses a dilemma. Cultivating compassion may reduce some of our experiences of immediate gratification, but it also rewards us by leading us toward a deeper and more enduring form of well-being. As mentioned, we feel internal rewards when we help others, and it gives our lives a sense of purpose and meaning.

To put it simply, the balance is in trying not to become overwhelmed on the one hand or to become overly complacent on the other. When you find that your openness to considering the suffering of others leaves you feeling depleted, it is a sign that some self-care strategies are in order. When you find that you are feeling detached, bored, unmotivated, directionless, but otherwise well, perhaps it is time to consider the needs of others around you. In the Buddhist tradition, there is an archetype of a bodhisattva, one who dedicates themself to the quest for enlightenment in order to rescue all beings from suffering and its causes. Often such figures are depicted as alternating between retreating into the forest to meditate, and then reemerging into society in order to work directly for the well-being of others. I find this to be a useful image in helping me discern a balance as I alternate between caring for myself and caring for others.

When practicing compassion in the context of a meditation session, it is good to begin with a brief period of mindfulness, followed by brief contemplations on equanimity, gratitude, and kindness. As before, settle your mind into a meditation on your breath while imagining breathing kindness and thoughts of well-being into yourself imagined as a soft light, and then breathing out that light of kindness and well-being to others. You can come back to this calming meditation to refresh yourself if you start to feel overwhelmed by thinking of the suffering others are going through. Doing this also moves you out of "identical empathy" in which your feelings mirror those of the people whose suffering you contemplate, and into compassionate care in which you feel concern for the suffering of others while still maintaining your own sense of well-being. This is a crucial skill for avoiding burnout and compassion fatigue.

Once your mind is established in a meditation on kindness, consider someone you know or someone in the news who is going through a distressing experience. Try for a moment to imagine what life might be like for that person. What feelings might they be experiencing? How would you react if it were you in that situation? How would the situation impact you? If you begin to feel a wish that they be freed from their distress and suffering, that is compassion. Hold that thought and feeling for a while.

Allowing yourself to savor moments of compassion fosters familiarity. Doing this frequently eventually helps your mind become accustomed to the feeling of compassion. Over time, compassion can become an emotional resting place. In the beginning, it is good to start with short periods of such contemplations, so that you feel inclined to return to them repeatedly. It is also probably useful to start with contemplating people in situations that are mildly distressing rather than only contemplating people in horrific situations. Otherwise, the practice might overwhelm you. Gradually, you can build up to imagining how people feel in more challenging situations as you feel ready.

Once you generate a feeling of compassion with a single individual, you can expand the circle of situations you consider. For instance, if you begin by trying to feel what it's like for someone you know who is struggling with an illness, once you start to feel the wish that they would be free of the illness, you can expand the radius of your compassion by considering other people affected by illness. One study indicates that 95% of the world's population suffer from some form of illness.[8] This means that your contemplation could potentially embrace all of humanity. Even the 5% who are not presently sick are vulnerable to becoming ill like the other 95%. Or, if you are contemplating the suffering of someone who is being exploited and treated badly, you can expand your contemplation to include everyone who is oppressed, abused, marginalized, or exploited.

By expanding the scope of your compassion, the feelings can deepen and widen. You might feel helpless to change the conditions for the people whose situations you consider, which is a natural response when facing things we can't change, but the practice at this point is aimed at producing the thoughts and feelings of compassion rather than forming solutions. Forming solutions will be discussed later. It is okay for now to allow yourself to just feel compassion even if you realize that you may be helpless to fix the problems you consider. The goal of this practice is simply to accustom your mind to dwelling in compassion.

Most of us imagine the way we would like things to be. For instance, in the United States, most us would like people to have equal opportunities, justice, and rights to life, liberty, and the pursuit of happiness. Despite the obstacles to achieving such equality, we continue to hold this as a value that is important to us. Similarly, we can hold the value that wishes everyone could be free from suffering and its causes despite the many obstacles to achieving it. Thus, compassion can become a steady thought and feeling as well as a fundamental guiding principle in our minds.

As you accustom yourself to contemplating the harsh realities faced by everyone who walks the earth, you can begin to appreciate how diverse we all are and how similar we all are at the same time. We are all vulnerable to the vicissitudes of impermanence, uncertainty, and complexity involved in trying to sustain and enhance our lives. We all have strengths and weaknesses. Most of us worry about economic security, health, the well-being and safety of our loved ones, and a variety of other unknowns that haunt our thoughts about the future. We experience various discomforts and unpleasantries each day as we navigate our existence.

Some people might take exception to this focus, fearing that contemplating suffering and its causes could lead to depression. To counterbalance this possibility, as we contemplate the various forms of suffering that we all go through, it is important to simultaneously contemplate our potentials. For instance, Steve and Sybil Wolin study teens who have survived troubled family situations, and in response to the challenges they have faced, developed inner strengths and resiliencies like insight, relationship skills, morality, independence, initiative, humor, and creativity.[9] Our potential to adapt, change, and grow in the face of adversity provides hope and possibility. In Buddhism, there is a belief that we all have the potential to free ourselves from internal factors that cause us to suffer, and that we can awaken and become enlightened. In most religions, there is a belief in a higher power, a greater purpose in life, and the possibility of salvation. For people who do not have any spiritual belief, we can all see instances where humanity prevails in the case of injustice, and where human integrity and ingenuity overcome daunting obstacles.

Compassion, rather than leading to depression, provides resilience by connecting us to our common ground with humanity. It reminds us of the potential that we and others share, and of our need to move forward in a positive direction by learning from our experiences and adapting through the insights gained. Researchers have found that one of the main factors promoting resilience is human connection.[10] Compassion strengthens our ability to empathize with people unflinchingly, even in their most vulnerable and painful times. It helps us to see reality more clearly because it helps us understand and accept both the positives and the negatives that are happening to others rather than avoiding the painful aspects of their situations or trying to sugarcoat them. The key is to become comfortable with seeing reality as it is. Rather than avoiding aspects of ourselves and others that are unpleasant, we can practice staying with whatever arises in ourselves and others. This in turn allows us to connect more deeply and develop hardiness in the face of adversity.

My experience is that most people respect and value compassion. When I work with families, I notice that all members tend to defer to whichever family member shows consistent compassion during family decisions and interactions. Insights offered that are based on compassion tend to resonate more accurately and therefore carry more weight. Often, when families find themselves in a crisis, or stuck in a cycle of conflict, it is by tapping into compassion that things start to move forward, and healing begins. So if you learn how to dwell in compassion, you might find that others start looking to you for guidance and leadership.

Participants in the January 3, 2015, presentation of COMPASS, after trying the compassion exercise, reported positive experiences such as feelings of calmness, peace, empathy, relief, compassion, goodness, giving, freedom, wishing to volunteer, gratitude, lightness, buoyancy, and being overwhelmed by compassion. Negative experiences that were reported included feelings of the weight of the cruelty of the world, sadness, concerns about whether such compassion can be sustained, the difficulty of giving, interfering self-focus, a need for wisdom, memories of when others have been mean, disappointment with humanity, and a lack of compassion for people who harm others.

Participants in the January 25, 2015, pilot study of COMPASS at George Mason University reported the following positive experiences after trying the compassion exercise: feelings of calm, gratitude for positives in life, happiness at wishing others not to suffer, good to connect to others rather than self-focus, accountability, being privileged, energized, pleasure at positive memories, empathy, hopefulness, compassion, and kindness. Negative experiences that were reported included feelings of sadness over the suffering of others, guilt, anger at those who ignore the suffering of others or stereotype the less fortunate, and "a bit of worry for my physical and mental health when I get older."

Tips for Helping Professionals

Choosing Compassion as your Moral Compass

Empathy, fortified with compassion, helps us to listen to the hardships of others with care and without becoming bogged down by emotional contagion. Rather than becoming depressed ourselves when listening to someone describe their depression, we can empathize with compassion while maintaining our own sense of well-being. Over time, this approach produces a resilient form of compassion. However, sometimes profit motives and worries about liability can encroach on compassionate motivation and compromise the integrity and effectiveness of helping professionals. Therefore, it is crucial to be aware of conflicting interests when faced with ethical dilemmas and bring ourselves back into compassionate motivations for our work each day.

In section 11 of the appendix, "A COMPASS Handbook for Helping Professionals," profit motives in the medical industry are explored along with suggestions about how to bring back a compassionate motivation when facing moral ambiguity.

It's interesting to note how some participants described very positive emotional experiences of compassion like calmness, peace, lightness, gratitude and so forth, while some reported sadness, guilt, and anger or disappointment with people who lack compassion. It is unclear whether some of the participants felt mixtures of both positive and negative affect at the same time, but it would not be surprising if this were the case. My personal experience of compassion is that it has a bittersweet quality to it. On the one hand it allows me to be open and in touch with the suffering of myself and others, and on the other, it gives a kind of inner strength and courage that makes me feel connected with humanity and the best part of being human.

As with similar concerns mentioned in previous exercises, the qualm raised about the difficulty of sustaining compassion can be mitigated with an assurance that it can be generated repeatedly and therefore restored at will. The experience that I have heard from people who continually practice these exercises over a long time is that repetition eventually leads to habit and that the feeling of compassion becomes more sustainable. Compassion can become a predominant emotional state and motivational force for accomplished practitioners. It is similar to the way someone who repeatedly focuses on worries eventually becomes consumed with anxiety, except that in this case you are focusing on a positive emotional state until it begins permeating your internal landscape.

The feedback that people gave about anger, disappointment, and lack of compassion for people who disregard or harm others is not uncommon. As you become more compassionate and aware, you might start to notice that many people do not share your perspective. I have found that teens with high levels of compassion sometimes feel that they don't fit in with their more narcissistically inclined peers. The important thing is to not take this as a personal flaw, but instead to see it as a strength. You might find yourself seeking out other more compassionate people for friendship and solidarity. Over time, as you grow more secure with your evolving compassionate nature, tolerance toward self-absorbed people can increase. Instead of focusing on anger and contempt for those regressed into narcissism, it can help to focus on their potential for emotional growth. A simple format for practicing compassion is as follows:

A. Contemplate the benefit of compassion and do a brief practice of mindfulness, equanimity, gratitude, and loving-kindness. Settle your mind into a meditation on your breath while imagining breathing kindness and thoughts of well-being into yourself imagined as a soft light, and then breathing out that light of kindness and well-being to others. You can return to this meditation periodically to refresh yourself should you feel overwhelmed at any point when contemplating the various forms of suffering others go through.

B. When settled, contemplate the following:

- Though I want only happiness and not to suffer, life is filled with difficulties and hardships.
- Others, just like me, want only happiness and not to suffer. Yet many face daily hunger, poverty, and homelessness.
- Many encounter conflicts, disrespect, living in fear, imprisonment, torture, abuse, or violence.

- Many experience sickness, frailties of body, and mental distress.
- Life is full of uncertainty and unpleasantness for all of us as we struggle to survive and thrive.
- If you feel a sense of compassion for yourself and others, focus on it for a while and sustain it. Think about how everyone is equal to you in not wanting to suffer, and about how wonderful it would be if everyone, everywhere, could be free from suffering and its causes.

Notes

[1] Pruzinsky, T., & Hurley, W. (2013, September 22). *COMPASS* [PowerPoint slides].

[2] Wisdom Library. *Definitions of Karuna.* https://www.wisdomlib.org/definition/karuna

[3] For a summary of some of the studies showing the many benefits compassion can bring, see Seppala, E. (2013, July 24). Compassionate mind, healthy body. *Greater Good Magazine.* https://greatergood.berkeley.edu/article/item/compassionate_mind_healthy_body

[4] Chopra, Deepak. (2015). The health benefits of practicing compassion. *Huffington Post.* https://www.huffingtonpost.com/deepak-chopra/the-health-benefits-of-pr_b_7586440.html

[5] Seppala, E. Top 10 scientific benefits of compassion. *Charter for Compassion.* https://charterforcompassion.org/defining-and-understanding-compassion/top-10-scientific-benefits-of-compassion

[6] Weiner, S. J., & Auster, S. (2007). From empathy to caring: Defining the ideal approach to a healing relationship. *Yale Journal of Biology and Medicine, 80*(3), 123-130, https://www.ncbi.nlm.nih.gov/pmc/articles/PMC2248287/

[7] For the nuances in the differences between these three, see Tend Academy. *What is compassion fatigue?* http://www.tendacademy.ca/what-is-compassion-fatigue/

[8] The Lancet. (2015, June 8). Over 95% of the world's population has health problems, with over a third having more than five ailments. *ScienceDaily.* https://www.sciencedaily.com/releases/2015/06/150608081753.htm

[9] Wolin, S., & Wolin, S. (1993). *The resilient self: How survivors of troubled families rise above adversity.* Villard Books.

[10] Levine, S. (2003). Psychological and social aspects of resilience: A synthesis of risks and resources. *Dialogues in Clinical Neuroscience, 5*(3): 273-280. https://doi.org/10.31887/DCNS.2003.5.3/slevine

CHAPTER 8

Giving and Taking

The form of compassion generated in the previous chapter is in a passive state. It is a compassionate feeling associated with a wish that others be free of suffering and its causes. The task at this point is to start to strengthen it and put it to use. A kind of lulling and complacency can occur if compassion remains passive and is not exercised. It is easy for self-centered concerns to retake center stage in the mind and disempower compassion if it remains passive and underutilized.

If you wish to actually engage in helping others, you will need a resilient form of compassion that can withstand the trials and tribulations that go along with directly working with others. For example, as a social worker, I am often met with anger, fear, or mistrust as I try to assess client needs, especially when delving into reactions to difficult circumstances. Sometimes the client might misinterpret my attempts at assessment as blame and react defensively or take offense at well-intentioned attempts to look at their situation from a different perspective. At such times, I often use a meditative strategy called giving and taking to help myself digest harsh feedback and use it to renew my compassionate focus.

Giving and taking is a practice that was formerly kept secret in Tibet. It was passed down privately by teachers to only their most worthy disciples until it almost was lost. Geshe Chekawa Yeshe Dorje (1101–1175), fearing that he was the only person alive who knew of the practice, finally wrote it down in his text "Seven Point Mind Training" and began to teach it openly so that it would survive for future generations. Later it became popularized in Tibet and now has begun to be understood and practiced around the world.

The tradition of mental development in which giving and taking practice is presented is called "exchanging self for others." Exchanging self for others does not mean that I become you and you become me, but rather that I exchange my preoccupation with always putting myself first with a preoccupation about you and what you need. It is a revolution of the mind. Normally, we refer to ourselves throughout each day as the most important person at any given moment, but the strategies put forth in the tradition of exchanging self for others help us to let go of this limiting perspective and begin to put others ahead of self. This might seem a bit scary, and it might elicit thoughts like, "What about me? Will this make me a doormat? Will others take advantage of me?" But as mentioned in previous sections, there is empirical evidence that caring for others benefits us as well as them, so this practice can reinforce self-compassion and self-care. We can also always set boundaries if someone starts to take advantage of our goodwill.

In preparation for the practice of giving and taking, there are four contemplations suggested in the tradition of exchanging self for others. The first is to remember that we are all equal in wanting to be happy and in not wanting to experience even the smallest suffering. The second contemplation has to do with considering the faults of predominantly just cherishing yourself. In Buddhism there is the belief in past and future lives, so the logic that they put forth in this contemplation focuses on how narcissistic self-focus has repeatedly led us to accumulating negative karmic actions, which in turn have caused us to endure repeated rebirth into miserable situations. Other religious traditions also teach in various ways that there are spiritual repercussions for a selfish lifestyle.

For secular audiences, we can simply observe how narcissism affects us and the people around us, how it leads to social rejection and isolation. We can also consider the research on how narcissism has been linked to depression, distress, health problems, anger, loss of satisfaction, and a diminished sense of well-being. Narcissists have a tendency for heightened impulsivity and pleasure seeking, which can lead to risky behaviors such as substance abuse, sexual acting out, aggression, and reckless driving. Narcissism has also been linked with heart disease and poor stress regulation.[1]

Grandiose narcissism, which some assert as a support to happiness, has been tied to underlying fears of rejection and loss of control as well as depression.[2] Otto Kernberg, a psychoanalyst who wrote extensively about ego psychology and object relations, hypothesized that narcissism was at the core of psychopathology.[3] Narcissism can become particularly painful in the later part of life, resulting in what Erik Erickson called "stagnation and self-absorption," producing depression, apathy, and feelings of emptiness.[4] Such contemplations on the faults of self-cherishing are meant to help us question our unexamined and misinformed assumptions about self-focus being self-protective.

The third step is to consider the benefits that come from cherishing others. Tibetans argue that we can realize the benefits of cultivating compassion by comparing ourselves to those who are believed to have become enlightened by dedicating their lives to others. They see such selfless service as the main cause for spiritual awakening. In Christianity, a similar trend of thought can be found in the popular expression, "What would Jesus do?"

From a secular point of view, as mentioned before, researchers have found that compassion training reduces anxiety, increases mindfulness, enhances empathic accuracy, and reduces worry and emotional suppression. Compassionate acts stimulate our brain's pleasure center. We are hardwired for empathy. Empathic children display more moral integrity, courage, imagination, ability to understand the feelings of others, and an enhanced ability to stay calm under pressure. They tend to go on to lead productive lives.[5] We can observe the social benefits of having compassion by watching how compassionate people become surrounded by people who care about them.

Having considered the faults of selfishness and the benefits that come from compassion, the fourth step is to attempt to exchange our habit of considering our own needs as primary with an attitude that sees the well-being of others as primary. This step is difficult to accomplish, but well worth the effort. When the Dalai Lama first visited the United States in 1979, I had the good fortune of being part of an organizing group that hosted a public talk by him at Constitution Hall in Washington, DC. In front of a packed hall filled with dignitaries and political figures, he gave a talk on the need for a compassionate heart. He asked everyone to imagine for a moment that they were a spectator, outside of themselves, observing themselves wanting to be happy and not wanting to suffer. Then he asked that everyone imagine that across from themselves, there were countless beings wishing for happiness and wishing not to suffer. He asked, from a neutral stance, which side was more important, the one individual seeking happiness or the group of countless others seeking happiness?

The stance of logically seeing that the well-being of countless others supersedes the needs of an individual is often voiced in public discourse. For example, coaches tell their players, "There is no I in team." Politicians are expected to consider the public good in their choices, and therefore face condemnation when they cater to big money or special interests. A good doctor is expected to put the needs of their patients ahead of their own needs. Such a selfless stance is possible. With practice, we can begin to replace our recurrent, trollish drone of "What about me?" with a calm, persistent awareness of the needs of others. This mental stance serves as a firm basis for giving and taking practice.

Giving in this context is the imagined sending of one's well-being to others, which ideally is done with a feeling of kindness and a wish that they have happiness and its causes. Taking is an imagined taking away of their hardships and suffering, done with thoughts and feelings of compassion. In practice, taking is done first to imagine others being free from suffering before imagining that they receive the well-being that you send. These two practices are linked with the breath. Breathing in, you imagine inhaling their suffering and its causes. Breathing out, you imagine sending well-being, taking the form of whatever they might need.

If this practice frightens you a bit, it is considered a good sign. Our habitual tendency to dwell in a narcissistic stance is being challenged. The inner troll of selfishness is being directly targeted for reduction. It is natural that self-centered fears and misgivings may arise as you consider such a practice. Therefore, it might help to consider some of the psychological benefits that can come from giving and taking.

Exposure therapy has been shown to be one of the most effective strategies available for treating anxiety disorders.[6] In this approach to treatment, the patient is gradually led, either directly or through imagination, to face their fears. By doing so under safe conditions, the patient gradually becomes used to the things that they previously found frightening, and eventually the fear is replaced by a calm confidence that they can handle whatever the feared scenario might be. This strategy has been used to treat people with a variety of phobias, from fears of spiders and performance anxiety to bigger and more entrenched fears. It has even been effective with people who suffer from post-traumatic stress.[7]

Giving and taking practice can be seen as a form of exposure therapy that is done by imagining taking on suffering and giving away well-being. The goal is to reduce self-centered fears and increase compassionate courage. In order to gradually build up a tolerance for doing this, the practice usually begins by imaging taking on the suffering that you fear might come to you personally in the future, and then to imagine sending well-being to your future self. This gentle approach allows us to feel that we are taking care of ourselves, and therefore tends to reduce self-centered fear. As we acclimate to this beginning level of giving and taking, we can then imagine taking on distress we see in others and expand our practice from there as we feel ready.

By imagining exposing ourselves to suffering rather than avoiding it, we are making ourselves more resilient and courageous. This is in line with the adage that growth happens just beyond our comfort zones. If you allow a socially phobic teen to stay in their room and play video games, their social phobia will just continue to grow and become more paralyzing. If, however, you gradually make the teen come out of their room and interact with others, the social phobia begins to wane in the face of exposure and mastery. Similarly, if allowed to shelter from considering the realities of suffering that others endure, our self-centered tendencies can cocoon into a cozy but stifling room of self-indulgent fantasies that picture only well-being for ourselves without considering the needs of others. Giving and taking practice helps us to step out of that process.

I often use giving and taking practice when faced with situations I would prefer to avoid or when flooded with anxiety about a situation that I cannot change. I have noticed that, instead of heightening my distress, giving and taking has a calming effect.

Brain researchers report that avoiding feared objects increases anxiety, whereas facing them enlists higher levels of brain functioning that have a calming effect.[8] Therefore, giving and taking practice is a handy strategy to enlist when times seem challenging, but also it is useful for daily practice in order to reduce narcissism and enhance compassion.

Another crucial concept that can help dispel apprehension about giving and taking practice is to imagine that as you inhale the suffering, you feed it to your internal source of suffering: the inner troll of self-cherishing. Self-cherishing, since it causes so many problems, can be considered a weed in our inner gardens. In old Tibet, they used to compare self-cherishing to "thief dogs," which were wild dogs that would roam the streets. If you happened to leave your door ajar for a moment, they would scramble in and take away any food that could be found. Similarly, the narcissistic attitude that predominates our thoughts and feelings steals away our potential for expanding compassionate insight and other positive qualities of mind.

By visualizing that we are inhaling suffering and feeding it to the selfish habits of mind, we are purposefully disentangling ourselves from identifying with our narcissism. In psychological terms, this is called making ego syntonic traits ego dystonic. Ego syntonic traits are qualities about ourselves that we feel good about. They are part of our ideal self-image. If someone feels okay about conceiving of themselves as the most important person alive, their narcissism is reinforced by being ego syntonic. In contrast, if we are uncomfortable about a personality trait, and want to disavow it or reduce it, it becomes ego dystonic. By making our habitual self-focus ego dystonic and seeing it as a habit that harms us rather than helps us, we won't mind trying to reduce our narcissism. Instead of identifying with our narcissism, we can identify with our compassionate nature and see ourselves as compassionate people. This will strengthen compassion.

From this perspective, giving and taking practice can be an aid in regaining inner health. When we are fighting an infection, strong medicine is sometimes needed. When fighting the long-term illness of narcissism, the strong medicine of giving and taking practice is needed. Tibetans have different ways of visualizing during giving and taking. For instance, in one tradition they imagine their selfish mind to be like a candle flame and the inhaled suffering to be like a dark cloud of smoke that snuffs it out. In another tradition, they visualize their narcissism as a cloud of darkness in their chest and the inhaled suffering as light that dispels the darkness. I have chosen the latter visualization for the COMPASS presentation of giving and taking because I think Westerners might feel more comfortable with it. But you can adapt the visualization to fit your preferences.

To begin, think of a situation that you currently face or one that is coming to you in the future that is a cause of distress. It could be a conflict, a financial dilemma, an illness, or any other form of unpleasantness that you would prefer to avoid. Instead of avoiding it, allow yourself to picture it in your mind and let yourself feel the discomfort that you have about it. You can imagine the discomfort as a dark cloud in your chest. Usually, such distress is linked with self-focused fears such as, "How will this affect me?" If so, imagine that the self-focus is the underpinning of the discomfort you are feeling.

Next, with self-compassion, imagine that the troublesome situation you are picturing dissolves into light, which you inhale as you breathe. As its light enters you, allow it to dispel the mass of darkness in your chest, filling you with calm light. Imagine that the act of facing your fears fills you with confidence and well-being, that your compassionate courage is renewed. Now imagine that, with kindness, you exhale that well-being in the form of light to your future self, giving you the courage and skills to face whatever challenges lie ahead and helping you to solve the problem or learn how to accept it. Repeat this exercise until you feel that you are ready to expand your focus. As you gain equilibrium with this level of the practice, first try expanding your focus by thinking of other situations in your own future that trouble you. Many of us worry about old age, illness, and all the uncertainties of living, which can be brought into this exercise as focal points for practice.

Once you have contemplated your own personal sources of concern, try to think of someone you know who is going through a difficult time. As you picture that person in front of you, do the same exercise with them. Imagine, with compassion, that their suffering dissolves into light, which you inhale. That inhaled light dispels the darkness of your own self-focused fear, filling you with confidence and well-being. With kindness, you then exhale that well-being as light that takes the form of whatever the person you have visualized in front of you needs in order to face and overcome the problems in their life.

Once becoming comfortable with this level of the practice, you can expand your focus to include family, friends, acquaintances, the community, your state, your country, and even the world. You can extend your contemplation to include everyone. No one is hurt by such a contemplation, and as mentioned above, your own self-focus can be reduced and its influence over your judgment and choices lessened. The resulting feeling of connection and compassion can be profound. I have noticed that when I am facing particularly painful client situations, and I secretly use this visualization to keep myself fully engaged with my clients, it seems to help both my clients and me. My clients seem to feel more supported, and I feel less distress and helplessness in the face of their suffering.

As you become more familiar with giving and taking practice, you can also use it when your mind becomes unsettled during your daily activities. For instance, if you become angered at someone, you can imagine inhaling the problems in the world generated by people's anger as light that dispels your anger and self-focus, filling you with patience and well-being that you exhale to everyone. Similarly, if overwhelmed with attachment, fear, or any other disturbing mental state, you can imagine inhaling problems in the world associated with that mental state, and visualize your internal distress being dispelled, exhaling well-being to others. In this way, you can begin to transform negative experiences into a path to mental peace and compassion.

It is crucial to maintain self-compassion when practicing giving and taking, so that it does not become self-punitive. It would be counterproductive to confuse reducing self-focus with self-hatred and to become overly hard on yourself. We all have a basic drive for self-preservation. Realizing that compassionate insight is an aid to self-preservation and that excessive self-focus detracts from our own well-being can help us to keep a balance with this practice. Our compassionate nature is well worth preserving.

We are in fact being compassionate with ourselves when we reduce the influence that narcissism has over us. It is unrealistic to expect that narcissism will simply go away. It is a tenacious force in the psyche, and reducing it takes time, self-awareness, and perseverance. We also must balance taking care of others with taking care of our own needs. The foundational practices of mindfulness, self-acceptance, self-compassion, and self-care can help us keep on track, so that giving and taking practice is safely and properly integrated as a support in the process of developing compassionate insight.

Participants in the January 3, 2015, presentation of COM-PASS reported the following positive experiences with the giving and taking practice exercise: feelings of acceptance, restful, compassion, a real wish for the happiness of others, peace, breathing to heal, repairing a relationship, personal healing, calm/complete, and a sense that you cannot go wrong by giving to the less fortunate. Negative experiences that were reported included feelings of the impossibility of imagining no suffering, blank thoughts.

Tips for Helping Professionals

Staying Compassionately Engaged in Challenging Client Situations with Giving and Taking

For helping professionals, excessive self-focus interferes with our ability to connect with our clients and thoroughly consider their situations. It can also lead to "the silencing response," which is an avoidance of traumatic or upsetting information that a client might be trying to communicate. The silencing response can manifest by a helping professional becoming distracted, changing the subject, minimizing client experiences and concerns, or even sarcasm. To bring ourselves out of self-focus, connect with our clients' distress, and bring ourselves back into compassionate responses, giving and taking practice can help. It targets self-focused fears for reduction and compassionate courage for enhancement. It is simple to practice once you become used to it, and it can help us keep engaged with our clients even during the most stressful situations.

Section 12 of the appendix, "A COMPASS Handbook for Helping Professionals," offers a detailed discussion about how to bring giving and taking practice into direct practice interactions.

Participants in the January 25, 2015, pilot study of COMPASS at George Mason University reported the following positive experiences of the giving and taking exercise: feelings of "a boost in confidence about myself and my skills as a 'helper,'" compassion for self and others, hope, calm, self-acceptance, return to mindfulness of breathing, curiosity, interest, encouraged at the possibilities, wishfulness, optimism, "a bit of lighter sensation in my body and mind," good "to give positive emotions to myself" and a sense that doing so might help to enhance giving to others, "a great amount of strength in envisioning the ability to help people," power, and love. Negative experiences that were reported included feelings of "a bit of worry about being able to handle others' stuff," "fear of all the negative going in . . . was calmed with the breathing out," "when I don't love and give to myself I become resentful of others, especially those who seek me out for help," "anxiety about my responsibilities," dread, discouraged at others' pain and inability to fix it by this exercise, and "a little bit of disengagement and doubt about the activity."

As mentioned, disengagement and doubts about this exercise, dread, and "fear of all the negative going in" are common reactions upon first considering it. I hope that I have addressed some of these concerns in the discussion on the logic, intended benefits, and procedures for giving and taking. In the short time allotted for explaining the practice in the pilot study, I was not able to go into as much depth about it as I have done here. I hope that the explanations above will allay some of these fears.

The observation from one participant that "when I don't love and give to myself, I become resentful of others" is especially important. It speaks to why self-compassion, self-acceptance, and self-care should be kept as the foundation for the practice of giving and taking. Resentment comes when basic needs go unmet and/or the part of us that is self-focused feels overly impinged. Each of us must judge for ourselves when we have overexerted ourselves and need self-care time. The participant who mentioned "anxiety about my responsibilities" and the other who mentioned worries "about being able to handle others' stuff" share a truth we all encounter when we tread a path of compassion. It is important to monitor ourselves and know when we have overstretched, so that we can set boundaries, seek support, and regain equilibrium.

The participant who mentioned having blank thoughts might have been distancing from the exercise due to feeling overwhelmed, or might have been struggling with difficulties using visualization exercises. If it were the former, a break and rest might have been helpful. If it were the latter, difficulties with visualizing are not uncommon. Some find it easier to use their imagination than others. We can only do as well as we can. Just thinking about taking away someone's suffering and offering them well-being serves a good purpose. Tibetans sometimes use prayers to help them think of turning hardships into compassionate thoughts. For example, one prayer a friend shared with me is, "Through enduring this hardship, may I empty the ocean of sorrow. Through having this moment of well-being, may I fill the ocean of joy."[9] If visualization is difficult for you, such prayers might take its place.

The participant who mentioned the impossibility of imagining no suffering, and the other participant who mentioned discouragement at others' pain and the inability to fix it with this exercise express important truths. Their realistic assessments set the stage for what is discussed in the next two sections of COMPASS. When faced by the reality of suffering, it is easy to feel helpless, ineffectual, and defeated. The exercises up to this point are meant to combat such obstacles internally, but as pointed out, do not get at the question of how to actually make a difference in the lives of others. We can imagine taking away suffering, but when we awaken from our meditation, suffering is still occurring within and around us. We can imagine giving others well-being, but when we encounter them, they are still dealing with the realities of their situations. Therefore, the next sections of COMPASS deal with turning your compassionate focus into an activated form of compassion that leads to actual engagement in helping others. A simple format for practicing giving and taking is as follows:

A. Contemplate the benefit of giving and taking and do a brief practice of mindfulness, equanimity, gratitude, loving-kindness, and compassion.

B. When settled, contemplate the following:

- My tendency to think only about my own needs limits my wish to develop my compassion and has other negative social, emotional, and health effects as well.
- My wish to develop my compassion is based on understanding that to do so will strengthen my social and emotional well-being and my ability to help others. Therefore, I will try for a moment to consider the needs of others before my own.

  - Imagine a future situation you face that is troubling you and picture your fears about it as being like a dark cloud in your chest.
  - Now, with compassion, imagine inhaling the future situation in the form of light. As it enters your chest, it dispels the dark cloud of your fear and fills you with confidence, courage, and a sense of well-being.
  - With loving-kindness, exhale that sense of well-being and confidence in the form of light to yourself in the future, imagining that it gives you confidence and the ability to overcome the troubling situation.
  - Do the same visualization for someone you care about who is going through hardship.
  - Do the same visualization for loved ones and friends.
  - Do the same visualization, extending it to everyone, everywhere.

- Rest in the visualization of everyone being freed from their suffering and filled with well-being, thinking how wonderful it would be if you could actually help others find happiness and freedom from suffering.

Notes

[1] Konrath, S., & Bonadonna, J. P. (2014). Physiological and health-related correlates of the narcissistic personality. In A. Besser (Ed.), *Psychology of Narcissism*. Nova Science Publishers.

[2] Jauk, E., & Kaufman, S. B. (2018). The higher the score, the darker the core: The nonlinear association between grandiose and vulnerable narcissism. *Frontiers in Psychology, 9*, 1305. https://doi.org/10.3389/fpsyg.2018.01305

[3] Kernberg, O. F. (1975). *Borderline conditions and pathological narcissism*. Jason Aronson.

⁴ For a discussion on this, see Marcia, J., & Josselson, R. (2013). Eriksonian personality research and its implications for psychotherapy. *Journal of Personality*, *81*(6), 617-629. https://doi.org/10.1111/jopy.12014

⁵ See chapter 3, notes 8-14.

⁶ See Norton, P. J., & Price, E. C. (2007). A meta-analytic review of adult cognitive-behavioral treatment outcome across the anxiety disorders. *Journal of Nervous and Mental Disease*, *195*(6), 521-531. https://doi.org/10.1097/01.nmd.0000253843.70149.9a; and also Tolin, D. F. (2010). Is cognitive-behavioral therapy more effective than other therapies? A meta-analytic review. *Clinical Psychology Review*, *30*(6), 710-720. https://doi.org/10.1016/j.cpr.2010.05.003

⁷ See Becker, C. B., Darius, E., & Schaumberg, K. (2007). An analog study of patient preferences for exposure versus alternative treatments for posttraumatic stress disorder. *Behaviour Research and Therapy*, *45*, 2861-2873. See also Foa, E. B., Zoellner, L. A., Feeny, N. C., Hembree, E. A., & Alvarez-Conrad, J. (2002). Does imaginal exposure exacerbate PTSD symptoms? *Journal of Consulting and Clinical Psychology*, *70*(4), 1022-1028. https://doi.org/10.1037//0022-006x.70.4.1022; and also Foa, E. B., Hembree, E. A., Cahill, S. P., Rauch, S. A., Riggs, D. S., Feeny, N. C., & Yadin, E. (2005). Randomized trial of prolonged exposure for posttraumatic stress disorder with and without cognitive restructuring: outcome at academic and community clinics. *Journal of Consulting and Clinical Psychology*, *73*(5), 953-964. https://doi.org/10.1037/0022-006X.73.5.953

⁸ See https://www.brainfacts.org/Thinking-Sensing-and-Behaving/Emotions-Stress-and-Anxiety/2018/Does-Facing-Your-Fears-Help-You-Get-Over-Them-080118

⁹ Thanks to Ani Tenzin Lhamo for this version of the prayer.

CHAPTER 9

Activation

If wishes were to come true, everyone would now be free of suffering and its causes because you visualized it happening. But as you can see if you look around, suffering is still alive and wreaking havoc all over the world. This does not mean that it is useless to wish for suffering to end and others to enjoy well-being. Such wishes propel the motivations of doctors, nurses, scientists, and others involved in trying to find solutions for humanity's problems. The pioneers of germ theory, vaccines, antiviral medications, immunotherapy, and other advances in medicine all worked tirelessly to find solutions to problems that were previously misunderstood and unaddressed. They did not give up. Their wish to understand and find solutions kept them going, and we are all better off for their efforts.

So how do we take our budding wish to help others and activate it into a strength that cannot be thwarted by discouragement and doubt? How do we fully embody our wish to be a compassionately engaged person and to make this world a better place? In the Tibetan traditions of mental training, the next step is called the "pure exceptional attitude."[1] It is a statement to oneself by oneself that "I will take personal responsibility to free others from suffering and its causes." In the context of COMPASS, it is an acceptance of responsibility to do one's best—a firm determination that, no matter what comes, "I will work toward helping others."

By making such a commitment to ourselves, we are fully identifying ourselves with our compassionate core values and choosing to embrace them. This process of defining self based on core values is discussed in Acceptance Commitment Therapy (ACT), developed by Stephen C. Hayes in 1982, which integrates cognitive and behavior therapy.[2] ACT has been extensively studied and empirically validated. It points out how we entangle ourselves emotionally by fusing with our thoughts, judging our reactions, avoiding discomfort, and thus defining ourselves in limiting ways based on our reactions to situations. To counter this trend, an ACT approach suggests defusing from our thoughts by being fully present and becoming accepting of, but not identified with, our thoughts and feelings through mindfulness practice. Then, upon seeing that our sense of self is based on changing contexts, we can define our sense of self by discovering our core values and making a commitment to let them guide our decisions and direction.[3]

This process is like being on a diet and being tempted by a piece of chocolate cake. If we dwell on our urges to eat the cake, there is a likelihood that we will cave and eat the cake. However, if we can recall our commitment to our diet and our reasons for it, we have a good chance of keeping on track. We can accept that we are having an urge to eat the cake while also committing to our healthy choice to forgo it for now. This requires some self-discipline.

In this case, the activation exercise is used to make a commitment to helping others, to commit to compassionate action in thought, word, and deed. This commitment helps us fully identify with our compassion, which increases its influence on us and our adherence to pursuing a compassionate direction in life. There is a kind of inner strength and fortitude in people who know their direction. In a way, it makes things clear. If we are facing a dilemma, it simplifies our choices by ruling out options that could be hurtful to self and others. It compels us to take the high road. Even if we feel an impulse calling us toward a destructive direction, by recalling our commitment to compassion we can accept how we are feeling while simultaneously choosing to follow what we know is truer to our values.

As mentioned, we can make our commitment simply by thinking, "I will work toward helping others." Recommitting to this thought daily strengthens it over time and helps us to identify with engaged compassion. In the Tibetan tradition of mental training, five strengths are mentioned to help practitioners be successful living compassionate lives. The first is called the strength of intention. Intention is required for any task that we choose to undertake. For instance, if you choose to make a cup of tea, that intention is what leads you to heat up water, soak the tea bag, and then enjoy your cup of tea. Similarly, when we wake each morning, we can set out an intention for our day by thinking, "I will try to work on carrying my compassion throughout my activities today and try to make a positive impact on the people I encounter."

The second strength is called the strength of habituation. By setting a time to meditate each morning, you can renew your motivation and make it increasingly firm. Coming back to meditation for brief periods throughout each day brings familiarity and makes your mind accustomed to the COMPASS exercises until they become second nature. Then your compassion becomes natural, activated, and ready as you enter your daily activities.

The third strength, the strength of virtuous actions, is to purposefully enter into positive actions based on your compassion. This can be done like a mitzvah, which is a Jewish tradition of doing positive or charitable acts. It can be fun to put this into practice. As you go through your day, you will see situations that could benefit from your help. Instead of letting such opportunities pass you by, you can let your compassion guide you into action. Maybe it's as small a thing as complimenting someone for one of their positive qualities. Or maybe it's a bit bigger action like offering some food to someone who is homeless or helping to de-escalate an argument between colleagues. As you engage in such activities, your compassion begins to have an impact on the world around you.

The fourth strength is called the strength of purification, which is a self-assessment at the end of each day to see how you did. If you feel you made mistakes, admit them to yourself and set your intention to learn from them, so that your future attempts go better. If you feel you did something well, let yourself feel good about it. This strengthens your wish to continue trying. And finally, the fifth strength is called the strength of dedication, which is to mentally dedicate your positive motives and actions from your day toward the deepening of your compassionate insight. These five strengths can help your practice of compassion become firm and steady, and for compassion to define your life's purpose.

We can see the impact of everyday heroes in the lives of others. These are people who rise up spontaneously to help others when the need arises. Jesse Lewis, a six-year-old at Sandy Hook Elementary whose last act before Adam Lanza took his life was to yell to his classmates to run, was such a hero. His mother, Scarlet Lewis, who in the aftermath of her terrible loss decided to dedicate her life to teaching others to choose love instead of hate, is such a hero.[4] First responders, teachers, hospital workers, and ordinary citizens who step forward to help others are all heroes. We too can become heroes by choosing to follow our compassion and by engaging in acts each day to benefit others.

When we act on our kindness and compassion:

- It makes us feel good, causing a release of endorphins and oxytocin.
- There is more likelihood that our activities will be successful.
- Our actions help others while also boosting our own mental health.
- It causes more cooperation in our social networks, encouraging others to help.
- We receive the psychological and physiological benefits that come from compassion.[5]

If we do not make this world a better place, then who will? Whose job is it? It is up to each of us, and we each have a particular role to play. Each of us has unique qualities that can be put into use for the betterment of ourselves and those around us. One of my teachers used to say, "It takes many straws to make a broom." Similarly, collectively, people with goodwill working together can have a positive impact on this world. It is up to us.

Participants in the January 3, 2015, presentation of COMPASS reported the following positive experiences after having been introduced to the activation exercise: feelings of being able to make a difference and wanting to write a list to be accomplished and sticking to it. Negative experiences that were reported included feelings of not knowing where to begin. Participants in the pilot study at George Mason University on January 25, 2015, reported positive experiences after this exercise that included feelings of agreement with the activity, satisfaction, hope, pleasure, and "a push to live life fully." Negative experiences that were reported included feelings of "a bit of self-punishment" for wanting change without acting.

Tips for Helping Professionals

Maintaining Self-Care and Active Compassion in Crisis and Disaster Situations

Relief workers and first responders in crisis and disaster situations are at high risk for secondary traumatic stress and burnout. The intensity and duration of exposure to traumatic situations contributes directly to the severity of impact on response staff. The sense of helplessness and loss that first responders feel when faced with disasters can be overwhelming. Therefore, emergency response professionals should be trained ahead of time about compassion fatigue and ways to guard against it. Supervisors need to think ahead about ways to provide appropriate supports and training for frontline staff. Self-compassion and self-care strategies are essential supports in this effort. Compassion-building strategies can be a useful resource for workers between shifts to help in regaining equilibrium and motivation.

Detailed recommendations for emergency response staff, including ways that compassion-building techniques can help, are discussed in section 13 of the appendix, "A COMPASS Handbook for Helping Professionals."

It's hard to tell if the person who felt "a bit of self-punishment" for wanting change without acting felt pressured by the activity itself or if their feelings were due to other internal dynamics, but they raise an interesting point. Some of these exercises might bring feelings of guilt and/or memories of times when we felt pressured by others to enlist in activities that we would rather have avoided. It is important that each of us go at our own pace, according to our own sensibilities. If we are not yet wishing to activate our compassion into actions, perhaps cultivating more passive forms of mental stability and compassion is more appropriate for the time being. It will backfire if we push ourselves to the point that we begin to resent our practice. At all times, it is good to be mindful and friendly toward yourself as you try to expand your compassionate focus.

The participant who reported not knowing where to begin with their compassionate activities brings up another good point. There is simply so much need in the world, and so many options as to how we might help, that it can be daunting to choose a direction to channel our activities. A simple response to this question about where to begin is to start with whoever you encounter and try to become more compassionate with the people you meet in your daily life. An additional strategy is to seek a goal for your compassion, which is the final topic of the core compassion skills in COMPASS. When our compassion finds its true goal, we have found our inner compass to guide us through life's wilderness. A simple exercise for generating activated compassion is as follows:

A. Contemplate the benefit of activating your compassion and do a brief practice of mindfulness, equanimity, gratitude, kindness, compassion, and giving and taking.
B. When settled, contemplate the following:

- Though I have imagined taking away the sufferings of myself and others, and then imagined us all filled with well-being, in reality the world is still full of suffering.
- If I do not accept any responsibility for making this world a better place, then whose job is it?
- If I want this world to improve, it is important that I do my part.
- Generate and hold the thought, "It is my responsibility to improve the conditions of myself and others."

Notes

[1] Tibetan transliteration: *hlagbsam rnamdag* (pronounced hlaksam namdak), translated here as pure exceptional attitude, is considered the direct cause of the mind of awakening (Sanskrit: *bodhicitta*), which is the aspiration for enlightenment in order to help all beings.
[2] Hayes, S. C., Strosahl, K. D., & Wilson, K. G. (2012). *Acceptance and commitment therapy: The process and practice of mindful change* (2nd ed.). Guilford Press.
[3] Ibid.
[4] Lewis, S. (2013). *Nurturing, healing love.* Hay House. See also https://choose lovemovement.org/.
[5] The Honey Foundation. *Kindness research and info: More research and case studies about the impact of kindness and compassion.* https://www.honeyfoun dation.org/research-info/

CHAPTER 10

Goal-Focused Compassion

By activating your compassion, you are ready to choose your own unique way of expressing it. But, as mentioned, finding a direction can be a puzzle because there are simply so many ways that we can express and enact compassion in the world. In the Tibetan tradition of mental training, compassion is directed at the spiritual goal of becoming enlightened in order to liberate all beings from suffering. This is called the mind of awakening (Sanskrit: *bodhicitta*) and is the fundamental motivation of bodhisattvas, spiritual beings who embody this wish and the activities it inspires. For the purposes of translating this aspect of mental training into a secular approach that everyone can use, no matter what their beliefs, I call it goal-focused compassion and suggest individual inclination as the key to finding one's own personal direction for compassion.

We all have different inclinations, perspectives, beliefs, assessments of reality, proclivities, and passions. Tapping into these brings out our full potential and the tremendous energy we have within us to pursue our goals. Erik Erikson (1902–1994), a psychoanalyst who developed a theory about the stages of life, noticed that we all go through an assessment period in our teen years about who we are, how we fit into the world, and what we want to become. He called this stage "identity vs. role confusion," which is sometimes also called identity formation and identity diffusion.

Erikson saw identity formation as being based on an individual's biological, psychological, and social context. Sometimes, people develop a negative identity stance in reaction to their context, as when a child of an overly controlling parent rebels by acting out and becoming defiant. In identity diffusion, rather than defining oneself, many of us drift along, letting ourselves be defined by whatever circumstances and people we encounter. In the case of role foreclosure, a teen allows themselves to be molded by a strong parental figure into becoming someone very different from who they truly want to be.[1]

My father went through the latter struggle. He was raised by a strong military man, who went on to become a diplomat and a high government official. My grandfather raised my father to follow in his footsteps. But my father was an incredibly creative, intelligent, and sensitive human being who did not comfortably fit into his father's mold. After my grandfather died, my father gave up his law practice and began to pursue artistic expression. This was an interest he had found during his childhood, and something he was good at. He went on to become a quite successful artist and was much happier following his natural inclinations.[2]

To find a comfortable fit between who we are at heart and the context of our lives, we need time and self-awareness. Erikson called this process a moratorium, which ideally takes place in adolescence when we can assess ourselves and our fit with the world.[3] However, we can reopen this process of self-assessment at any time. By noticing our natural interests and inclinations, we can link them to our emerging compassion as we consider how we want to direct our efforts at helping others.

I chose to become a social worker because it is a career based on compassionate action. I also have always been fascinated with trying to understand people, how they think, how they feel, how they see the world. I wanted my working life to be helpful to others. In addition, my ability to listen to people and understand their needs and intentions has been a relative strength. So combining these factors, I embarked on educating myself and building a career in social work. Now, nearing the end of that career, I have no regrets about my choice. If I had let myself be foreclosed into another career path by well-meaning friends and family who told me things such as "that's a depressing profession" and "you'll be poor if you go into social work; you should do something that earns more money," I doubt that my working life would have been as productive and fulfilling as it has been.

Each of us must choose based on our own inclinations and self-assessment, for we are the ones who will have to live with our choices. So my suggestion is to give yourself time, a moratorium, in which you see where your inclinations and compassionate actions take you. Which expressions of compassion seem significant to you? In what sorts of compassionate activity do you feel most fulfilled and do others seem most benefited? What sorts of change do you think are most important? What kinds of changes do you want to see happen in the world? What are the realities of your livelihood that you need to consider? What kinds of external supports are available to you for pursuing activities that interest you?

One principle to keep in mind as you consider such questions in your pursuit of goal-focused compassion is the importance of being realistic. If I were to make my main goal to eliminate war, it would be a noble goal, but very hard to accomplish. There is a likelihood that I would eventually feel defeated, which might lead to discouragement and giving up. On the other hand, if I were to tweak my goal a bit by aspiring to bring peace to my own mind while pursuing making the world a more peaceful place, there is much more likelihood that I might see signs of progress over time. The realism comes by seeing which factors we can control and which factors are simply beyond our ability to control.

Therefore, there are many internally focused goals one might choose. For example: "I want to become a more patient person." Or "I want to increase my knowledge about medicine and how to care for people suffering from illness." Or "I want to become more generous with what I own in order to help people struggling financially." The list of options for what you might choose to work on is vast. Coupling internal goals with external objectives is optimal because doing so offers a combined approach of helping self and others at the same time. An example of a coupled goal is, "I want to increase my insight into how my own mind works while I also work on helping others gain more insight into how their minds work."

Having a goal and purpose in life is good for our health and well-being. One study by the Centers for Disease Control and Prevention found that four out of ten Americans do not have any sense of meaning or purpose in life.[4] Researchers have found that having a purpose in life is linked to positive mental and physical health outcomes. People report higher life satisfaction and sense of well-being when they feel their life has meaning. Depression is lessened; self-esteem and resilience are thus enhanced.[5] While the pursuit of happiness is good, if it is done solely for oneself it tends to lead to more narcissism, thus ultimately defeating our pursuit of happiness.[6] Therefore, developing our own mission statement for our life's direction gives us an internal compass with which we can keep ourselves on track even in the toughest of times.

In Erikson's model of human development, the penultimate developmental crisis we all face in life is called "generativity vs. stagnation." Generativity refers to efforts to help oneself and others. From the viewpoint of compassion, it is perhaps the most important dilemma because it determines how useful our lives will be to ourselves and to others. We can help others in each phase of life, but once we have established our identities and achieved a degree of intimacy, we can afford to devote ourselves more fully to the service of others.

Truly generative people balance self-care with caring for others. As their sphere of who they are helping expands, so do stress levels, and therefore self-care is crucial. However, many people lapse into a sort of pseudo-generativity in which they care for others outwardly while covertly doing so to receive favors or reciprocal care from them.[7] For example, an aging relative might offer to make his nephew a beneficiary in his will, while not so subtly implying that this would be contingent on the nephew's catering to his whims and needs. In short, such tainted overt acts of care are just an extension of narcissistic preoccupation.

Stagnant, self-absorbed individuals indulge themselves with all the care a mother would afford her only child. We can see this in many people who amass a fortune, only to hoard it and then procure the most expensive and fancy items they can find in attempts to feel self-worth. However, often such individuals find that they feel increasingly worthless and empty, lapsing into depression and apathy.[8] This is the legacy of following narcissism. It seems that it has your best interests at heart, but it deceives you. If you have been vigilant over time in reducing your narcissism and in increasing your compassionate insight, by the time you reach middle age and embark on your own missions of generativity, you are more likely to find increasing satisfaction and well-being. Research has shown that prosocial goals in midlife help us:

- find purpose and meaning in life;
- enhance our cognitive abilities;
- improve health, dexterity, and longevity; and
- produce psychological well-being by developing:
  - empathy
  - wisdom
  - generativity
  - gratitude
  - joy and happiness[9]

Participants in the January 3, 2015, COMPASS training following the exercise on goal-focused compassion reported the positive experiences of the possibility of doing something and remedying previous inaction. Negative experiences that were reported included feelings of fear of failure. Participants in the January 25, 2015, pilot study of COMPASS at George Mason University following the exercise on goal-focused compassion reported positive experiences including feelings of hope, encouragement, and empowerment. Negative experiences that were reported included feelings of "just a bit of frustration because I put pressure on myself to come up with the 'perfect' goal to live my life with."

Fears of failure are frequently a response to attempts at major habit changes. Many of us predict that we will give up and return to whatever pattern of behavior we are used to should we be tempted to make a change. One style of counseling that has arisen in response to this pattern is called Motivational Interviewing.[10] It was developed in the context of helping people with substance abuse issues to develop a motivation for sobriety. Researchers noticed that when counselors used the traditional model of confrontation, clients tended to resist, dig in their heels, and take away their own addictive logic rather than consider the therapist's advice. This is an important truth to consider when working with your own motivation for change.

Tips for Helping Professionals

Finding Hardiness in Your Compassion and in Your Sense of Mission

Goals give direction to our efforts. They help us prioritize and clarify what is essential when making tough decisions. They also provide motivation, enhance productivity, and increase confidence. Forming career goals that increase compassion satisfaction can help sustain us when facing adversity in the workplace. Eventually, resilience in bringing ourselves back on course when challenging situations block or distress us will contribute to a hardiness in our cores that will fortify us and ward off compassion fatigue.

In section 14 of the appendix, "A COMPASS Handbook for Helping Professionals," there is an overview of how the core compassion skills can be used to bolster a resilient and compassionate career focus.

Our internal dialogue is instrumental in either pulling us toward healthy decisions and positive change or in shutting us down and encouraging us to slide back into old habits. Self-defeating logic like "this is too hard" or "I can't do this, it takes too much effort" can derail us from goals we have set for ourselves. Corrective self-messages like "one step at a time" and "I can spend at least a little time today on this" encourage progress and the development of new habits. As mentioned before, it is an important skill to set an intention each morning to work toward your compassionate goal and then try to stick to it during the day.

Motivational interviewers just listen with acceptance to their clients as they talk about their habits. The interviewer listens carefully for signs of "change talk." Often, when people talk about their habits, you will hear "sustain talk" in which they justify or even glorify their habits. This is a sign of precontemplation, which is a stage lacking in a motivation to change. When clients begin to talk about problems they experience due to their habits, counselors notice it as "change talk" and begin to point out the discrepancy between where things are for the client and where the client is saying they want things to be. This helps the client slowly move toward contemplation, a stage of considering real change.[11]

Similarly, we can listen to our internal dialogue with attention to the parts of ourselves that want to develop more compassionate insight versus the parts of ourselves that just want to stay the same. With a little self-encouragement, we can gently nurture our motivation for change until it begins to show up in actual changes in our actions. Once we begin to experience the benefits of engagement in compassionate activities, the ensuing rewards will motivate us to continue our journeys toward our compassionate goals. We are destined to fail at something only if we never give ourselves a chance to try it in the first place.

The participant who mentioned frustration in trying to find the "perfect" goal for their life brings up another important point. It can be difficult to settle on a single direction for your compassionate efforts, and that is okay. Perhaps your goals will change frequently, or perhaps they will gradually become more clear, steady, and focused. Because they are unique to you, you get to decide what they are and when you want to change them. When you have a sense that you have not yet found the perfect life goals for yourself, it might just mean that you have more questioning and searching to do. As you look for a goal that resonates with your core values, you can still try other shorter-term compassionate directions and activities in your search for something that captivates you. A simple exercise for generating goal-focused compassion is as follows:

A. Contemplate the benefits of goal-focused compassion and do a brief practice of mindfulness together with a brief contemplation on the equanimity, gratitude, kindness, compassion, giving and taking, and activation exercises.

B. When settled, contemplate the following:

- To sustain compassionate efforts over time, it is important to develop my internal capacities and begin to put my compassion into action.
- Take a moment to consider what internal qualities you want to make stronger and what direction in life is important to you.
- Set a goal to develop the qualities you identify as important to be of best help to yourself and others. Also consider what types of compassionate activities might be of interest to you.

- Hold your goals single-pointedly while thinking, "I will develop these capacities and enter into these activities in order to benefit myself and others."

Consolidating the Core Compassion Skills

We have gone over several exercises at this point, and it might seem a bit daunting when you consider incorporating all of them into a daily practice. So in the beginning, you might want to focus on just a few and then slowly build your familiarity with the others. At the end of the appendix, "A COMPASS Handbook for Helping Professionals," I have put the exercises in order so that you can have an easy guide for daily practice. My suggestion is to follow your own pace and inclinations as you try them out. While there is an emotional logic to how they are sequenced and how they build on each other, you do not necessarily have to practice them in order. You can try one at a time if you wish.

As you become more familiar with the exercises, you might find that sequencing them in order has a more profound effect on your emotional states, and that it is easier to develop a strong sense of goal-focused compassion by the end of your meditation sessions by following the sequence. When they become natural and habitual, they might resurface during your daily activities and refresh your compassionate courage. If so, this is a sign that you are beginning to integrate them. The key is regular, consistent practice. Make friends with your practice by keeping it short and sweet at first, only lengthening it as you feel comfortable in doing so.

Notes

[1] For an overview of Erikson's theory about identity formation, see Kroger, J. (2017). Identity formation in adolescence and adulthood. *Social Psychology Online.* https://doi.org/10.1093/acrefore/9780190236557.013.54

[2] Hurley, R. (2019). *Celebrating the richness of reality: The life and art of Wilson Hurley.* Fresco Books.

[3] Kroger, J. (2017).

[4] Kobau, R., Sniezek, J., Zack, M. M., Lucas, R. E., & Burns A. (2010). Well-being assessment: An evaluation of well-being scales for public health and population estimates of well-being among US adults. *Health and Well-Being, 2*(3), 272-297. https://doi.org/10.1111/j.1758-0854.2010.01035.x

[5] Smith, E. E. (January 19, 2013). There's more to life than being happy: Meaning comes from more complex things than being happy. *The Atlantic.* https://www.theatlantic.com/health/archive/2013/01/theres-more-to-life-than-being-happy/266805/

[6] Kashdan, T. (2011). The problem with happiness. *Huffington Post.* https://www.huffingtonpost.com/todd-kashdan/whats-wrong-with-happines_b_740518.html

[7] Marcia, J., & Josselson, R. (2013). Eriksonian personality research and its implications for psychotherapy. *Journal of Personality, 81*(6), 617-629. https://doi.org/10.1111/jopy.12014

[8] Ibid.

[9] Suttie, J. (2018). How to find your purpose in midlife. *Greater Good Magazine.* https://greatergood.berkeley.edu/article/item/how_to_find_your_purpose_in_midlife

[10] Miller, W. R., & Rollnick, S. (2013). *Motivational interviewing: Helping people change.* Guilford Press.

[11] Ibid.

CHAPTER 11

Core Practices for Developing Analytical Insight

All the practices presented up to this point are designed to help reduce narcissism and enhance a calm, focused sense of compassion. They are conducive to emotional well-being. As you become accustomed to them, you will be shaping your sense of identity in a positive way of your own choosing. At first this might only seem superficial, but with time it can grow deeper. There is a quote that pertains to this that is often attributed to the great psychoanalyst Carl Gustav Jung (1875–1961), "I am not what happened to me. I am what I choose to become." Whether or not Jung said this might be contested, but its truth rings clear.

Unexamined, our pasts can define who we are and how we respond to our present circumstances. This is because the reactions that we have had to past events and the conclusions about ourselves and the world that we form as we go through life's experiences are all carried with us.[1] They begin to color our perceptions of ourselves and our world just like sunglasses color the appearances of the sky and scenery when we wear them. Our cognitive constructs about reality can help us navigate through the complexity of the world, but they can also limit us and distort our perceptions. When they do the latter, they are called cognitive distortions.[2]

Insight, as I am using it in the context of COMPASS, can be defined as the ability to see through and dispel cognitive distortions in order to gain a more realistic sense of ourselves and our situations. In particular, the analytical exercises in COMPASS focus on identifying and uprooting distortions about how we see ourselves because such distortions can limit or even undermine our progress in developing compassion and accomplishing our goals.

Take for example a young child, who is often left on her own due to her parents having to work multiple jobs. She might develop a sense of being unimportant or even unworthy due to circumstances. This distortion about herself could then continue to affect how she sees herself in other situations as she grows older, leading to low self-esteem, feeling undervalued, and resulting in depression. This kind of cognitive distortion affects many of us. I call it a negative or diminished sense of self, which can sap motivation by leaving us feeling helpless and avoidant. A variety of problems have been associated with low self-esteem including depression, anxiety, suicide, obesity, substance abuse, joblessness, financial difficulties, and higher rates of criminal behavior.[3]

Another kind of distortion of self can arise when someone's good fortune turns into feelings of entitlement. Take for example a young boy who is indulged by his loving parents who provide him whatever he wants, telling him he is stronger and better than his peers. There is a possibility that he might grow up feeling entitled and superior to others around him. I call this an overly positive or inflated sense of self. Such a distortion could lead to feeling invulnerable and could result in him becoming inconsiderate, self-indulgent, and/or having unrealistic expectations about how he should be treated. Such a stance becomes an obstacle to developing empathy and compassion. Grandiosity and entitlement are associated with different kinds of self-serving behaviors, but in general, an entitled view of self has been linked to unethical behavior in which one's own needs are promoted at the detriment of the needs of others.[4]

Both extremes in perceptions of self, diminished and inflated, are based on circumstance, and therefore are not real in the sense of being valid perceptions. They are conjured based on time, place, status, and other factors beyond the control of the individual who experiences them. And yet, because of our innate tendency to define our sense of self based on what happens to us, we construct a sense of ourselves based upon our reactions to situational factors that we encounter in our lives. A bad string of events can diminish our sense of self. A lucky chain of circumstances can elevate it. Our diminished or inflated sense of self then shapes our feelings, thoughts, and behaviors. Rather than being defined by circumstance, we can choose to take over this process by defining ourselves based on our compassionate goals.

To accomplish this task, we need to develop our insight. Insight comes by peering into the deeper levels of our mental functioning and keeping track of how we see our ourselves as we go through life, looking for and dispelling distortions when we find them. This process can be likened to walking next to a friend. Part of your mind is focused on where you are going, and another part of your mind is aware of your friend walking next to you. Similarly, during your daily activities, a part of your mind can monitor how you are seeing yourself as you encounter various challenges during your day.

You might notice that a solid sense of indignation and self-righteousness arises if someone falsely accuses you of something. At such times, many of us will get a clear mental picture of who we imagine ourselves to be along with thoughts about how to vindicate ourselves. Or, if you happen to be credited with an accomplishment, a bit of pride might ensue together with a positive image of yourself. On the other hand, if we encounter several setbacks and disappointments during the day, we might start to despair and have a sense of ourselves as being ineffectual or helpless. It is important to remember that all these fluctuations in how we see ourselves are based on concepts that our minds conjure in reaction to circumstance. They do not constitute something real, only something imagined.

The good news is that, since these self-images are imagined, we can also dispel them and then reimagine them as wished. We can develop a sense of playfulness with them in which we determine which parts of them to hold onto and which parts to let go. Doing the groundwork in developing your goals and a sense of direction in which you want to go in life helps you determine what attributes about yourself are important. The fundamental question is: What kind of person do I want to become? By imagining yourself as the kind of person you aspire to be, you are forming a concept of yourself based on your own willpower.

Some might object to this and say, "Just be yourself, anything else isn't genuine." But are the fluctuations in your sense of self based on circumstances a genuine reflection of who you really are?

Aren't your core values more genuine and constant than your fluctuating mental pictures of yourself? By identifying with and defining yourself based on your core values, aren't you being truly genuine? By identifying with your core values, you are coming closer to the person you intend to be. You are developing a solid internal compass to come back to when life throws you off course.

Values are convictions that we hold dear about how things should be. They inform our sense of right and wrong. Sometimes we might develop our values based on how we were raised, what religion we were exposed to, or things we learned in school, from friends, and via the media. However, sometimes values also seem to naturally arise from within us. For example, when I was about seven years old, I had a dream one night that I had killed my brother. I woke up horrified, with a deep remorse and guilt. I was relieved the next morning to find that my brother was alive and well, that it had just been a dream, but it took days before I felt okay again. My deep-seated sense that it is wrong to take life has eventually become a guiding force for me, and to this day, I try to preserve and respect life.

My father went through something similar. When he was young, he had a special colt to look after and became quite fond of him. However, the horse was injured, developed tetanus, and had to be put down. My grandfather, in his efforts to make my father more of a man, insisted that my father be the one to shoot the horse, which my father did.[5] However, my father never wanted another horse after that, and once he was grown and parenting my siblings and me, he refused to teach us how to hunt. His natural values seemed to lead him toward protecting life rather than toward taking it.

So part of the task of finding your inner compass is to discern your true values. You might choose to put aside some of the values you unwittingly absorbed during your upbringing, or you might reaffirm them as you consider what you want to take forward. As you practice the exercises in this book, from mindfulness up to goal-focused compassion, you will start to sense what resonates within you. Perhaps you resonate with the exercise of equanimity most easily, or perhaps kindness comes more naturally. As you find dissonance and internal images of yourself that conflict with your core values, the analytical exercise in this section might help you to resolve them and to build a more integrated and resilient sense of self based on your chosen direction for your life.

The three core analytical exercises of COMPASS are designed to be done in a single session. These three steps are:

1. identifying distorted self-concepts,
2. analyzing and debunking them, and
3. reidentifying with one's compassionate goals.

Ideally, it is good to start with a brief session of mindfulness followed by briefly reviewing the core compassion skills until renewing your sense of goal-focused compassion. This sets a good basis because at the end of the analytical exercise you will want to reidentify with your compassionate goals.

Identifying Distorted Self-Concepts

In one way, we can say that all self-concepts are distortions in that they are built on conceptual thoughts. Since concepts are mental constructs, their very nature is that they are approximations of reality, not reality itself. Reality is complex and constantly changing. Concepts are a bit like internal maps that we create to help us navigate in the real world. The more accurate our concepts, the better our chances for successful interactions with the world.

Take, for example, entering a new job. If you approach your new job with an idea that you will be evaluated for how well you fit in and do your job, that accurate idea will help you to be careful to learn the requirements of the new tasks you will be expected to do, listen closely to what your new boss and colleagues tell you about what is important to accomplish, and strive to integrate this information with each task you face. Then there will be a likelihood that you will keep your job and perhaps even eventually be promoted. If, however, you approach the new job with a distorted idea that you can collect the paycheck but disregard the tasks at hand, you will likely soon be out of work. The mistaken idea is too far out of line with reality, and it will sabotage your ability to function in the new work setting.

Similarly, as discussed previously, inaccurate ideas about self can get in the way of optimal functioning. Diminished or inflated concepts of self can interfere with our ability to develop and maintain compassionate insight. These distortions tend to arise as we face the ups and downs of daily life and the various ways we feel as we go through them. In order to try to identify distortions in self-concept, I find it helpful to begin by becoming aware of whatever emotional issues seem to be predominating my thoughts and feelings as I am sitting down to meditate. Often, it is possible to trace the origin of strong emotions to events that have occurred or to future events that I might be facing.

Tips for Helping Professionals

Weeding Out Self-Defeating Thoughts

It is important for helping professionals to self-monitor thoughts that can lead to burnout or vicarious trauma. Our nervous system has a negativity bias, which can cause us to focus more on negatives than positives. If left unchecked, this can lead us into negative rumination about ourselves and our work, especially if we are repeatedly facing challenging cases. To combat this trend, it can help to analyze and debunk distorted thoughts about ourselves and about our clients when they arise. An accurate appraisal of ourselves, our capacities, our clients, the realities of their situations, and about what might help is essential for effective intervention and for maintaining our own well-being as we provide care.

Section 15 of the appendix, "A COMPASS Handbook for Helping Professionals," explores this topic in more detail and suggests ways to recognize and dispel cognitive distortions.

For example, suppose a friend or loved one has said something insensitive or unflattering, leaving you feeling disrespected and angered. As you sit with those feelings and remember the encounter, you can notice that behind the emotions, or mixed in with them, are concepts about yourself. Thoughts such as, "How dare they say that about me" might come up. Often, people get caught up in internal dialogues between themselves and their imagined antagonist when remembering negative encounters, but in this context, rather than allowing that to happen, focus on the image of yourself that comes to mind. Notice how your concept of yourself appears in your thoughts. The more clearly you can picture that image of yourself the better.

Next, ask yourself about whether the image of yourself in this context fits or does not fit with your image of the kind of person you want to be. If there is a discrepancy between the currently held self-image of yourself and the image that you have for yourself within the context of your compassionate goals, you have found the distortion in self-image to use for the next step of the exercise. So try to keep that distorted self-concept in mind as you move to the next section. It will make the exercise more effective if you can also remember the emotions you are having in connection with that self-image. For instance, if you are feeling angered, hurt, and/or betrayed, you can keep those associated feelings in mind as well.

Analyzing and Debunking
Distortions in Self-Concept

While mentally holding the distortion in self-image from the first step of the exercise, the second step is to begin to analyze it with a corner of your mind. One Tibetan text likens this process to "a tiny fish flashing about in a lucid pond and not disturbing it."[6] The analytical part of the mind, like a tiny fish, subjects the distortion in self-image to a thorough analysis without disturbing the calm focus holding your self-image in mind. This strategy is derived from Tibetan traditions steeped in a rich context of philosophical thought and inquiry into the nature of the self.[7] Their strategy for debunking false concepts about the self dovetails nicely with techniques found in cognitive behavioral therapy used to challenge and overcome cognitive distortions.

For example, one strategy used by cognitive behavioral therapists is cognitive restructuring, in which clients write down evidence either supporting or refuting problematic thoughts.[8] The analysis of the cognitive distortion helps the client to see for themselves that the distortion is untrue. When the thought is thus shown to be invalid, it tends to lose its grip over the client's emotions and behaviors. Similarly, in the exercise we are doing here, by subjecting the distorted self-image to analysis you can see the unreality of the image, thus helping it lose its power over your thoughts and feelings.

One way to do the analysis is to mentally search for the distorted image of yourself among the different components of your body and mind. For instance, our bodies are made up of different systems: cardiovascular, nervous, pulmonary, digestive, reproductive, lymphatic, etc. Is the distorted sense of self to be found in any one of these systems, or separate from them? Is it a physical or mental thing? Can you find it at a cellular level? Or is it hovering in any particular organ of the body? It is not the skin, or the bones, or the blood: having analyzed the body, no dwelling place for the distorted sense of self can be found.

Therefore, is it to be found in the mind? If so, is it a feeling of pleasure, pain, or indifference? Or is it the mind's ability to discriminate between things and discern their features? Or is it an impulse of the mind? Is it one particular emotion of the mind? If so, which emotion is it? Where does that emotion dwell? Is it your thoughts, and if so, which thoughts in particular? Is it an aspect of awareness and cognition like eyesight, hearing, smell, taste, or touch? Is it mental awareness itself? Or is it merely a concept?

As you analyze the distorted image of self in this manner, you can start to see for yourself that it is only a mental construct, and that it does not have any real validity of its own. As a concept that is invalid, there is no need to hold onto it or to let it define who you are and how you feel. Tibetans liken this process to a person who sees a coiled rope on the floor at dusk and mistakenly thinks the rope is a snake. At first the person is filled with fear at the mistaken perception of a snake. But once the person retrieves a flashlight to shine some light on it and sees that it is just a rope, their fear disappears along with the misapprehension of the snake.

Similarly, when feeling stuck in a negative emotional state that is bound by a negative perception of self, using an analytical process like the one described above can free you from the distorted sense of self and allow you to reframe who you are on your own terms. You can imagine the distorted self-image dissolving like a cloud into the sky, leaving you free from its influence. In its place, you can imagine yourself as you want to be, in the image of your compassionate goals, which is the third step of the exercise.

Reidentifying with One's Compassionate Goals

Once you have dispelled the distorted self-image, it is time to rebuild your sense of who you are. This time, you can do so on your own terms instead of doing so as an automatic reaction to circumstances beyond your control. A good way to start this process is by recalling your compassionate goals and identifying with them. Identification with your core values and goals helps to build a competent sense of self based on your own convictions. Therefore, one way to envision yourself is to remember a time when you were living in accord with your core values and bring that image of yourself into focus, holding it clearly in mind. It is important to identify with that positive self-image, thinking, "This is who I really am." Hold that thought and image for a while.

When the Tibetans practice meditation, they use visualization to supplement this process. For example, they might imagine themselves being filled with a light that has the nature of compassionate insight. I have adopted this approach for COMPASS because I find that visualizing light has an uplifting effect on the mind, and it gives your mind a focal point and an image that you can associate with your compassionate goal. I have also found that visualizing light is a universally accepted practice in most major religions, and therefore seems to have resonance with people of various faiths and beliefs.

If you wish to add this visualization, you can imagine that your compassionate goals take the form of a small orb of light in your chest and that it has a calm, healing effect on your mind and body. You can then imagine that this light becomes brighter, strengthening your compassionate insight, melting away doubts, confusion, misgivings, afflicted states of mind, and disturbing concepts, filling your entire body with a soothing radiance. From there, you can imagine that light radiating out from you and healing family, friends, your community, and eventually everyone, everywhere.

By settling into this imagined well-being for a few moments, you are resetting your internal focus and reclaiming your chosen direction for your life. Once you finish meditating and go on with your daily activities, you can occasionally come back briefly to the above visualization of your compassionate goal as an inner light.

This can help you to sustain your intention throughout the day and rekindle it from time to time as needed.

Participants in the January 3, 2015, COMPASS training reported the following positive experiences after trying the analytical exercise: feelings of being okay, being intrigued by the idea of debunking cognitive distortions, and focus. Negative experiences that were reported included feelings of uncertainty and restlessness. Feedback on this exercise was not obtained in the formal pilot at George Mason University on January 25.

The feelings of uncertainty and restlessness reported by at least one of the participants are most likely felt by many of us when we try more complex forms of meditation. Personally, when I began trying more complex forms of meditation, I too had some difficulties gaining certainty about how to do the practices and in getting my mind to settle on them. However, I found that by sticking with them, seeking clarity about how to do the practices, and repetition, eventually the more complex meditations became more effective in settling my mind than other simpler practices. The core practice for developing analytical insight can be summarized as follows:

❖ Purpose: to turn back internal obstacles to compassion through analytical insight.

   A. Cognitive schema: patterns of concepts about reality inform our judgments/reactions.
   B. Distortions in personal schema can occur based on our reactions to and interpretations of our unique experiences, thus affecting self-concept.

   ➤ Overly negative/diminished sense of self can lead to feeling:

   • worthless,
   • helpless, and
   • hopeless.

   ➤ This can sap motivation by exacerbating

   • depression,
   • anxiety, and
   • avoidance.

➤ Overly positive/inflated sense of self can lead to feeling:

- superior,
- entitled, and
- invulnerable.

➤ This can block compassion by exacerbating

- inconsideration,
- self-indulgence, and
- unrealistic expectations.

❖ Practicing the analytical core skills:

- After contemplating the rationale for the analytical core skills as described above and a brief practice of mindfulness, do a short review of the core compassion exercises.
- When settled into goal-focused compassion, contemplate the following:

A. Identifying a cognitive distortion:

- Within a calm and clear state of awareness, recall an incident that is troubling to you. Focus on your reactions to the situation, looking for how the situation affects your self-concept.
- If you identify any distortion in self-concept, hold it clearly in mind.

B. Analyzing the self-concept:

- Ask yourself whether this concept of you is of mental or physical nature.
- Mentally search for such a self within the various parts of your body and mind.
- Recognizing that this concept is just that, a concept, allow it to dissolve along with the reactions it has aroused.

C. Defining self-concept using compassionate insight:

- Within the clarity of your awareness, recall your compassionate goal. Recall a time when you were living in accord with your core values and identify with that positive image of yourself, holding it clearly in mind for a while.

- If wished, you can imagine that your compassionate goal takes the form of a healing, soothing ball of light in your chest.
- As you focus on your compassionate goal, imagine the light getting brighter, filling your body with light and melting away all your internal obstacles to reaching your goal.
- Imagine that light going out from your pores, dispelling the problems of your loved ones, friends, acquaintances, and eventually, everyone, everywhere. Hold that image single-pointedly while identifying with your compassion and insight.

Overall Feedback on COMPASS

When asked about their overall experience of COMPASS, one participant from the January 3, 2015, COMPASS training noted feeling "inspired by the revelation that I can choose to be defined by my goals and not my afflictions," and "after each module I got more and more relaxed." Another noticed the importance of repetition.

Participants in the January 25, 2015, pilot study at George Mason University gave more extensive feedback about their overall experience of COMPASS, including:

- "I definitely had a positive experience, but as I lost energy, I had difficulty feeling the present moment with vivacity. I also feel there was a lot of form to the training whereas I'm more comfortable with longer periods of just meditation."
- "I enjoyed the training overall; wish it was shorter though. At the same time, I wish we had enough time to practice all the modules."
- "Grateful that I was able to attend. Encouraged at having another set of doable tools to empower myself as a new helper—and later on as a more experienced helper."
- "I find myself filled with a renewed sense of energy and motivation to pursue more acts of mindfulness and self-reflection. I particularly liked the guided imagery and use of concrete examples to attend to and reflect upon. Moreover, I liked the idea of creating a 'mission statement' of my own attainable compassionate goals."

- "Really enjoyed this training. I definitely enjoyed the practices of meditation. I [think] this is a great tool for those in mental health."
- "Impressed with the vast amount of information and techniques shown through the training. I particularly enjoyed the inclusion of positive feelings and compassion toward others as part of such feelings for ourselves. I thought the research data showing the positive effects of following such a model to be inspiring and motivating."
- "The training helped me practice thinking of a wider perspective of my life. I felt less restricted afterwards and like there is more opportunity. I would suggest, however, to make it shorter because it became harder for me to pay attention."

When participants in the George Madison University pilot study were asked about which part of the training had the biggest impact on them and about what the impact was, they responded with the following:

- "Practicing the meditative, contemplative aspects was most impactful in that it relaxed both my mind and body. They allowed me to slow down and have a wider perspective of things. I also liked the exploration of self-acceptance/self-care being the foundation of compassion."
- "The meditative parts—the experientials; allowing us to practice what we are learning adds to experience some of the positive outcomes."
- "The video and explanation on empathy vs. sympathy. It helped me to reflect on my interactions with others and my clients."
- "I enjoyed the idea of a mental garden, one in which I can plant more compassionate beliefs and empathy while trying to remove unneeded distortions and sense of helplessness. I think it really captured one's ability to find acceptance with all parts of the self while feeling free to bolster our better aspects. This metaphor I also think will be helpful with future clients."
- "Explaining the various steps—they are basically common sense and pieces of other concepts and training, but I don't think we can have enough of."
- "I think that 'giving and taking' module had the biggest impact on me. After this module, I felt confident and hopeful. I can see

how this practice can help to go through difficult times personally as well as professionally."
* "The self-compassion was very beneficial as well as the equanimity, much metta."

I have received a lot of positive informal feedback from students and workshop participants over the years when I have presented COMPASS or parts of it. One of the most informative interactions I can remember came after a presentation to social workers. A woman approached me and told me that if she had known ahead of the symposium that the strategies for compassion building we would present were derived from Buddhist sources, she would not have attended. She confided that she had a deep faith in Christianity. I asked if there were strategies for developing compassion within her tradition that might be useful for secular audiences, and she responded that it was only through faith in Jesus that it is developed. Another woman, who had been listening to us, joined the conversation, saying that she was Muslim. As we discussed the intersection of compassion and faith traditions, we eventually concurred that a secular approach to compassion development might have a place within our diverse culture.

The conversation reminded me of the deep convictions many people hold toward their systems of faith, which might cause reluctance to try strategies derived from traditions other than their own. I have met people equally emphatic about their disbelief in all faith traditions, who indicate that they are likely to reject anything derived from religious thought. There is a common boundary between science and spiritual traditions, which I have tried to walk while writing this book. I do not know whether I have walked it successfully, but that has been my intent. It seems crucial now more than ever that we have empirically validated approaches available to help people overcome narcissism and develop their compassion.

Integrating COMPASS in Tough Times

All the COMPASS exercises can be integrated into a daily practice. Mindfulness practice sets a foundation and can be likened to preparing the soil and climate for your inner garden, contemplation of the core compassion skills is like planting good seeds in your mind's garden, the analytical skills can be compared to weeding your garden, and regular practice is similar to tending to your garden by watering it and nourishing it. If you maintain these practices daily, you might find that your compassionate insight begins to grow and flourish.

As people become fully dedicated to compassionate activity, they often face increasing challenges as they encounter the complexities of the world and the realities of the conditions that plague humanity. This keeps life from being boring, but it also tests the resilience of one's compassion. The danger is in becoming overwhelmed and giving up. In Tibet, there was a great practitioner of mind training named Langri Tangpa Dorje Seng-ge (1054–1123), who wrote a poem of eight verses for training the mind. In his poem, which reads as a prayer, he speaks to some of the most challenging situations a practitioner might face in the pursuit of compassionate insight.

One of his verses addresses the dilemma of how to view people who are either completely devastated and/or completely off track and pursuing destructive lifestyles:

When I see beings with a bad nature,
Overwhelmed by their misdeeds or suffering,
May I care for them as if I had discovered
A jewel treasure, for they are so hard to find.[9]

His verse addresses an impulse that often strikes people when they encounter someone whose suffering is so intense or whose negative actions are so troublesome that an urge to avoid and distance from them arises. Some of us might notice this, for instance, when passing by a homeless person who is requesting money. A discomfort and sense of apprehension immediately arises. There are many levels to consider in such reactions. Am I uncomfortable with this situation because I fear that it might be a threat to my immediate safety? Am I worried that I too am vulnerable to ending up in this person's unfortunate condition? Am I concerned that if I try to help this person, I will become overwhelmed, they will want more from me than I can give, and things will become unmanageable?

Such worries trigger our fight/flight response and often lead to disengagement, leaving the person seeking our help abandoned and alone again. Langri Tangpa's verse can help to change this dynamic by offering a different way to see such situations. If our main goal is to develop our compassion, such situations are rare opportunities. Usually, we don't have a chance to directly help others in such dire conditions, but in this instance, we do. Even if we don't have all that the person needs in the moment, we can at least imagine taking away their suffering and giving what they need. Or perhaps, just by giving a little, it can help them for a moment to feel hope, inclusion, and well-being.

It is more complex when the encounter is with someone whose behavior and attitude make them dangerous. Of course, our first concern should be seeking safety for ourselves and others. Once safety is secured, it is still helpful to consider this verse. It can remind us of the humanity of even the most deranged and incorrigible among us. We see stories in the nightly news of atrocities that can engender hatred and condemnation for the perpetrators. It is natural to feel compassion for the victims and anger/fear toward those who harm them. Langri Tangpa is challenging us to go deeper and consider the perpetrators as well as their victims in order to move ourselves beyond hate and fear.

Often, when we look into the lives of perpetrators of violence and abuse, we find a sad early history of victimization leading to a cycle of abuse.[10] Buddhists, who believe in karma, predict that such cycles of abuse will continue for perpetrators who are sowing the seeds of future suffering with their current behaviors. Even if we do not share this viewpoint, from a secular point of view, we can see that most perpetrators lead lives of misery. If our hearts can turn from hate and fear to compassionate concern for them as well as for their victims, there is a chance that encounters with such individuals, whether direct or indirect, will lead us to deepen our compassionate insight.

As a social worker, I have had times when I have worked with clients whose values and lifestyles were very different from my own. This verse has helped me time and again to get past impulses to distance from such people, and instead, to try to understand their histories, what led them to their behaviors and to their current stance, and how to help them reconsider their future responses and actions. I have considered these to be some of my most useful learning experiences as a clinician. I cannot convey the joy it has brought to me when I notice even the slightest shift in my client's self-awareness and intentions to change destructive patterns of thought and behavior. Even a slight shift often means a better future for my client and the people they will impact. Thus, such clients become like a jewel treasure for me.

Langri Tangpa continues to challenge us with his next verse:

May I accept any loss from such unfair treatment
As being attacked and belittled
By those who are jealous of me; and
May I give every gain to others.[11]

Life offers many opportunities for this practice. Personally, I find it has saved me from needless escalations many times during my career. Once, a colleague decided to say some belittling things about me to other staff and seemed to be trying to undermine their confidence in me as a professional. It was something that the person had done to others in my field, so it appeared to be driven by a sense of rivalry and need to feel secure. After much anxiety, and some sleepless nights worrying about my employment situation, I had a revelation while sitting on my meditation cushion. This tormentor was not in the room with me, and I had no idea of the person's real motivations. The only thing tormenting me in the moment was my internal image of the person based on past encounters. So I settled into giving and taking practice, coupled with deconstructing my damaged images of the person and of myself. Once I regained my internal equilibrium, the external situation no longer troubled me, and it eventually resolved on its own.

In cases where we escalate in response to insults to our characters, new cycles of attack and counterattack are initiated. This sometimes ends in tragedy or major obstacles to our goals. Whereas a quiet acceptance can help us move past the situation, learn from it, and continue with our journeys. Tibetans see this as a form of purification. They call it "turning hardships into the path." The negative things that happen to us can be used to deepen our compassionate insight.

At first take, you might think that accepting defeat and offering victory to your detractors will render you helpless and victimized. Indeed, it is important to contemplate whether the situation you face would be better addressed through setting boundaries or employing this method. It is possible to employ both methods simultaneously, to set boundaries with a detractor while not counterattacking or defending yourself. The main thing this practice is meant to help us with is deescalating from anger.

When someone insults us or treats us unfairly, there is a natural tendency to feel hurt and outraged. Such reactions are protective of self, and most of us automatically respond with counter-insults and self-defensive statements. This is the way of the world. You can see it played out in politics as well as on the street, where it often leads to violence. This pattern is often the cause of marital and family conflict. Developing the skill of acceptance when others are hurtful brings a sense of serenity that fortifies you in your journey toward compassion, so that you don't become sidetracked into anger and cycles of conflict.

A fellow clinician, Dr. Lorne Ladner, calls this skill "joyfully losing an argument," and tells a story of a man whose neighbor damaged his new car, leading to an escalation of accusations, denials, and legal actions culminating in the man getting paid for some of the damage to his car. However, once he had repaired his car, he found that someone had scratched it again, and suspected that this had been done by his neighbor in retaliation for their dispute. A friend taught the man the skill of joyfully losing an argument, after which the man approached his neighbor with a gift of golf balls, having heard that his neighbor was a golf enthusiast. He offered the gift and apologized for his part in their conflict. The neighbor later apologized as well and promised to be a good neighbor.[12] Sometimes enemies can become friends if you treat them with respect over time.

Langri Tangpa's next verse goes to an even deeper challenge:

May I view one who I have helped and
Whom I greatly hoped would help me in return, but
Instead mistreats or even harms me,
As my greatest spiritual teacher.[13]

Some of the most venomous anger I have witnessed has come from people who once trusted and helped someone who then betrays or hurts them. I've noticed as a mental health provider that the deeper people bond with each other, the more vulnerable they become. When there is a violation of the trust in such relationships, it leads to deep-seated rage and resentment. This is especially true when someone sacrifices a lot for another person and takes care of their needs over time. Such outrage is often verbalized in words such as, "After all I've done for you, this is how you repay me?"

Langri Tangpa is suggesting a way to help overcome the narcissistic wounds and ensuing rage that such situations can provoke. In the spirit of transforming hardships into a path for increasing compassionate insight, he is suggesting that we try to see such betrayals as opportunities to grow, step beyond our narcissism, and learn from the experience. I have often heard clients reflect on particularly painful relationships by saying, "I learned a lot from going through that."

Tibetans tend to see hardships as created by past misdeeds, so when they've helped someone who turns around and hurts them, they think things such as, "Maybe this happened to me because I've done similar things to someone else in my past." Such thoughts remind them to be vigilant about repaying kindness with kindness, trust with trust, and receiving help with giving help. Instead of getting stuck in cycles of rage and retaliation, such thoughts allow them to move forward and put the betrayal behind them. In this way, they see the betrayer as a spiritual teacher who reminds them to choose compassion over anger.

We can do something similar by noticing when our anger has been triggered by a betrayal, and then looking into the root of our reactions. What are the psychological underpinnings to the intensity of our anger and disappointment? Often, we might find that when we have given help to someone with a hidden expectation of receiving help in return, our expectations turn into resentment if unfulfilled. Alcoholics Anonymous has a saying that "expectations are premeditated resentments." Therefore, the bigger our hopes that we will be rewarded for our good deeds, the more we are setting ourselves up for disappointment. The implicit lesson that we can therefore take away from such letdowns is to learn how to help others without expectations of rewards or gratitude.

This is easier said than done. To let go of hopes of rewards for our good deeds means to let go of our narcissistic focus and to replace it with a compassionate motivation. When narcissism motivates positive actions, there is always an underpinning of "what's in this for me?" When this motivation is decreased and replaced by compassionate thoughts and feelings, there is less concern about what the outcome will be for ourselves. Instead, there is more genuine concern about what the outcome will be for the person we are helping. Then, whether they help us in return is less significant to us. If we can gain such a perspective, then when we are betrayed by someone we have benefited, we can monitor our emotional reactions. If our anger is triggered, the betrayer is serving as a spiritual teacher pointing out where our narcissism has been hiding and influencing our decisions. This allows us to let go, rekindle a compassionate motivation, grow from the experience, and move forward.

The above strategies are just a few ways that we can start to use—whatever happens to us—as grist for the mill as we try to focus on our compassionate goals, whatever they may be. The more skills we learn, the more resilient we can become in recovering from bouts of narcissism, and the more robust we can become in building our compassionate will. Eventually, whatever happens to us, good or bad, can strengthen our resolve.

Geshe Chekawa (1101–1175), who wrote the classic Tibetan text *Seven Points for Training the Mind*, included several pledges and precepts for practitioners to follow at the end of his writings.[14] They were meant to help practitioners stay on track and not lose direction. I will mention a few of them here in the hopes that they might be useful. One in particular, "Change your aspiration but remain natural,"[15] would have helped me had I followed it early in my attempts to develop compassion.

When I first started studying and practicing meditation, I was a bit overeager in explaining my new interest to family and friends. It seems that my overzealousness alienated some people and I wish, in hindsight, that I had been more vigilant to use what I was studying internally rather than trying to convince people around me about it. Tibetans love to tell stories about great practitioners who appeared to be ordinary people, but later showed extraordinary qualities. The skill in this case is to be yourself and approach relationships in your normal manner externally, while internally making strides to deepen your compassionate insight.

Another pledge says "remove your worst mental affliction first."[16] Keeping a daily practice of mindfulness will help you to stay in touch with your internal world. Over time, you will become more aware of your own patterns of thought and behavior. By addressing the most disturbing patterns disrupting your mental well-being first, you will slowly notice progress. Even a slight improvement can feel like a huge accomplishment. The key is to keep plugging away one day at a time.

To bolster diligence, the next pledge says "give up all hopes of achieving results."[17] Hoping for immediate results from meditation can lead to disappointment and giving up on our practice. Therefore, we need a more down-to-earth attitude. For instance, we don't expect to avoid cavities by brushing our teeth once or twice. We realize that we have brush our teeth on a regular basis to maintain them. A similar attitude toward your COMPASS exercises will help.

One of the precepts says "do not practice sporadically."[18] This speaks to the importance of making these exercises a part of your daily routine. I once heard someone ask a great meditator, "Why do you tell us to practice an hour a day?" The meditation teacher replied, "Ideally, you should be practicing 24-7, but for beginners, I suggest an hour a day." In the COMPASS approach, I recommend starting with meditation sessions that are much shorter than an hour, even limiting your sessions to a few minutes. The idea is to keep them short and sweet, so you want to return to them. However, it is crucial to practice them daily, even several times each day. Once you familiarize yourself with them and they become second nature, you can extend your sessions easily as wished.

The last four precepts are also quite useful. "Do not be conceited"[19] keeps us from getting puffed up about our practice, so we do not start to imagine ourselves as somehow superior to others because of our growing compassion. "Do not be resentful"[20] helps to remind us not to hold onto grudges when criticized or scolded. "Do not be fickle"[21] is a call to try to keep our minds steady rather than let them go up and down like a roller coaster. And "do not hope for gratitude"[22] guards us from clinging to expectations that others will be grateful to us for our compassionate activities. By letting go of such expectations, we can protect ourselves from disappointment.

Endings Are Beginnings

Whenever something ends, something else begins. Falling autumn leaves fertilize the ground for spring's new growth. Erik Erikson (1902–1994) called the last crisis in life integrity versus despair.[23] He characterized integrity as coming to full acceptance of oneself, one's life, and the inevitability of one's death. He noted that a failure to find acceptance leads to despair and fear of death. If we have lived our lives fully and well, there is a better chance that we will navigate this last challenge with integrity.

I remember my mother on her deathbed as T-cell lymphoma ravaged her body. She told me with a wry sense of humor that she would come back and haunt me if I did not start to have more fun. Even at the end of her life, she was taking care of the people she loved. She said that she believed that her mind would continue after her death and told me some unusual things that she had experienced when her father died that made her think he was communicating with her. I have heard of similar experiences from many people over the years when they lose a loved one.

It happened to me with my mother. The morning she passed, I had a dream of calling her on a pay phone, but not being able to get through, which left me with feelings of panic and loss. My father, who had been divorced from my mother since 1964, told me later that he too had a dream of her on the morning of her death telling him, "I'm leaving now." A week after she died, I had another dream. My mother was smiling, youthful, and radiant. She recited a phrase from a sacred Tibetan liturgy and said, "That stuff really works." I found out during the day after that dream that my teacher had performed a ritual ceremony on my mother's behalf the previous evening, the same practice she had quoted to me in the dream. Of course, such things can be brushed aside as coincidences, but it's hard to know.

There are many different views about death and dying and about whether it constitutes a final end of consciousness or a transition into something else. What really happens is beyond the ability of most of us to discern, but many of us have strong convictions about it. Materialists maintain that the mind is totally dependent on neural functioning and therefore ends with physical death.

Religious and spiritually inclined people tend to have other beliefs that may vary depending on which traditions they follow.

The secrets of death have yet to be unlocked by scientific method, though a few areas of research have led to debates among scientists. For example, research on near-death experiences has opened questions about whether consciousness survives death.[24] Another ongoing area of research focuses on children who talk of memories of a previous life.[25] There does not yet seem to be much consensus among scientists about how to understand these phenomena; nonetheless they are intriguing and thought-provoking.

The reason I am bringing this topic up here is to highlight one more practice from the mind-training tradition that is focused on helping us through the dying process. Tibetans see death as an important transition, and therefore use the last moments of their lives for practicing compassion. They believe that doing so provides the best possible condition for one's future journey. One practice that they use to prepare their minds for death is to recall the five strengths mentioned before in the section on activation, except in this case they are called the mental training transference instruction. Because this practice can be used to supplement whatever religious or spiritual tradition a person is following, I thought that it might be appropriate to share. Even if you do not adhere to any religious or spiritual traditions, you might be interested in at least knowing about it, should you want something to focus on when death approaches.

The strengths of intention, virtuous actions, purification, dedication, and habituation take on slightly different meanings in the context of preparing for death than they do when used for enhancing daily practice. The strength of intention when dying is to focus the mind on never giving up on compassionate insight. Instead, one attempts to develop a strong intention to carry compassion through the death process and into the future. It is said that this intention calls up the virtuous states of mind one has cultivated throughout one's lifetime, which propels the mind in a positive direction. Since compassion is a valued trait in most major religious and spiritual traditions, it should coincide with whatever faith one follows, so that you can add it to whatever prayers or traditions you find to be of comfort.

Tips for Helping Professionals

Assisting Clients with End-of-Life Issues and Coping with Our Own Mortality

End-of-life issues are challenging at both a personal and a professional level. Helping professionals are frequently called upon to assist people facing death and dying. This can provoke our own fears of mortality and raise ethical issues over how to approach the fit between our own spiritual beliefs and those of our clients. Many helping professionals are also put in harm's way as they serve the public. Maintaining compassionate courage as we help clients go through end-of-life issues can help us master our own fears. Accommodating the spiritual beliefs of our clients as they face their own mortality need not conflict with our own preferred beliefs.

In section 16 of the appendix, "A COMPASS Handbook for Helping Professionals," these issues of working with death and dying are explored in more detail.

The strength of virtuous activities at the time of death consists of letting go of your attachment to your belongings, giving them away to others. My teacher used to recommend having a will, so that you don't spend your last moments fretting over who will get what. If you have enough time and strength left, you can give valued things away yourself. It is also good to say your goodbyes and seek closure with loved ones. This is a kindness to them, and it also allows your mind to be more at peace, helping you to let go and move forward without clinging.

The strength of purification at the time of death is focused on removing obstacles from your mind that otherwise might cause problems as you journey forward. These obstacles include things that you may have done through the course of your life that were hurtful or patterns in your thoughts and behavior that you wish were different. Tibetans think that feeling regret, atoning, applying virtuous antidotes, and forming an intent to restrain from repeating such patterns can reduce their potency and hold over us. Therefore, they put a lot of effort into purification practices as they or their loved ones approach death. Most religious traditions have similar confession ceremonies or purification practices. You can employ whatever spiritual traditions appeal to you at this time as a support. Alternatively, by simply noting patterns that you wish to overcome in the future, you can direct your mind toward your compassionate goals and becoming the kind of person you aspire to be.

The fourth strength at the time of death is dedication, which is a form of prayer. Since death often is associated with physical discomfort and pain, the prayer in this case is for any suffering we go through in the dying process to become a cause for removing suffering from everyone. Praying in this way strengthens one's compassion in the face of the inevitable suffering that death brings. I once heard a mother describe giving birth; she said that as she was feeling the intense pain of childbirth, she focused on all mothers throughout history who have endured such suffering to bring children into the world. She said that as she thought of this, her own pain lessened, and she was able to bear the birth process more courageously.

The final strength is that of habituation. It consists of focusing your mind on your compassionate goals and keeping it there. You can also rely on whatever spiritual practices you have familiarized yourself with throughout your life. Doing so calls forward the best of your aspirations and hopes, which then become your internal guiding force for your journey through the death process.

This last practice of the five strengths is a clear step into the spiritual, but I hope that it can be useful for people with or without a spiritual bent. In any case, I felt that the book would be incomplete without including it. I hope that you find the COMPASS exercises helpful in your daily life. At the end of his text called the *Seven Point Mind Training*, Geshe Chekawa wrote this verse:

Motivated by the great wish,
I have ignored suffering and criticism
To be able to receive instructions
That overcome self-grasping.
Now I am ready to die without any regrets.[26]

Notes

[1] Leahy, R. L. (1997). Introduction. In *Practicing cognitive therapy: A guide to interventions*. Jason Aronson. http://cognitivetherapynyc.com/docs/arosnonintro.pdf

[2] For examples, see https://psychcentral.com/lib/15-common-cognitive-distortions/

3 McClure, A. C., Tanski, S. E., Kingsbury, J., Gerrard, M., & Sargent, J. D. (2010). Characteristics associated with low self-esteem among US adolescents. *Academic Pediatrics, 10*(4), 238-244.e2. https://doi.org/10.1016/j.acap .2010.03.007

4 Tamborski, M., Brown, R. P., & Chowning, K. (2012). Self-serving bias or simply serving the self? Evidence for a dimensional approach to narcissism. *Personality and Individual Differences, 52*(8), 942-946. https://doi.org/10.1016/j .paid.2012.01.030

5 Hurley, R. (2019). *Celebrating the richness of reality: The life and art of Wilson Hurley.* Fresco Books.

6 Gyeltsen, Losang Chokyi, the Fourth Panchen Lama. (1997). *The Gelek/ Kagyu tradition of Mahamudra* (A. Berzin & H. H. the Dalai Lama, Trans.). Snow Lion.

7 Shiah, Y. J. (2016). From self to nonself: The nonself theory. *Frontiers in Psychology, 7,* 124. https://doi.org/10.3389/fpsyg.2016.00124

8 Boyer, A. (2013, January 21). Cognitive restructuring: Six ways to do cognitive restructuring. *Psychology Today.* https://www.psychologytoday.com/us/blog/ in-practice/201301/cognitive-restructuring

9 Langri Tangpa Dorje Seng-ge, Geshe. (1998). Quoted in *The essence of Mahayana Lojong Practice: A commentary to Geshe Langri Tangpa's mind training in eight verses,* by Sermey Khensur Lobsang Tharchin, p. 59. Mahayana Sutra and Tantra Press.

10 Glasser, M., Kolvin, I., Campbell, D., Glasser, A., Leitch, I., & Farrelly, S. (2001). Cycle of child sexual abuse: Links between being a victim and becoming a perpetrator. *British Journal of Psychiatry, 179,* 482-497; discussion 495-497. https://doi.org/10.1192/bjp.179.6.482

11 Langri Tangpa Dorje Seng-ge (1998), 67.

12 Ladner, L. (2004). *The lost art of compassion: Discovering the practice of happiness in the meeting of Buddhism and psychology,* 225-229. HarperCollins.

13 Langri Tangpa Dorje Seng-ge. (1998). I changed the translation as it appears above slightly from that in the original found on page 75 in order to bear out its fuller meaning.

14 For a complete list and commentary on these, see pp. 154-232 of Tharchin, Sermey Khensur Lobsang. (1999). *Achieving Bodhicitta: Instructions of two great lineages combined into a unique system of eleven categories.* Mahayana Sutra and Tantra Press.

15 Ibid., 157.

16 Ibid., 177.

17 Ibid., 179.

18 Ibid., 224.

19 Ibid., 228.

20 Ibid., 229.

21 Ibid., 230.

22 Ibid., 230.

23 Kroger, J. (2017). Identity formation in adolescence and adulthood. *Social Psychology Online*. https://doi.org/10.1093/acrefore/9780190236557.013.54

24 Lichfield, G. (2015, April). The science of near-death experiences: Empirically investigating brushes with the afterlife. *The Atlantic*. https://www.theatlantic.com/magazine/archive/2015/04/the-science-of-near-death-experiences/386231/

25 University of Virginia School of Medicine. *Children who report memories of previous lives*. https://med.virginia.edu/perceptual-studies/our-research/children-who-report-memories-of-previous-lives/

26 Quote adapted from a translation found in Tharchin, Sermey Khensur Lobsang. (1999). *Achieving Bodhicitt*, p. 252-253.

A COMPASS Handbook for Helping Professionals

In this handbook you will find a detailed discussion of the brief tips for helping professionals found in the text boxes interspersed throughout the book. At the end of this handbook is a section that contains all the main exercises set forth in the COMPASS approach to developing resilient compassion. It is hoped that the handbook will provide an easy-to-use reference for helping professionals seeking to prevent or recover from compassion fatigue and hoping to renew and strengthen their compassion insight.

The sections are as follows:

1. Empathy and Compassion
2. Compassion Fatigue
3. Regaining Equilibrium
4. Finding Acceptance and Self-Compassion When Something Goes Wrong
5. Cultivating Self-Care and Healthy Professional Boundaries
6. The Benefits of Compassion in the Workplace
7. Focusing on Strengths and Solutions When Working with Addictions
8. Equanimity and Honoring Diversity
9. Filling Your Cup with Gratitude When Taking Care of Others
10. Maintaining Patience and Kindness When Confronted by Workplace Bullying
11. Choosing Compassion as Your Moral Compass
12. Staying Compassionately Engaged in Challenging Client Situations with Giving and Taking

Section 1. Empathy and Compassion

Empathy and compassion are crucial elements of the helping process. For example, the majority of studies on positive therapeutic outcomes indicate that the relationship between a therapist and client is a primary factor in the healing process, and that this alliance is strengthened by the therapist's ability to be empathic, helpful, and understanding.[1] Empathy facilitates practitioner abilities to form successful psychotherapeutic relationships and can manifest in an ability to accurately assess, understand, listen to, and respect client perspectives.[2] Clients are more likely to trust a therapist who displays empathy and compassion.[3] Empathy is the ability to recognize what another person is going through and compassion is the wish that the person be free from suffering and difficulty.

Psychologists describe two types of empathy: cognitive and emotional.[4] Cognitive empathy allows us to imagine what another might be experiencing but may not compel us to act on their behalf. Emotional empathy causes us to feel a similar experience to what another is feeling and may motivate us to act but can lead to emotional depletion.[5] Merriam-Webster defines compassion as "sympathetic consciousness of others' distress together with a desire to alleviate it."[6] The consciousness of others' distress is the empathic aspect of compassion. It is the sympathetic wish to alleviate that distress that turns empathy into compassion. Compassionate empathy offers a strong resource for people intent on helping others.[7]

Researchers have begun to map the parts of our brain that engage when we tap into empathy and compassion.[8] For instance, when we are processing cognitive empathy, three regions of the brain begin to interact with each other: the dorsal medial prefrontal cortex (dmPFC), the posterior circulate cortex (PCC), and the temporoparietal junction (TPJ).[9] When we experience emotional empathy, two different areas of the brain become engaged: the dorsal anterior circulate cortex (dACC) and the anterior insula (AI).[10] As we consider the relationship between ourselves and the person to whom we are focused, a third part of the brain is activated: the ventral medial prefrontal cortex (vmPFC).[11]

These empathically engaged neural circuits compete with "vigilance-to-threat" networks like the amygdala and can easily be dominated should fear and distress steal our focus away,[12] which is why COMPASS begins with mindfulness and self-regulation strategies as the foundation for building compassionate insight. Compassion and love engage the brain's limbic motivation and rewards systems, causing the release of neurotransmitters like dopamine and endorphins, the hormones vasopressin and oxytocin, and adrenal corticoids, morphine, and nitric oxide, thus reducing stress and suffering and activating the mirror neuron system, which allows us to mirror what we perceive in others.[13] While compassion is a positive emotion, the experience of compassion can heighten negative affect, so self-care is important.[14]

Compassion is crucial for well-being and effectiveness in the helping professions. For instance, teachers with a compassionate approach to teaching create classroom environments with increased cooperation and enhanced learning in their students.[15] A professional climate in which teachers express compassion for each other promotes commitment to the school, job satisfaction, and vigor.[16] Empathy and compassion have been linked to patients having positive medical outcomes.[17] Doctors even briefly expressing compassion to their patients reduces their patient's anxiety.[18] Compassion helps motivate patients suffering from chronic illnesses and their nurses to cooperate in achieving relevant treatment outcomes.[19] Volunteers engaged in compassionate activities experience better health and well-being.[20]

All helping professions consider empathy and compassion to be a crucial part of their respective callings. For instance, according to Supervisory Special Agent William Beersdorf of the FBI, "Having compassion and empathy for fellow human beings is essential for successful law enforcement personnel."[21] In healthcare professions, provider empathy and compassion are associated with better patient outcomes, fewer malpractice complaints, less likelihood of mistakes, enhanced patient satisfaction, better adherence to medication protocols, and even symptom reductions including a lessening of pain.[22] Firefighters exhibit selfless courage in their compassionate bravery to rescue people from burning buildings.[23] Without empathy and compassion, helping professionals can become uncaring or even inept and harmful. Therefore, teachers, childcare providers, nurses, military personnel, civil servants, employers, doctors, service industry personnel, therapists, social workers, and frontline workers from almost every aspect of our society must rely on empathy and compassion as core motivators for providing competent services to the public.

The exercises set forth in the COMPASS approach are designed to establish equilibrium and self-care, evoke emotional states conducive to compassion, strengthen compassion resilience, and reduce obstacles to maintaining a compassionate heart. It is hoped that they will provide a useful tool in strengthening helper dedication, performance, and well-being.

Section 2. Compassion Fatigue

Compassion fatigue is a term coined by Charles Figley, PhD, an author, professor, and researcher of traumatology at Tulane University.[24] It is defined as an "emotional and physical exhaustion that can affect helping professionals and caregivers over time."[25] It has been linked to depression and anxiety in caregivers along with emotional depletion, substandard care, clinical errors, and a negative working climate.[26] Compassion fatigue has come to be used as a generic term that describes conditions like secondary traumatic stress, vicarious trauma, and professional burnout. While in a sense these terms are describing the same phenomenon of helper fatigue, they have subtle differences as well as many similarities.

Secondary traumatic stress refers to a condition that is similar to post-traumatic stress disorder brought on not by a direct experience of trauma, but by listening to the accounts of trauma victims.[27] It can have a negative impact on behaviors and emotions in caregivers and can lead to avoidance and other forms of functional impairment. Vicarious trauma is similar, but some say that it is also more complex and potentially more lasting.[28] It focuses on cumulative negative impacts to cognitive schema and caregivers' emotions and sense of self as they repeatedly listen to the accounts of trauma victims over time. It can cause caregivers to question their spirituality, core beliefs, and view of the world, leading to a loss of meaning and hope.[29] If a therapist and their client have similar histories of traumatic experience, for example in response to a collective traumatic event or to having endured similar types of trauma, it is called shared trauma, which adds another level of complexity in countertransference reactions in the helping relationship.[30] Professional burnout is linked to excessive institutional demands on caregivers who are faced with chronic and stressful client situations, economic insecurity, uncertainty about job position, and loss of control or helplessness about choices in patient care issues.[31]

Some argue that compassion fatigue is, more accurately, a combination of secondary traumatic stress and professional burnout.[32] Its symptoms can include such things as recurrent and distressing thoughts and feelings about clients and work, work avoidance, feeling harshly judged, irritability and anger, sleep disruption, problems concentrating, errors in judgment, depression, loss of interest in important activities, anxiety, loss of hope, helplessness, and emotional distancing.[33] This can have a negative effect not only on helping professionals themselves, but also on the clients they serve. For example, many nurses report feeling that they are "running on empty."[34] It is thought that this can lead to errors in client care. Often malpractice claims involving nurses are due to breakdowns in communication, errors in assessing needs of clients for medical interventions, and/or failures to report changes in patient conditions to other practitioners. According to the American Association of Colleges of Nursing, 13% of newly licensed RNs left their profession within the first year of becoming licensed and 37% reported thinking of doing so.[35]

High levels of work-related stress seem to have a negative impact on physical health, psychological well-being, and job satisfaction.[36] In one study, the worst scores in these three factors were found among ambulance drivers, teachers, social services workers, customer service call workers, police, and prison workers.[37] There is a relationship between the intensity of work-related stress and vulnerability to burnout, anxiety, and mood issues.[38] Healthy coping strategies for work-related stressors can foster resiliency and increase job satisfaction.[39]

In the sections that follow, various nuances of compassion fatigue and ways to remedy or prevent it will be explored. It is hoped that helping professionals will find a useful arsenal of strategies to employ in maintaining well-being and compassion resilience. Because everyone is different, some strategies might work better for one person than they do for another. Ideally, it can be helpful to have a wide array of self-care methods at one's disposal and to use them regularly. If you don't use them, they can't help you. It is important for helping professionals to establish a daily routine of the self-care exercises for preventing compassion fatigue and for maintaining and developing compassionate courage.

Section 3. Regaining Equilibrium

As biological systems, we humans constantly seek homeostasis or equilibrium.[40] Our bodies and minds seek a pleasant temperature, enough nourishment and hydration, adequate sleep and rest, and a sense of well-being. Life can be challenging and can throw us obstacles each day that send our bodies and minds into disequilibrium, causing us to feel stressed and uneasy. This is particularly true for helping professionals, who face unpredictable and complex challenges each day that frequently trigger the fight/flight response and lead to emotional overload. If this occurs repeatedly, it leads to chronic stress, which can compromise our digestive, cardiovascular, immune, and nervous systems.[41] Therefore, it is crucial for us to develop daily routines we can use to regain homeostasis and equilibrium.

In one study, psychiatric hospital workers who demonstrated empathic concern and communicative responsiveness to their clients were more prone to burnout and obstacles to responsiveness when emotionally flooded by emotional contagion.[42] Emotional contagion is a term coined by Miller, Stiff, and Ellis, who noticed that helping professionals who feel sad or anxious when hearing troubling client stories are more vulnerable to burnout than workers who can maintain empathic concern without their emotions paralleling those of their clients.[43] In other words, a professional with empathic concern might feel compassion for a client who is experiencing intense depression without becoming depressed themselves, whereas a professional who becomes depressed themselves when listening to a depressed client is more prone to burnout.

Most of us are vulnerable to emotional contagion. When working around others who are stressed, we can easily react with our own stress responses, thus absorbing and taking their stress into ourselves. When our clients feel helpless, hopeless, and depressed, we can easily start to feel the same way. This is called identical resonance:[44] when our emotional reactions mirror those we perceive in others. While this can lead to reactive resonance,[45] which is when you begin to sympathize and wish to help, it can also lead to emotional depletion, contagion, and becoming overwhelmed. Therefore, we must learn how to de-escalate ourselves each day, inoculate ourselves against emotional contagion, and learn ways to regain equilibrium. This is particularly true when working in stressful environments.

As a clinician, I have often noticed how teachers and students become more stressed and burned out as the school year enters its third month. Sometime around mid to late October, students start to report falling behind in tasks and feeling that there is no point in trying. Teachers often report similar feelings. Many students report waking up with a sense of dread and a wish to avoid the toxic stress of their schools. Teachers often report feeling hit on every side by students who want to avoid tasks by disrupting class, parents who expect special attention for their child, and administrators who want them to take on additional tasks on top of their teaching demands.

Therefore, I often advise school-involved clients and anyone working in a stressful environment to begin a regular regimen of self-care each day that includes adequate sleep, a healthy diet, exercise, and some form of mind-body self-regulation routine. Mind-body equilibrium can be maintained and regained in many ways. Yoga, tai chi, and mindfulness are all empirically validated ways to self-regulate.[46] Progressive relaxation, body scan practices, biofeedback, prayer, and guided imagery can also help, along with hobbies, art, music, dance, gardening, taking a walk, journaling, and other forms of restorative activities. Humor and spending time with friends and family are helpful as well.[47] The important thing is to pick a routine that works well for you and to come back to it each day. It helps to get back into equilibrium and well-being before the challenges of the next day send you back into disequilibrium.

Setting a Daily Routine

A morning self-care routine can help you prepare for the day ahead. This is the time when using the COMPASS exercises can be particularly beneficial to set your motivation for the day. Brief mindful moments throughout the day can also help. For instance, doctors and nurses might find it helpful to take a mindful breath when entering a patient's room to calm themselves and become open to fully engaging with their client. Teachers can pause between lessons to lead their class and themselves through a calming technique or exercise. Counselors can take a moment to center between clients. At the end of the day, it is useful to mentally scan your body to assess your stress level and then engage in self-calming strategies until you regain composure and equilibrium. While doing so, you can also take stock of unresolved work issues and think about what future steps are needed to resolve them. If you write down what you need to do the next day, it can clear your mind of worries so that you can get a good night's sleep.

Grounding

Research is unclear about whether mindfulness practice can help during active stressors once the fight/flight system has been activated.[48] Mindfulness is useful for gaining equilibrium once a stressful situation has passed, but when helping professionals encounter more stress than their systems can handle, symptoms of panic can set in. These can include a shortness of breath, increased heart palpitations, sweating, trembling or shaking, nausea, discomfort in the chest, and thoughts of losing control or fears of dying.[49] It is important to seek medical attention if you begin to have such symptoms because they might be signs of more serious health conditions. However, as you seek medical attention, there are also strategies called grounding exercises that you can try to use to regain composure. In a panic attack, three factors collide that unleash your

fight/flight response: high levels of anxiety and stress, reactive physical symptoms, and an escalation in fears and worries about loss
of control. In order to break the escalating influence of these three
factors with each other, grounding strategies can be used in order
to pull your awareness into the here and now, so that you can begin
to de-escalate the panic and regain equilibrium.

One useful grounding strategy is to focus on your sensory fields
of awareness, which helps to bring you out from your concepts and
worries.[50] For example, you can tune into how it feels to have your
feet on the floor and how the chair feels beneath you and at your
back. You can pick up something nearby and notice how it feels in
your hands. Let yourself take a few deep breaths and notice how
it feels to take the breath in and then release it. Breathe in through
your nose, then out through your mouth. Listen to sounds around
you. Notice the various colors and shapes in your field of vision.
What scents can you smell in the room? What is the taste in your
mouth? It can also help to take a walk, move your body, or talk
with a trusted friend. Sometimes people report finding it helpful to
repeat a reassuring phrase or prayer to themselves. If you have a
daily self-calming routine in place, this would be a suitable time to
use it.

When Self-Calming Strategies Are Not Working for You

If you find that you are unable to regain equilibrium with self-
soothing strategies alone, it might be time to consider adding therapeutic support. There are a variety of therapeutic approaches from
individual psychodynamic and cognitive behavioral interventions
to group and family therapies that you can consider. Some employ
exposure approaches in which you try to face causes of distress and
learn to desensitize yourself to them or approach them from a different perspective. Others may employ strategies that allow decom-
pression or self-expression, and/or enlist your creativity. There are
also pharmacological options. A short, five-session strategy called
the Accelerated Recovery Program (ARP) has also shown promise
in helping workers recover quickly from compassion fatigue.[51] As a
consumer, you can explore which modalities are available and best
suited to your needs.

Section 4. Finding Acceptance and Self-Compassion When Something Goes Wrong

When helping professionals are involved in a client case that goes wrong, not only do they worry about liability and licensure issues; they also must deal with internal distress, guilt, and doubt. Client misfortune can also cause provider misfortune. As helpers, our mission is to help our clients, not to hurt them. Therefore, when an intervention does not save a client or even misfires and a client's condition worsens or ends in death, helping professionals often feel distressed or even devastated. For instance, when a clinician loses a client to suicide, reactions can include being stunned and traumatized, disbelief, fear, anger, humiliation, and a profound sadness that can last for a long time.[52] I sometimes wonder whether reactions to client tragedy contribute to the alarming rate of suicide among emergency medical technicians.[53] Therefore, it is important that you check in with yourself when things go wrong with clients, seeking collegial and therapeutic supports, and tuning in to your reactions with acceptance and self-compassion.[54]

Finding Acceptance

The first stage of processing tragedy is usually denial.[55] It can manifest as a feeling of unreality, as if it didn't really happen, which is then usually followed by intense emotions and thoughts that can include anger, blame, obsessing about ways that the tragedy might have been avoided, and sadness. Some frontline workers try to compartmentalize client tragedies by stuffing their feelings and moving on instead of taking the time to process what happened and to mourn. Stuffing feelings just buries grief, which will come back to haunt you over time. Grief is not something one gets over.[56] It sends us reminders that it is there even years after a loss. When we stuff our grief, hoping it will go away, it often turns into depression and can contribute to compassion fatigue. Therefore, it is important to be open to your emotions and to investigate what they are communicating.

Who or what is to blame? As we process client tragedies, it is important to be honest with ourselves and to avoid the extremes of self-condemnation and overlooking mistakes. It is by realizing and learning from our errors that we can become more skilled in providing competent help. However, it can also incapacitate us to take on too much blame for tragedies, and therefore, we must be honest with ourselves. In the case of client suicide, the choice of whether to end one's life is in the hands of the client, not the clinician. Clinicians must become proficient in risk assessment, making safety plans with at-risk clients and their families, referrals to higher levels of services when necessary, and crisis intervention and/ or detention procedures. However, clinicians cannot read minds. If the client does not share their level of distress or their intention to complete suicide despite a clinician asking the appropriate questions, the possibility of a suicide might be beyond a clinician's ability to foresee or to forestall. Also, the factors in a client's life that drive the client toward contemplating suicide might be beyond the clinician's ability to control.

All we can do as clinicians is our best. If you have done your best and taken appropriate steps to ensure your client's well-being at each step of the helping process, self-condemnation for a client tragedy serves no purpose and can be self-injuring. After examination, if you find that there are things you might have done differently, it is important to be more diligent in those areas in the future. However, often clinicians overcompensate following a client suicide, becoming hyper-vigilant, which can get in the way of forming trusting therapeutic bonds, which is counterproductive. So it is useful to develop self-compassion and remember your own humanity. Balance and acceptance are crucial components in moving forward from a tragedy in a healthy way.

Acceptance of a tragedy does not mean one's feelings about it disappear. The intensity of your feelings might lessen over time, but you may continue to feel some sadness when things happen that remind you of the loss. Being in touch with your own reactions to tragedy can help you become more empathetic and compassionate when working with your clients and with their friends and family when they go through tragedy. After all, as a professional, in the wake of client tragedy you must take care of the impact of the tragedy on your client's family and friends while you take care of yourself. It is a challenge like no other. Acceptance gives you courage to look at all aspects of tragedy with clarity and full awareness. Mindfulness practice can help in this process by allowing you to calm your reactions while maintaining nonjudgmental awareness of whatever comes through your mind. Having the tools to then regenerate self-compassion and compassion for others can give you the courage and strength you need to address the aftermath of client tragedy.

Contemplating the Pros and Cons of Being a Hero: What Kind of Hero Do You Want to Be?

The self-esteem model of heroism tells us that we must be the best provider. Our confidence is boosted by positive client outcomes, so we can start to see client successes as our own successes. But what then are client failures? If we build our sense of being a good provider based on client successes and our model of being a hero is that we should be able to solve any problem and fix any situation, what happens to our self-esteem when we encounter factors beyond our ability to control? The suicide rate in the United States has risen 30% since the 1990s with an estimated 129 people taking their lives each day and more than 47,000 people having completed suicide in 2017.[57] Between 20% and 60% of psychiatrists experience a client loss to suicide at some point in their career.[58] If we build ourselves up by taking ownership of client successes and by conceiving ourselves as perfect and unerring, we are setting ourselves up for a big fall when things go wrong.

The self-compassion model of heroism focuses on doing our best rather than being the best. If we renew our commitment to compassionate service each day, and if we do our best to stay current in our field and connected empathically with our clients, responding to their needs to the best of our abilities, then if tragedy strikes we will know that we did the best we could. If our model of being a hero is to persevere compassionately even in the face of adversity, we protect ourselves from overestimating our abilities and thus we become more able to recover from tragedy and process it in a realistic light. We can see that we have our strengths and weaknesses, that like everyone else we have to take care of ourselves in order to be effective, and that we are living in an imperfect world where tragedy can strike despite our best efforts to avert it. It is not within our power to save all clients from tragedy, but it is within our power to do the best we can. If we do the best we can, we can afford ourselves self-compassion when things go wrong.

Holding Your Injured Inner Hero with Self-Compassion

Along with seeking collegial and therapeutic supports following a client suicide or tragedy, it is helpful to hold your own heart within a self-compassionate stance. This can be like tending to an injured child because our core emotions may regress. At first, it is important to try to regain equilibrium. Regular sessions of mindfulness in conducive settings can help. For example, you can practice breathing meditation in a forest, beside a lake, or in your own room. As you practice, try to notice the internal turmoil of reactions to the client tragedy rise in your mind and tend to them with a gentle kindness as you would with a troubled friend. Breathe in reassurance, acceptance, and kindness, while breathing out your sadness, self-blame, and fear. Let your inner hero start to heal within the warm embrace of mindful self-compassion.

Learning from Tragedy and Becoming Stronger

It is possible to grow from traumatic events.[59] Richard Tedeschi and Kelli N. Triplett found that people reported five areas of personal growth in the aftermath of trauma, including improved personal relationships, more appreciation of life, finding new opportunities and life pathways, more resilience in facing life's challenges, and spiritual growth.[60] As helping professionals, other areas of growth might be a renewed vigor to learn more about the research that pertains to the type of trauma we or our clients encountered, enhanced awareness of what can go wrong and what can be done to prevent it, and a deepening of self-compassion and compassion for others. We all have blind spots. You don't know what you don't know. Traumatic experiences can wake up us up to things we had not considered before. It is important not to let hardships defeat us and cause us to give up on our compassionate goals. If we can develop our compassion and learn strategies for strengthening it, hardships can be used to strengthen compassion resilience.

Turning Self-Compassion into Compassionate Courage

One technique for turning self-compassion into compassionate courage is to consider others in your profession who have encountered similar client tragedies and their courage in moving forward rather than giving up. By moving forward with self-acceptance, self-compassion, and professional growth, you are sharing the legacy of the heroes of your profession and with heroes everywhere who work to make the world a safer and better place.

Section 5. Cultivating Self-Care and Healthy Professional Boundaries

The Green Cross Academy of Traumatology is a nonprofit humanitarian organization composed of traumatologists and mental health professionals dedicated to helping trauma victims and those who serve them. It was organized following the bombing of the Alfred P. Murrah Federal Building in Oklahoma City in 1995. They have developed a guideline of standards of self-care for care providers. The first guideline is "do no harm to yourself."[61] They delineate the following ethical principles of self-care:

Ethical Principles of Self-Care in Practice

These principles declare that it is unethical not to attend to your self-care as a practitioner because sufficient self-care prevents harming those we serve.

1. Respect for the Dignity and Worth of Self: A violation lowers your integrity and trust.
2. Responsibility of Self-Care: Ultimately, it is your responsibility to take care of yourself and no situation or person can justify neglecting it.
3. Self-Care and Duty to Perform: There must be a recognition that the duty to perform as a helper cannot be fulfilled if there is not, at the same time, a duty to self-care.[62]

Doing no harm to oneself is crucial because as helping professionals we must be at our best to do our best. It is estimated that about 30% of police officers, firefighters, and emergency medical personnel develop mental health issues including anxiety, depression, and post-traumatic stress disorder during their careers. Of those, about 50% develop a coexisting substance abuse disorder.[63] An estimated 11% of male police officers and 16% of female police officers engage in at-risk drinking, which is attributed by researchers to both social and stress-related drinking.[64] It is estimated that 29% of firefighters abuse alcohol and 10% abuse prescription drugs.[65] Drug abuse is more prevalent among paramedics and emergency medical technicians than among other emergency personnel.[66] In one study it was found that 37% of fire and emergency medical services (EMS) professionals have contemplated suicide, which is about ten times the rate of the general population in America.[67] In another study, police officers who reported burnout were 117% more likely to contemplate suicide than their peers.[68]

The Substance Abuse and Mental Health Services Administration (SAMHSA) recommends that organizational structures be put in place for first responders "protecting them from overwork and excessive stress and supporting them in seeking help when needed."[69] It is the responsibility of administrators to monitor staff stress and burnout, and to ensure that frontline staff have adequate time off from work for sleep, connecting with family, and rejuvenation. When a worker is showing signs of compassion fatigue, administrators need to take notice and intervene supportively, which might include making referrals for appropriate therapeutic intervention. Agencies should schedule regular break times throughout the day and arrange for adequate supervision and special accommodations for workers following intense traumatic exposure. However, not all administrators and agencies live up to this task. One study indicates that 69% of emergency medical services personnel do not receive adequate time between traumatic events to recover.[70]

Until all agencies establish reasonable procedures for identifying and addressing signs of compassion fatigue in frontline workers, first responders need to become aware of their own limitations and needs, setting boundaries as necessary in order to recover from intense schedules, case overloads, and stressful traumatic client events. A message sent to Vermont emergency responders at a wellness conference in December 2019 said, "It's okay not to be okay."[71] This is a good message because the first step in encouraging first responders to take their self-care seriously is to remove any stigma they might feel for being adversely affected by the traumatic scenarios they encounter each day. The next step is to encourage healthy ways to express and address the feelings generated by the intensity of the work they do. Stuffing feelings or trying to drink and drug them away adds to the problem and leads to burnout and incapacitation.

The Green Cross Standards of Humane Practice of Self Care state that providers have rights to wellness, rest, nourishment, and "sustenance modulation," which refers to the need to use self-restraint when it comes to unhealthy forms of coping strategies like poor food choices, alcohol, and drugs, all of which can compromise their competence as helping professionals.[72] The standards state that providers have a right to expect appreciation for their service, which under ideal circumstances should be fair and appropriate. However, in real-life contexts, providers often receive blame and criticism for attempts to help. I personally deal with this harsh reality by lowering my expectations for such rewards. Low expectations for such rewards mean less disappointment and a pleasant surprise when someone does show appreciation. This said, it is a positive thing for recipients of care to express their gratitude. It is also an essential thing for supervisors and agencies to acknowledge and reward the courage and service of their workers. Frontline workers must advocate for themselves and their coworkers when agencies show reluctance to show support or arrange for adequate self-care accommodations.

The Green Cross Standards of Humane Practice of Self Care specify the need for frontline workers to commit to self-care and to let go of work during break times, recommending that workers set deadlines and goals for using strategies for rest and relaxation, body work, a good sleep routine, a healthy diet, creative expression, gaining competence in effective calming meditation or spiritual practices, and effective methods for self-assessment and awareness.[73] The methods outlined in this book are directly aimed at enhancing the goal of developing self-awareness through mindfulness and go further by introducing strategies for renewing and strengthening compassion resilience.

Frontline workers would be wise to focus on the following healthy boundaries:

- Advocating for adequate work leave.
- Disengaging from conflictual or taxing relationships.
- Not attempting to fit in with working peers by engaging in counterproductive coping strategies like excessive drinking or drug use.

Another important boundary to set is with yourself:

* Instead of pushing yourself past your limits, recognize when you are starting to become overwhelmed or depleted and seek appropriate supports.

Section 6. The Benefits of Compassion in the Workplace

Toxic work environments disrupt our ability to maintain equilibrium and engage in normal restorative activities like sleep, healthy eating, and connecting with friends and family. As a result, such environments foster a high rate of employee turnover and illness, lack of enthusiasm about the work being done, and interstaff hostility, mistrust, and gossip. Often such environments are exacerbated by narcissistic leadership styles such as bosses who make unreasonable demands of staff while having low standards for themselves.[74] Such environments exacerbate burnout, making compassion fatigue more likely.

To reduce the dangers of compassion fatigue and substandard service to clients, it is crucial that helping professionals and their agencies strive to build healthy work environments focused on mutual support and effective service delivery. A compassionate approach to administration and staff communications can help. Several studies have indicated benefits that come from having a compassionate work environment including enhanced job satisfaction, interoffice cooperation, staff engagement, dedication, better health, staff retention and loyalty, reduced stress, and better interactions between employees.[75] In order to transform toxic environments into healthy ones, administrators should engage in developing staff team building, consciously developed structures to provide staff support, and supportive styles of supervision. Staff team building can be developed through active listening, demonstrating concern for staff welfare, accepting feedback, offering encouragement, and being considerate.[76] In cases where attempts to remedy toxic work environments are disregarded or discouraged by administrators, staff might have to organize, document, and register complaints with higher levels of administration or to appropriate state licensing authorities.

Creating Compassionate School Cultures

In many communities, children come to school burdened with traumatic backgrounds.[77] Their conditions are often exacerbated as they enter toxic school environments. Signs to look for that indicate a toxic school environment include:

- There is no well-defined school mission, so staff have different agendas.
- Teachers and staff are overburdened, underpaid, and unsupported.
- There is mistrust and hostility between staff, students, and parents.
- There is a sense that the environment is unsafe, and therefore self-preservation is primary.
- Instead of honest communication, recognition, and incentives for learning, there is an emphasis on control, rules, regulations, and punishment.
- Teachers do not feel empowered to do what is needed for their students, and there is little incentive to make the curriculum relevant to student interests and needs.[78]

In such environments, no one feels safe and old wounds are reopened. To transform toxic school cultures into compassionate environments, and in order to keep positive school cultures moving forward, it is important to keep compassionate principles in mind. There are several strategies available to accomplish this. For example, Scarlett Lewis, the mother of Jesse Lewis, who lost his life courageously saving his classmates from the Sandy Hook shooter, developed a Social Emotional Learning (SEL) program for schools called the Jesse Lewis Choose Love Movement, which contains strategies for developing courage, gratitude, forgiveness, and compassion in action.[79] Another approach is called SEE Learning, which stands for Social, Emotional, and Ethical Leaning. It was developed at Emory University under the guidance of His Holiness the Dalai Lama, and contains components for attention training, compassion and ethical discernment, systems thinking, and resilience and trauma-informed practice.[80] There are many other helpful SEL programs available as well.

Whichever approach you use, the key is to begin each morning by working on your own reactions using self-calming, renewing your compassionate goals, and bringing them with you to school and into your classroom. The following are some additional tips for creating a positive and caring school environment:

- Encourage parents to communicate with you when they have concerns about how their child is doing.
- Let students know that is important for them to let you and/or administrators know if they are experiencing difficulties with other students or with people in the community.
- Form positive bonds among the teaching staff with ongoing mentorship and open communication about mutual concerns.
- Cultivate engaged leadership in which administrators move in and out of the classroom frequently and are available to staff as needed.
- Have weekly school assemblies focused on conveying prosocial messages about topics like compassion, kindness, mutual respect, and consideration. The more these engage students in role playing acts of kindness, the better.
- Do intermittent short surveys on how staff and students are feeling in terms of safety and well-being.
- Celebrate diversity.
- Promote respectful language.
- Weave themes about compassion into topics covered in your curriculum.
- Involve parents in community building using principles of safety, respect, and compassion.[81]
- Model and teach definitions of compassion and compassion-building strategies to students.[82]

Section 7. Focusing on Strengths and Solutions When Working with Addictions

To accurately assess and intervene, helping professionals must be trained in what can go wrong for the populations they serve. Sometimes this can lead to only seeing the impact of past trauma, pathology, and illness while overlooking strengths. Steven Wolin,

MD, and Sybil Wolin, PhD, call this approach the damage model and suggest that, if helping professionals engage in treatment using only this model, it can disempower clients and make them more prone to succumbing to adverse life experiences.[83] In contrast, they recommend a challenge model in which helping professionals focus on resilience and strengths that clients have developed in response to adverse circumstances. Focusing on resilience empowers clients and helps them build on their strengths, leading to more successful treatment outcomes.[84]

A strengths approach is especially crucial when working with people with substance abuse issues. Evidence is emerging indicating that a strengths approach leads to reductions in substance use, fewer arrests, and better social functioning.[85] In a strength-based approach, one does not ignore the client's challenges and struggles. Instead, one selectively focuses on solutions, on client capacities, skills, knowledge, potentials, connections, and systemic supports in order to strengthen and empower them.[86]

People who have experienced adversity and trauma are more at risk for substance use disorders and mental health issues.[87] Therefore, in addition to a strength-based approach, it is crucial that professionals use a trauma-informed approach and avoid intervention strategies that might retraumatize clients rather than support their recovery.[88] A classic example of a treatment approach for substance disorders that backfires and triggers traumatic memory is the confrontation model, in which substance abuse counselors aggressively confront the denial in clients with substance use issues, attempting to get the client to acknowledge that they have a problem and therefore make efforts to overcome it. Confrontation easily degenerates into power struggles in which clients dig in their heels to oppose, reject, and resist change and provider help.

Currently, there are several other modalities being used to respond to substance abuse. A moral model for addressing substance abuse emphasizes crime and punishment. However, this approach can lead to adverse reactions in clients due to shaming, marginalizing, and stigmatizing, thus retraumatizing them and doing further damage. Often, clients relapse following perceived defeats and blows to self-esteem. Incarcerating them puts them into close contact with others caught in addictions, thus deepening connections with people addicted to substances and usually in environments without proper treatment modalities available.

Medical models offer a neurophysiological view of addiction along with pharmacological and detoxification strategies. Client compliance is a key factor in maintaining sobriety during and following medical interventions, so client motivation is a pivotal piece. Another standard mode of intervention is the spiritual model, which encourages clients to call on a higher power using 12-step programs. This has been a helpful model for many, but it depends on faith, connection with mentors, and motivation to change.

There are also psychological and sociocultural models, which offer a variety of insights into the inner dynamics and origins of substance use along with therapeutic and behavioral approaches to intervention.[89] For example, one emerging modality is the use of mind-body therapies such as meditation, hypnosis, relaxation, guided imagery, therapeutic suggestion, and cognitive behavioral therapy for reducing pain and opioid dependence.[90]

The possibility of having successful outcomes using any of the above strategies hinges on client cooperation, and therefore, enhancing client motivation for change is the most vital part of addressing substance abuse. There is an empirically validated method for doing this: the motivational interviewing strategy developed by William R. Miller, PhD, which focuses on developing an empathic relationship with substance abuse clients and recognizing, connecting with, and empowering the client's own reasoning and motivations for change.[91]

In this approach, the provider expresses empathy by using nonjudgmental active listening, developing the discrepancy between the client's goals and values and their current behaviors, avoiding arguments and confrontation, adjusting to client resistance rather than trying to confront and overpower it, and supporting the client's strengths, resilience, efficacy, and sense of hope. Thus the client is supported in moving from precontemplation to contemplating change, and from there to taking action steps toward recovery and sobriety maintenance.[92] Therefore, the most effective approach for providers to take in helping clients with substance abuse issues combines focusing on client strengths, using a trauma-informed approach, and maintaining an empathic connection in order to enlist motivation for change, treatment cooperation, and chances of success in helping them overcome addiction.

Tips for Keeping You Afloat Emotionally While Working with Clients Impacted by Addictions

There is a saying that is often used in Alcoholics Anonymous that expectations are premeditated resentments. Holding high expectations for positive client outcomes can increase your disappointment and disillusionment when things go wrong. Most addicted clients will relapse multiple times before finding their way to steady sobriety. Therefore, professionals working with clients with addictions can protect themselves from discouragement and burnout by adjusting expectations while simultaneously seeing their clients' potential. Some suggestions for tweaking your expectations include:

- See your clients not as addicts, but as human beings suffering from addiction.
- See relapses and manipulations as part of the pattern of addiction while recognizing, pointing out, and staying focused on your client's strengths and potential.
- Accept your helplessness in protecting your client from relapse while trying to also empathize with your client's feelings of helplessness against their addiction. At the same time, keep consistent in your positive regard for your client and in your support for your client's efforts to recover and free themselves from relapses.
- Remember that this is your client's struggle and journey. Your role is as a guide to help them find their way and encourage them when they are lost or feeling hopeless.
- Hold your client's wish for overcoming their addiction even when your client temporarily gives up on it.
- When your client relapses, you will have to go through the steps of helping your client remotivate themselves for sobriety. Consider this as a normal routine, like reminding yourself to brush your teeth each day.
- Remember that recovery takes different amounts of time for different people. Never give up.

- Each morning, it can help for you to renew your compassionate motive for going to work. Do the best you can with each client during your workday. At the end of the day:
  - mentally review how you did with clients during the day and list what you need to address the next day;
  - engage in self-care activities to regain your equilibrium; and
  - reset your compassionate motivation for facing the next day.

Section 8. Equanimity and Honoring Diversity

The National Association of Social Workers (NASW) code of ethics states:

Social workers respect the inherent dignity and worth of the person. Social workers treat each person in a caring and respectful fashion, mindful of individual differences and cultural and ethnic diversity.[93]

According to the code of ethics for psychologists:

Psychologists are aware of and respect cultural, individual, and role differences, including those based on age, gender, gender identity, race, ethnicity, culture, national origin, religion, sexual orientation, disability, language, and socioeconomic status, and consider these factors when working with members of such groups. Psychologists try to eliminate the effect on their work of biases based on those factors, and they do not knowingly participate in or condone activities of others based upon such prejudices.[94]

One of the core values for counselors is:

Honoring diversity and embracing a multicultural approach in support of the worth, dignity, potential, and uniqueness of people within their social and cultural contexts.[95]

The code of ethics for teachers says that teachers:

Shall not on the basis of race, color, creed, sex, national origin, marital status, political or religious beliefs, family, social or cultural background, or sexual orientation, unfairly exclude any student from participation in any program, deny benefits to any student, [nor] grant any advantage to any student.[96]

Police pledge to uphold the following standard:

> I will never act officiously or permit personal feelings, prejudices, political beliefs, aspirations, animosities, or friendships to influence my decisions.[97]

Other professions have similar codes, but the question is, how well do we live up to the values of our respective professions in honoring diversity and maintaining equanimity? We are all hardwired for survival, and our flight/fight systems make quick assessments each moment when in the company of others about whether they are safe. Sometimes mistrust can be triggered by differences and the unknown. We also have our own unique family, genetic, ethnic, cultural, and socioeconomic backgrounds. Differences can enrich us or set us apart depending on how we process and relate to them. Values promoting tolerance and acceptance can guide us but helping professionals should go deeper because even slight bias shows in our interactions and can trigger adverse reactions in our clients. It is crucial that helping professionals be aware of status, power, and privilege and how they impact the helping relationship. Therefore, it is important to:

- Know yourself and be mindful of how your thoughts and emotions react to diverse client populations.
- Work to counter bias within yourself by learning about races, cultures, gender expressions, religious beliefs, etc. that are different from your own.
- When working with a client whose culture or background is different from your own, take the stance of a learner and let your client educate you about their background and culture, and how they perceive it.
- Avoid judgments and stereotypes about things unfamiliar to you. Look for reactions in your client during interactions and check in with them should you sense a negative response to something you say or do, seeking to clarify and correct any unintentional miscommunications or microaggressions.
- Maintain mindfulness and recall repeatedly that, just like you, your client wants to be safe, respected, happy, and valued. Like you, they do not want to be neglected, dismissed, disrespected, controlled, misled, or harmed.

Section 9. Filling Your Cup with Gratitude When Taking Care of Others

Emotional depletion can occur in people who are taking care of the elderly, disabled, children, or people with chronic health conditions. Over time, caregivers can start to withdraw, lose motivation, and feel depressed, hopeless, helpless, irritable, and/or resentful.[98] A colleague and friend, Dr. Lorne Ladner, points out that it is not the compassion that becomes fatigued, but more the sense of self and well-being that reacts and begins to feel depleted.[99] Compassion is a resilient trait that gives us strength and perseverance when caring for others, but self-focus can cause us to neglect compassionate thoughts and instead start to think things like, "Why do I have to do this, I need a break, I can't stand this." When such thoughts and feelings of depletion start to arise, it is a sign that we need to take care of ourselves and rejuvenate. If you continue to focus on what you don't have and on the negative aspects of your situation, you will continue to increase your resentment and emotional depletion. Remember, it is your choice what you focus on. You can focus on aspects of your situation that make you feel more miserable, or you can choose to focus on aspects of your situation that uplift you.

Mindful self-compassion and other forms of self-care that have been mentioned previously are a good place to start. Ideally, you can take a break to refresh yourself, but if circumstances do not allow for a break, you can do some mindfulness practice in the place where you are providing care. Since mindfulness is a quiet exercise, no one around you will be able to tell that you are practicing it, and since it is a practice that engages your full awareness, it will have a positive impact on your ability to stay aware of your surroundings and keep vigilant to the needs of people for whom you are providing care. By replenishing yourself with mindfulness practice, you can regain your equilibrium. Once equilibrium is regained, a good way to start the process of reconnecting to compassion is to contemplate equanimity by thinking, "Just like I want to feel okay, so does this person to whom I am giving care." Breathe in care for yourself, breathe out care for them.

When you have regained a mindful sense of equanimity, an easy step to replenish your sense of well-being is to simply count your blessings. For instance, it is fortunate to have the health and stamina to be a person providing care instead of being in the condition of being unable to care for yourself and therefore being in the position of the person for whom you are providing care. We are all vulnerable to becoming incapacitated, but for now, you can care for yourself and for others. Another way to count your blessings is to remember times when you were in the position of needing care and to remember those who took care of you when you were most vulnerable, rekindling your sense of gratitude and wish to pay it forward. You can also recall things in your current situation and life for which you are grateful, particularly focusing on people for whom you feel gratitude. Researchers have found that gratitude can

- increase happiness, confidence, well-being, and positive emotions;
- improve relationships and social support;
- make us more optimistic and less anxious and depressed; and
- improve sleep, reduce blood pressure, and enhance overall physical health.[100]

By focusing on people and things that make you feel grateful, you are refilling your emotional cup, replenishing your heart, and giving yourself the emotional resources to continue more happily in your caregiving role. I personally feel tremendous gratitude to be able to work and make a living in a profession that is focused on caring for others.

Section 10. Maintaining Patience and Kindness When Confronted by Workplace Bullying

Hostile work environments have a negative effect on employee productivity, absenteeism, and healthcare costs.[101] Despite this, one survey indicates that

61% of bosses are bullies;
29% of targets remain silent;
40% of targets are believed to suffer adverse health effects;
71% of employer reactions are harmful to the targets;
60% of coworker reactions are harmful to the targets; and
65% of bullied employees lost their jobs trying to stop the harassment.[102]

There is a trickle-down effect of bullying. If leaders bully employees, it creates a hostile working environment that easily filters down to impact client care. Employees who are targets of bullying may experience increased emotional distress, disrupted sleep, fatigue, loss of vigor, depression, anxiety, or work-related suicide.[103] Medical complaints can include neck and musculoskeletal pain, fibromyalgia, and cardiovascular issues.[104] Bullying creates a work climate of anger and fear, which can be contagious and dangerous. Recently, three executives in a French company were successfully prosecuted for purposefully creating a hostile work environment in an attempt to push out employees to reduce their deficit, resulting in death by suicide of 35 employees.[105] Workers in male-dominated professions, service providers, and unskilled workers are most at risk for being bullied.[106] Some settings also pose a particular risk for helping professionals:

* Workplace bullying in healthcare settings is a serious problem that affects a growing number of healthcare workers.[107] One study reports that 44% of nurses have been bullied at work, particularly novice nurses.[108] Another study found that 38% of US healthcare workers have experienced some form of harassment.[109] Factors that contribute to this include inadequate staffing ratios, excessive workloads, imbalances of power, stress, lack of organizational fairness, and poor managerial skills.[110]
* Bullying among police officers is thought to be significant but underreported because of a code of silence and officers wanting to maintain an appearance of strength.[111] Bullying creates a climate of fear in which fellow officers may feel afraid to step forward on behalf of their peers because of possible reprisal from the bully.[112] However, bystanders, especially when they are trained in how to intervene, can have a positive impact on bullying:

  ° When a trained bystander steps in to stop a bully, half the time the bullying stops within ten seconds.
  ° Bystanders who stand up for a peer are 50% more likely to end offensive behaviors.[113]

Bullying can take the form of excessive teasing, withholding information to undermine a fellow officer's performance, badmouthing, being slow to offer backup, intimidation, threats, or even physical abuse.[114] Adding self-regulation, patience, and compassion exercises to police training curricula might be an effective prevention strategy to enhance morale, reduce incidents of aggression and counter-aggression, and reduce burnout.

- Bullying is also problematic among teachers. A study in the United Kingdom found that 15.5% of teachers reported currently being bullied, and 35.4% reported being bullied over the past five years.[115]
- In one study, almost three out of five agency-based social workers (58%) reported being subjected to rude, demeaning, and hostile work interactions in the past year.[116]

What Helping Professionals Can Do About Workplace Bullying Externally and Internally

External/behavioral responses to bullying that can help include the following.

- Document each incident of bullying.
- Look up your agency policies about workplace harassment and bullying and contact your union about it.
- Try not to react. Bullies enjoy a feeling of power when their targets become upset. They also use victim reactions to justify their acts of bullying and to blame their victims.
- Consider whether to confront the bully.

If the bully is your boss, it is important to consider your options carefully because confrontation could imperil your job security. Therefore, check with your union and HR representatives before deciding how to proceed. In some cases, it might be important to obtain legal counsel.

If you sense that the bully is potentially dangerous to you and others, don't try to handle it on your own; it is important to consult with administrators, HR, and security about how best to proceed.

Or, if you feel safe to do so, you can choose to confront the bully in a calm manner using I statements. For example, you could say, "I feel (state your feelings) when you (state what the bully did or said). If it happens again, I will begin to take informal and formal action." This sets a boundary. Many bullies are not used to someone setting a boundary on their behavior and might react with anger, so use caution and consider having a supportive person nearby. It is okay to be ambiguous about exactly what steps you will take should the bullying behavior continue because that leaves the bully in uncertainty, which can help them to consider being more cautious in avoiding future transgressions.

* Confide in people you trust about the situation. And take more formal steps if necessary.
* If upon analysis you see that there are things you have done or said that have contributed to the problem, it is important to learn from the experience and modify your behaviors as appropriate.
* Take care of your mental and physical health.[117]

Internal Ways to Regain Peace, Patience, and Kindness

* Remember your routines for regaining equilibrium and spend time doing them.
* In order to regain equilibrium, recall that like you, the bully is seeking well-being. So reflect on possible motives for the bully's behavior. Some bullies just want to feel powerful and superior, which belies an undercurrent of insecurity. Others can be people with good hearts who just get easily angered when things do not go the way they wish or expect. Ask yourself: What kind of bully are you dealing with?
* In this case, the practice of gratitude can be done by reflecting that it would be impossible to practice patience without encountering troublesome people. If everyone were always nice to us, there would be no occasion to practice patience. So in a way, this disturbing coworker is like a teacher who is showing you your vulnerability to anger and fear, thus giving you a chance to practice self-calming, tolerance, courage, and forgiveness.
* With a motive to free your mind from anger and fear, and to regain your mental peace, engage in the practices of forgiveness and kindness, breathing in well-being and peace to yourself and imagining breathing out well-being and peace of mind to your antagonist. If your antagonist were more at peace, they would

torment you and others less. While this might be a challenging practice, it can bring internal relief and help you to let go of your anger. It can also help you to restore a calm composure that will fortify you in taking skillful steps toward resolving the workplace challenge.

Section 11. Choosing Compassion as Your Moral Compass

A friend and excellent physician, Dr. John Tedeschi, wrote the following:

> We are now drawn into a world without an honest, sincere interest for human wellbeing . . . the true intent of compassion seems to be losing its ground. . . . This new healthcare world, the so-called healthcare industry . . . is now180 degrees in the opposite direction. . . . With the advancement of technology and AI there is no room nor time for compassion. In the last few years, life expectancy has dropped in the US, especially for the 30-45-year-old. Underlying medical conditions are being ignored and chalked up to either behavioral or emotional needs with a pill to cure. . . . People are becoming detached, having a difficult time trying to express their feelings in a short amount of time to a physician resulting in misdiagnosis and frustration on both sides. Being aware of this transformation/process is so important for everyone involved. Now we see clients, providers, members shuffled from one certified micro specialist to another, then placed on some medication thinking that the practice of medicine or even healthcare is only about giving a magic pill. Not realizing that pharmacology is only a small fraction of the practice of medicine. Underlying conditions are ignored because of time constraints or limited dollars. It's not surprising that one would expect a tremendous frustration and sadness related to anyone trying to honestly assist in this field. Today trained physicians, the masters of healthcare, are being told what to do, they are forced to limit their knowledge-base, their expertise, and marginalize their conscience, their ethics, all to satisfy stockholders and business.[118]

The dilemma between the profit motive versus doing what is best for clients is a real one. We all need to make a living to survive, but how do we know when we have enough? And how do we choose between our needs and the needs of our clients? We can see instances where CEOs seem to sacrifice public well-being to make a fortune. For example, large pharmaceutical companies made huge profits aggressively marketing opioids even though they knew that their product was leading to widespread addiction and death in the general public.[119] Also, healthcare insurance CEOs make as much as $26 million a year.[120] Where does all that money come from, and at whose expense? How much comes from limiting client benefits? Is the primary motive for providing healthcare insurance compassion or greed? Due to profit-driven business interactions, the price of insulin has gone up 64% since 2002, leaving many people with diabetes unable to pay for this life-saving medication.[121] Cancer patients are twice as likely to declare bankruptcy than the general population.[122] Is that how things should be?

Being mindful of your motives for doing your job is important because motive plays a major role in compassion fatigue. If greed overshadows your compassionate wish to help others, you are growing your neediness and narcissism instead of your compassion. You are also being drawn toward considering your own wants and needs as more important than your clients' well-being. It is hard to feel good about the work you are doing if you know that it is causing harm and/or that it is unethical. If you are doing harm to your clients with a profit motivation, you cannot honestly call yourself a helping professional. If you were to be honest, you might have to call yourself a professional predator.

Greed at the top of the healthcare industry has a negative impact on the entire healthcare system, from clients to nurses and frontline staff up through doctors and administrators. Doctors, nurses, and emergency medical services staff are trying to provide healthcare to the public at a time when costs are increasing while coverage is being slashed and human problems are becoming more complex. When helping professionals feel pressured to cut corners and deliver substandard services, they have misgivings about their work. Therefore, it is not surprising to see alarming rates of compassion fatigue and burnout among providers in systems headed up by profit-making CEOs with little compassion for their clients and workers.

What Helping Professionals Can Do to Keep Compassion as Their Inner Guide

- Choose compassion over fear and self-focused worries when facing ethical dilemmas. As a helping professional, you must consider codes of ethics, laws, and personal values when facing ambiguous ethical situations in treating clients. Agencies also have policies for how to handle challenging situations. If agency policies go against laws, ethical codes, and/or your personal values, you might have to make some tough decisions about whether to keep your current job or look elsewhere. Alternatively, you can also try to help administrators see the value in changing policy in order to better serve clients, enhance agency reputation, and avoid possible litigation and censure. If you only follow your fears, you are increasing internal factors leading to burnout. However, if you can stop, relax, and rekindle your compassion each day as your motive for doing your job, you will be building internal resiliency and a healthier motive for facing ethical dilemmas and stressful work situations.
- An example of how to move from self-focused fear into compassion when facing tough choices follows.

  - After regaining equilibrium through mindfulness of breathing, regenerate a sense of self-compassion and self-care. Breathe in well-being and breathe out your stress.
  - Recall that just as you want to be treated fairly and with compassion, so does your client. Just as you deserve effective treatment, so does your client.
  - Generate gratitude to be in a profession dedicated to helping others instead of harming them.
  - Breathe in peace, courage, and well-being to yourself. Breathe out peace, courage, and well-being to your client.
  - Generate a compassionate wish to solve the problematic situation facing you and your client. Ask yourself, "What are possible ethical ways to solve this?"
  - Pick your best ethical choice and see how it works.

Remember, if you keep compassion as your main motivation for going to work each day, you will still be making an income and thus be taking care of yourself and your own needs. At the same time, you will be increasing your effectiveness in your profession. If your income is insufficient or unfair, there is a place for advocating, enlisting union support, and seeking better employment opportunities, but for your own well-being it is good to make compassionate service the focus of your work. By making compassion the center of your moral compass you will be taking care of yourself and your clients at the same time.

Section 12. Staying Compassionately Engaged in Challenging Client Situations with Giving and Taking

Therapists and others working with clients who are going through adverse life experiences and trauma may attempt to avoid and distance from the client's distress by changing the subject, mentally retreating, minimizing, blaming the client, disbelief, or by having difficulty staying attentive. When a therapist avoids or changes the topic away from what the client is sharing because the material is troubling to the therapist, it is called "the silencing response."[123] I see this as a self-protective response that leads therapists to close down instead of opening up to important areas of dialogue with clients. The therapist might respond this way if feeling helpless to do anything about the problem, feeling vulnerable or triggered by what the client is expressing, and/or feeling that the material threatens their worldview.[124] In cases of shared trauma, the client's description of traumatic events might trigger the therapist's memory of similar past trauma.

Therapist avoidance of the client's traumatic material may delay client recovery, weaken the therapeutic bond, and interfere with providing treatment approaches that could provide relief.[125] Therapists who struggle with their reactions when listening to client descriptions of trauma might need to seek therapeutic supports in order to desensitize themselves and resolve their own traumatic issues, so that they can become more effective and overcome the silencing response.[126] In addition to working on one's own triggers and practicing ways to regain equilibrium and compassion, giving and taking practice can provide an effective way to stay fully and compassionately engaged with clients when they are expressing intense emotions and/or difficult material. It also can alleviate feelings of helplessness, which otherwise might contribute to secondary traumatic stress.[127] I find that giving and taking practice helps me tune in emotionally and cognitively when clients express distress and describe traumatic experiences. It also helps me face, process, and self-regulate during other stressful work-related challenges.

Procedure for Using Giving and Taking Practice in Challenging Client Situations

- It is helpful for you to have already done the work of regaining equilibrium and generating equanimity, gratitude, kindness, and compassion as your motive for your workday. Additionally, it is best if you have made a regular practice of giving and taking ahead of time, so that you are familiar and comfortable with the practice. If you are not fully comfortable with the practice of giving and taking, it is fine to focus on just the kindness contemplation described in the next step.
- If you find yourself in a client situation that is triggering you, causing you to become tense or wanting to avoid, remember the practice of breathing in well-being to yourself and breathing out well-being to your client while staying aware of what your client is telling you.
- Repeat out loud parts of what the client says, especially parts relevant to the emotions your client seems to be having about the material they are describing. Try to also identify the emotions your client is expressing and put them into words.
- As you breathe in with compassion, imagine your client's distress dissolves into light, which you inhale into you, calming your own fear response. Imagine that facing the fear enhances your courage, dispels your fear, and fills you with a calming light, bringing you peaceful confidence and well-being.
- As you exhale with kindness, imagine well-being and courage going out with your breath as light to your client, giving them calming reassurance and confidence.
- You can continue this visualization for as long as needed while being careful to listen and verbalize what the client is telling you. Doing so can give you a feeling that you are doing something for your client. It also keeps you compassionately

engaged with your client rather than reacting with avoidance or the silencing response. Over time, your resilience can become enhanced through exposing yourself to the difficult material your clients share with you and thus the practice of giving and taking can become a support for building your compassionate courage.

* When you see that the challenging situation with your client is resolving and you've taken whatever steps are necessary to ensure your client's well-being, it is useful to return to imagining breathing in well-being to yourself and breathing out well-being to your client and to others as a way to regain equilibrium.

Section 13. Maintaining Self-Care and Active Compassion in Crisis and Disaster Situations

First responders, disaster relief workers, and emergency mental health workers are all vulnerable to secondary traumatic stress. Often when a crisis or disaster occurs, frontline workers start out intervening with optimism and the hope for a quick recovery, but this can turn into disillusionment as their work and strong identification with the victims pull them into grief reactions, fatigue, and irritability.[128] Long-term disaster work can contribute to cumulative stress, anxiety, depression, and other physical, mental, and interpersonal difficulties.[129] Indeed, the duration and intensity of exposure to crisis and disaster work is predictive of the severity of compassion fatigue and burnout in emergency service workers.[130]

Therefore, therapeutic supports and stress-management routines for long-term emergency service workers are essential for their well-being. Wee and Myers have recommended several strategies to help mental health workers cope with the stress of treating people working with crisis and disaster situations.[131] I have adapted some of their recommendations below, which I believe are useful to consider for all emergency service workers whether they are engaged in short-term crisis situations or longer-term disaster relief situations:

* Encourage emergency service workers to prepare a personal emergency plan before a crisis or disaster strikes. This plan should include details about who will take care of the worker's

family members and how the worker's family will maintain safety should a crisis or disaster occur that suddenly calls the worker away from home. Having a plan ready ahead of time can give frontline workers peace of mind from knowing that their family is safe and secure.

* Mental health agencies should prepare plans for sending out trained therapists to sites of disasters to provide crisis intervention, and in addition, prepare community outreach initiatives for screening and intervening with people in the community who might suffer from longer-term impacts of disasters. Screenings should be done in agencies ahead of time in order to select crisis intervention teams of seasoned mental health workers who are not exhibiting signs of compassion fatigue or burnout because workers who are inexperienced or already traumatized are more at risk of developing symptoms if exposed to disaster work.[132] Frontline workers should be equipped with necessary training and supplies ahead of time. They might be called away for an extended period into challenging and dangerous circumstances, so every step should be taken to ensure that they have what they will need and that there is an abundant network of collegial support.

* During the crisis interventions themselves, supervisors and coordinators should track shifts of frontline workers, so that shifts are no more than 12 hours and so that frontline staff have at least 12 hours between shifts to recuperate, sleep, and rest. If a worker has a rough shift, the supervisor should rotate them into a less demanding task for their next shift. Regular supervision should be provided with short briefings at the beginning and short debriefings at the end of each shift. Supervisors should monitor for signs of compassion fatigue in their staff and ensure staff access to therapeutic supports and activities to help staff restore equilibrium between shifts. Establish a buddy system so that workers look out for each other. As crisis intervention activities begin to wrap up, arrange closure activities to help staff share experiences, integrate what they have learned, and acknowledge each other supportively. It is important to recognize, acknowledge, and honor workers for their contributions and personal sacrifices. This is true for all levels

of emergency service workers, but especially for first responders who put themselves in harm's way to protect and serve.

- Advance training for emergency mental health personnel should include the following:

  ○ A thorough education in all factors, phases, and treatment modalities for disaster intervention.

  ○ A systems perspective on how best to network with and mobilize micro, mezzo, and macro resources for disaster relief as well as how best to coordinate with other agencies and disciplines. Many communities develop crisis intervention teams (CITs) and mobile crisis units based on partnerships between law enforcement, local mental health agencies, and the community to intervene in situations before they escalate.[133]

  ○ Knowledge of how to intervene with special populations affected by disaster including children, elderly, homeless, disabled, local ethnic and cultural groups, and others who might need special considerations.

  ○ A specialized knowledge of how stress and trauma impact the mental health of victims and frontline workers, including an understanding of post-traumatic stress disorder, secondary traumatic stress, vicarious trauma, burnout, and shared trauma.

  ○ A strong repertoire of stress management strategies for regaining equilibrium including getting enough sleep, good nutrition, exercise, social support, humor, relaxation, creative expression, meditation, and other mind-body techniques.

  ○ Logistical training on all details of the disaster site, procedures, assignments, and how support systems will be set up so that frontline workers can help each other with self-care, emotional support, and stress management.[134]

If you are called into a crisis or disaster situation to help, it is particularly important that you have accustomed yourself ahead of time to regularly using a good repertoire of self-regulation skills in order regain equilibrium and restore yourself. I hope that the COMPASS exercises can help you in this process. The following is an example of how they can be adapted for crisis work.

- Be mindful not to fall for the self-esteem model of being a hero by thinking that you are superhuman, you do not need support, or that you can save everyone. Such thoughts are a setup for burnout, discouragement, and compassion fatigue. Instead, I suggest that you use the self-compassion approach of accepting your strengths and weaknesses, being friendly with yourself in acknowledging when you need a break or support, giving your best efforts with full awareness that you might not be able to keep bad things from happening to everyone you are trying to help, and make time for self-calming, sleeping, eating, connecting to support staff, exercise, meditation, and other activities to restore equilibrium.
- Mindful equanimity while you work can keep you open to whoever needs your help. By remembering that those you are helping are just like you in wanting to be safe and secure and in not wanting to suffer, you will feel a natural urgency in responding to the victims of disaster and to those who are in peril.
- Gratitude can lift your spirits when you notice small victories or successes. There are many people involved in crisis interventions and disaster relief efforts for whom we can feel grateful. We can also feel gratitude for all forms of material assistance that are brought in to help with emergency situations and to our opportunity to serve our community and the greater good. There can be a tremendous sense of gratitude in looking back and remembering people we have helped in some way. When I hear of a client doing well, it gives me encouragement and helps me continue my efforts to serve others.
- When anger and frustration well up due to something going wrong during a relief effort, it can be helpful to recall the benefits of patience and contemplate kindness. As you are working, remember to breathe in well-being for yourself and breathe out well-being to others around you. Anger might also set in if you are starting to become overtired or hungry, or if you are feeling unsupported. If so, it is an indication that you need to take a break and restore yourself.
- Remember to keep focused on compassion and to use giving and taking practice to cope with complex or overwhelming situations as you work. Sometimes people we try to help become

angry with us because of their situation, fear, grief, and/or suf-fering. If so, compassionate giving and taking practice can help you take it in stride without resentment or a wish to retaliate, and instead it can help you respond by giving help and comfort.

* When fatigued, give yourself permission to rest, remembering that you need to restore yourself to continue and be at your best. Once replenished, you can reengage your will to wade back into the helping process with an activating thought like, "Now it's time for me to put my compassion into action again. These people are counting on me. I will do whatever I can to help them."

Section 14. Finding Hardiness in Your Compassion and in Your Sense of Mission

Compassion satisfaction is a "sense of fulfillment you feel for the work you do."[135] It is an internal resilience that comes from finding your purpose in life through developing compassionate goals and pursuing them. When you develop compassion satisfaction, no one needs to build you up because, internally, you know that your heart is in a good place and that you are doing the best you can for your-self and for others. It helps if you can find a good fit between who you are as a person, your values, and the profession you choose. Sometimes it might take a few tries before you find the right job, but once you do, it is important to fully embrace the mission of your profession and agency in order to properly serve your clients. Remembering your compassionate goals will bring you fortitude, well-being, and resiliency in doing your best work.

Compassion satisfaction doesn't arise without causes; it comes from hard work over time and from being steadfast in repeatedly generating compassionate thoughts and feelings. It is a produced thing and you must nurture and support it in your daily practice. In my early adulthood, I had to fight with anxiety, depression, and dread because my pattern of self-focus was well developed, but my emerging interest in developing compassion was newly forming. I was also unsure about what career path I wanted to follow, though I knew that I liked working with people and that I wanted to do something that helped them. The good thing is that I never gave up trying to develop my compassionate insight or on trying to find the right fit between my values and my career. Each day, I made mindfulness and compassion practices my priority, returning to them for guidance and support when facing challenging work situations. I used them repeatedly during my career until I felt them gain traction and start to bring well-being.

As mindful self-compassion and compassionate insight began to develop and my career path became clearer, anxiety and depression along with the dread that they evoked began to wane. Compassion builds resilience and insight helps in discerning your next steps. When you become accustomed to compassionate insight by renewing it when you wake up in the morning, your compassionate goals can get you out of bed and pull you through your job each day. And at the end of the day, you can begin to experience the satisfaction that comes from knowing that you followed your goals and tried your best to help your clients that day.

While 60.7% of men and 51.2% of women have encountered life events that fit the criteria for post-traumatic stress disorder, only 7.8% of us develop the symptoms of PTSD.[136] Compassionate goals and the practices leading to them will help you enter into, face, and persevere with challenging situations. By facing challenges and persevering, we can build hardiness, and hardiness is a protective factor that can shield us from PTSD and compassion fatigue.[137] Hardiness combines a sense of control, commitment, and seeing change as a challenge.[138] In reality, the world is beyond our ability to control. However, if we can begin to self-regulate our reactions to the world, over time we can begin to feel a sense of internal control. By renewing our compassionate goals each day and doing our best in carrying them out, we are committing to following our own direction for our lives. By accepting the inevitability of change, we prepare ourselves for whatever life brings next. Instead of seeing the future as a scary unknown, we can begin to see it as an exciting journey that is anything but dull. Challenges can become opportunities to test our skills, learn new things, and expand our connections.

Helping professionals feeling helpless and ineffectual can lead to burnout.[139] If you stay negatively focused on the costs of caring and unsure of your purpose and meaning for your work, you are unwittingly depleting yourself. This process is exacerbated should you choose to try unhealthy coping strategies like avoidance, numbing your emotions, the silencing response, or excessive drinking or using drugs to drown out your distress. But remember, you can always choose to change your focus. By starting and ending each day with activities to help you regain equilibrium, focusing on mindful self-compassion and self-care, you can detoxify from the stress that most jobs bring with them. In addition, if you rebuild your compassion each day, using the COMPASS exercises to renew your compassionate goals, you are restoring your sense of efficacy, commitment to your work, and compassion satisfaction. In this way, whatever your helping profession and whatever activities you engage in during each day of your career, you are contributing to the well-being of yourself and others. So I suggest that it is as important as brushing your teeth each morning to remember to take a few moments to do the following:

1. Regain equilibrium with a few mindful breaths and recall that you and others are equal in wanting well-being and to avoid suffering. The people you will encounter and work with today are the same.
2. Recall your gratitude to be working in a job that encourages you to help others and for everyone who directly or indirectly brought you to this moment and career path as well as for those who sustain you in it.
3. Practice kindness by wishing well-being for yourself and others, imaging soothing light carrying well-being comes into you with your in-breath and back out to others as you breathe out.
4. Recall the difficulties that your clients and others are going through, developing a wish that they be free of them.
5. Imagine with compassion their sufferings dissolve into light, which you breathe into your self-focused fears, dispelling them. You are filled with light, courage, and confidence, which you breathe out as light to your clients and others, giving them what they need to find well-being.
6. Decide to take responsibility for trying to help your clients and others find internal and external resources to secure well-being.

7. Set your goals for how you will try to help them today. As you end your session and head to work, a simple strategy to help you recall your compassionate goals periodically throughout your workday is to silently repeat to yourself, "Remember your purpose," as a way to recommit to your goals when something bogs you down, distracts you, or temporarily throws you off course.

Section 15. Weeding Out Self-Defeating Thoughts

Our neurology causes us to have a negativity bias, which is a tendency to notice, think about, learn from, and make decisions based more on negative thoughts and information than on positive thoughts and information.[140] Researchers attribute this bias to an evolutionarily derived survival strategy that helps us to predict danger and protect ourselves. However, it can also become problematic because focusing too much on negative thoughts and events can start to affect how we feel, how we see ourselves and the world, and how we choose to respond to challenges and opportunities in our lives.

In the case of vicarious trauma, helping professionals who repeatedly listen empathically to the traumatic events that their clients share with them can sometimes develop a sense of hopelessness and helplessness, damaging their sense of meaning, purpose, hope, and faith.[141] This can have an adverse impact on our view of the world and self, spiritual beliefs, our sense of vulnerability, social relationships, behavior, and emotional/physiological well-being.[142] It is thought that high expectations of oneself and about desired treatment outcomes may contribute to the development of vicarious trauma.[143] Personal styles of trying to cope with troubling emotions by avoidance, blaming, or withdrawing make helpers more vulnerable.[144] Providers with a personal history of having experienced trauma, lack of social or agency support, an excessive work load, insufficient time off, and/or poor boundaries are also at risk.[145]

In order to reduce and prevent the chances of developing vicarious trauma, helping professionals are encouraged to find ways to take time away from work for rest and play. It is also possible to transform vicarious trauma by contemplating life's meaning from a deeper vantage point, connecting with people, remembering the benefits of compassionate work, noticing even small positive things in your life, being creative, and identifying and debunking cynical beliefs.[146]

The trifecta of cynical beliefs, negativity bias, and inaccuracy of conceptual constructs of reality can easily trap us in unproductive and destructive ruminations. Cynical beliefs can include thoughts like "nothing matters," "people are evil," "only a fool cares about anyone but themselves," "I'm never safe," and other self-defeating reactions to life's darker side that can arise from hearing traumatic stories over time. Such thoughts are self-defeating because they lead to inaction and to retreating into narcissism or despair. When cynical beliefs lead to a low opinion of yourself or to devaluing your skills, you might find that this a reaction to a previous overestimation of what is possible. For example, if you begin your career thinking that you should be able to cure everyone and make everyone's life better, you can easily begin to feel defeated and think you are incompetent when clients do not respond immediately to the treatments you offer. This too can be related to an initial underestimation of the tenacity and depth of client problems you are trying to address. When you sense that a distortion in your self-concept might be making you feel powerless or too powerful, it can easily be dispelled by:

a. identifying the distortion in self-concept;
b. analyzing and debunking it; and
c. defining your self-concept based on your compassionate goals.

Thoughts and concepts are often inaccurate and can easily fluctuate between overestimating and underestimating reality. For instance, when people see or hear of a terrible crime perpetrated on someone, it is possible for their reaction to generalize and lead to global fear or to a loss of hope for humanity. This can also happen to therapists when they listen to repeated accounts of traumatic events that their clients have experienced at the hands of perpetrators. Over time there can be a cumulative effect on a therapist's views of the world and of humanity, which can lead to helplessness, hopelessness, and fear. Meichenbaum recommends that professionals use calming strategies and cognitive restructuring to deconstruct triggering distortions in thought that can contribute to vicarious trauma followed by reimagining more positive self-talk focused on resilience.[147]

When you find a cluster of thoughts or beliefs about yourself or your world that are bogging you down and sapping your energy, insight and analytical skills can help you debunk them. You can use a similar formula to the three steps for analyzing distortions about self-concept, but adapt them as follows:

a. Recognize the cynical or distorted thought.
b. Debunk it using analysis.
c. Restore your compassionate goals.

For example, the thought that nothing matters can be debunked by remembering that you do not want to feel suffering and pain, and that the same is true for others. So it matters that you and others take steps to avoid unnecessary causes of pain and suffering. The thought that all people are evil is easily debunked by remembering times that people have benefited you and others. The thought that only fools care about anyone but themselves can be debunked by remembering the benefits that compassion brings psychologically, physically, and interpersonally to people who cultivate it. And the thought that whole groups of people or humanity do not deserve our care or respect is easily debunked by recalling that people are individuals and that crimes perpetrated by one person do not reflect on anyone but them. Factors that drive people to heinous crimes are complex and vary, but usually have a major component of narcissism and disregard for others. So if we work on reducing narcissism in ourselves and share ways for others to do the same, we are actively working to better humanity and create a safer world for ourselves and others.

Pearlman and McKay recommend that, in order to combat cynical beliefs and other factors that can lead to vicarious trauma, helping professionals should develop awareness, balance, and connection.[148] In particular, try to become aware of when something is troubling you or making you tense. I find that a regular practice of scanning your body and practicing the four foundations of mindfulness can heighten self-awareness and tune you in to your reactions. Acceptance and self-compassion can help you to digest your reactions in a supportive way as you contemplate ways to address your concerns. Try to balance your work life with time away from work so that you can tend to your home life. And while you are working, make sure to take breaks when you need them, especially if you are involved in crisis work. Make sure to also forge healthy connections with the people you work with and with your family and friends. A support network at home, at work, and in the community provides a protective shield to prevent burnout, secondary traumatic stress, and vicarious trauma.

Pearlman and McKay also recommend that you forge a spiritual connection in order to give you a sense of meaning and purpose. For some people, a spiritual connection might be to believe in a higher power. For others it might be a connection to humanity, to the natural world, or to something greater than the self.[149] Meaning and purpose give you the resiliency you need to move forward and to persevere in your compassionate work. Insight gives you the vision to see through false and destructive thoughts as well as to discern your best choices for moving forward in a positive direction. Feelings of being unsafe, mistrustful, and helpless, which characterize vicarious trauma, can be reduced by time spent on self-care and using coping strategies.[150] I hope that the above analytical skills will add a useful strategy to therapists' arsenal of self-care tools.

Section 16. Assisting Clients with End-of-Life Issues and Coping with Our Own Mortality

We all fear rejection, abandonment, loss of control, harm, failure, and death. We can tell what we are most attached to by noticing what we are most fearful of losing. Of all that we have, many of us consider our lives and health as our most cherished possessions. Ernest Becker (1924–1974) was a cultural anthropologist who argued that most human endeavors are unconsciously driven by attempts to deny our mortality or to try to transcend it.[151] Helping professionals are often called upon to assist clients and/or client families in dealing with the stress that surfaces with end-of-life issues.[152] We must not only face our own vulnerability to death and dying, but also those of our clients.[153]

Along with helping clients make decisions about practical matters during end-of-life cases, we are sometimes called upon to help clients search for spiritual meaning in order to cope with the fear and uncertainty that comes with death and with the dying process.[154] Mental health professionals tend to be less religious than the public they serve.[155] However, most are supportive of clients' use of prayer and other spiritual practices to cope with dying.[156] Personally, I believe that it is important to support a person's spiritual beliefs when they are in the process of dying. It will only cause distress or anger to try to convince someone of a faith they do not follow or with which they are unfamiliar when they are in the process of dying. As helping professionals, it is our responsibility to comfort people going through the death process, not to frighten or agitate them further in an already frightening situation.[157] A Jungian approach to helping clients through the death process shares this perspective in suggesting that therapists embrace the client's spiritual views, whatever they may be.[158]

There are some who argue that it is okay for helping professionals to use their own religious convictions to motivate themselves in their work with clients.[159] However, often people tend to resort to their own cultural worldviews when reminded of their mortality, and become distrustful of people who hold worldviews that differ from their own.[160] Therefore, while it is true that workers can use whatever spiritual perspectives appeal to them in order to keep themselves motivated and cope with their own fears and vulnerabilities, helping professionals need to be careful not to overstep bounds by trying to convert clients to their preferred spiritual beliefs. If a client asks us about a spiritual perspective with which we have familiarity, that is different. By responding with the information that they ask of us, we are respecting their wishes.

Our ethical code of supporting our client's right to self-determination is paramount, especially when it comes to their most vulnerable time—their approaching mortality. Surrogates who are charged with making decisions for hospitalized older adults also need to consider spirituality in their decision process.[161] It is suggested that surrogates consult with spiritual advisors for whom the older adult in their care has faith when making decisions about end-of-life care.[162] In short, spirituality can be a source of comfort and support for our clients who are dying. It is important that we make sure to use it that way.

Heightened fears of death and dying are associated with lowered self-esteem.[163] However, Kesebir and Pyszczynski wrote that only by facing up to the inevitability of our own death can we live "happier, wiser, more authentic lives."[164] Exposure to things we fear helps our nervous systems habituate to them, thus making us less afraid of them. By repeatedly facing our fears, we can eventually gain the confidence that comes from mastery. In contrast, avoidance of things we fear causes us to feel more anxiety about them, a sense of failure and weakness in reaction to them, and a lack of confidence. Confidence comes from mastery, and mastery comes from the practice of facing our fears.[165] For example, novice nurses exposed to patients experiencing serious illness and death report more distress and fear of death than more seasoned nurses.[166]

Frontline emergency workers put their lives on the line every day. Such heroism has been traditionally recognized and honored in military service and among police and firefighters, but it has also been applauded during the COVID-19 pandemic among many other professions including medical personnel, food producers and providers, and transportation and delivery workers. We all put ourselves at risk at times in doing what we must do for our clients. This is part of being a helping professional. For our own well-being as helping professionals, internally restoring ourselves by our preferred spiritual beliefs, mindfulness, self-compassion, self-care, and exercises to restore and enhance compassionate insight is our own prerogative. I hope you will find the strength to care in whatever combination of approaches works best for you. Your life and the lives of those you impact will be better for it.

Section 17. The Core COMPASS Practices in Simple Form

For beginners, rather than trying to do all these practices every day, it is suggested that you try to engage in a regular practice of mindfulness and then add one or two more practices per session. As you become familiarized with the different contemplations, you can review some briefly and spend more time with others as preferred. Eventually, the emotional logic of the practices in the sequence laid out below will become more evident, and you may want to incorporate all of the contemplations with each session.

Foundation Skill: Mindfulness

1. Mindfulness of body:

   a. Begin by noticing your breath as it leaves your nostrils and returns, noticing if it's a short breath or a long breath.
   b. Be aware of your whole body as you breathe.
   c. Breathe in calm and breathe out stress.
   d. Let your body start to calm and settle.

2. Mindfulness of feelings:

   a. As you notice your breath, also notice your feelings.
   b. Be aware of the present moment as you breathe.
   c. Breathe in joy and breathe out sorrow.
   d. Let your feelings start to settle.

3. Mindfulness of awareness:

   a. As you notice your breath, also notice your awareness.
   b. Focus your awareness on the present moment.
   c. Notice the clear nature of your awareness, freeing it from worries.
   d. Concentrate your awareness on your breath.

4. Mindfulness of mental objects:

   a. As you focus on your breath, notice thoughts come and go.
   b. Notice the changing and impermanent nature of thoughts.
   c. Let disturbing thoughts and feelings fade away.
   d. Let go of thoughts and return your focus to your breath.

Core Compassion Skills:

Equanimity can be defined as an unbiased mind focused on our shared humanity and everyone's equal wish to find happiness and to avoid suffering.

- Desired effects of this practice:

  ○ Counteracting bias, intolerance, alienation
  ○ Fostering connectedness, expanded social focus

A. Contemplate some of the benefits of equanimity mentioned above and begin with a brief practice of mindfulness.

B. Once settled, consider the following points:

1. We are all equal in wanting to be happy and in wanting to avoid suffering.

2. Just like I want to be loved, valued, and respected, everyone wants to be loved, valued, and respected.

3. If people treated each other with equal friendship and respect, it would reduce conflict and strife. The world would be a happier and more peaceful place.

4. Think, "How wonderful it would be if everyone abided in equanimity. In order to make my own mind more peaceful, and in order to help reduce conflicts, I will try to develop an equal sense of friendliness for everyone." Hold this thought for a while.

Gratitude can be defined as a recognition and appreciation of the help we have received that engenders thankfulness and a wish to repay kindness.

- Desired effects of this practice:

  ° Counteracting self-preoccupation, low self-esteem, poverty mentality
  ° Fostering hope, meaningful direction of wishing to help others, and thus confidence, fortitude

A. Contemplate the benefit of gratitude and begin with brief practice of mindfulness and equanimity.

B. When settled, bring to mind someone for whom you feel grateful and imagine him or her in front of you. Think of ways that this person has helped you.

- Surrounding you, imagine others in your life who have been helpful to you. For example, consider the following:

  ° How many people helped construct the building you are now using?
  ° How many people help directly or indirectly to sustain your daily life?

- Now ask yourself the same questions about how many people have contributed to:

  - The food you've eaten?
  - The clothing you've worn?
  - Your health care?
  - Your education?
  - The technology you've used?

- How many have been a friend, a parent, an ally, a protector?
- If you feel a sense of gratitude, focus on it for a while and sustain it. Then, think of ways you might be able to repay some of the kindness you've been shown.

Kindness can be defined as the wish for all beings, including ourselves, to have happiness in all of its many forms.

- Desired effects of this practice:

  - Counteracting anger, resentment, bias, intolerance
  - Fostering openness to relationships, tolerance, sense of belonging, shared humanity

A. Contemplate the benefit of kindness and do a brief practice of mindfulness followed by a short review of equanimity and gratitude.
B. When settled, contemplate the following:

- May I be happy, healthy, and peaceful; may I have joy, contentment, and security; may I have strength, determination, and success in overcoming the difficulties in my life.
- Make the same wishes for loved ones.
- Make the same wishes for friends.
- Make the same wishes for those who upset you (if they were calmer, happier people, they might be better company).
- Make the same wishes for everyone, everywhere.
- As you contemplate these kind thoughts, imagine a soft light of kindness travels in with your breath, bringing well-being to yourself, and then travels out with your out-breath bringing well-being to others. Meditate this way for however longs feels comfortable.

- If you feel a sense of loving-kindness, focus on it for a while, thinking how wonderful it would be if everyone could have happiness and its causes.

Compassion can be defined as the wish that others be free from suffering and its causes.

- Desired effects of this exercise:
  ◦ Counteract self-centered focus
  ◦ Foster universality, empowerment, humility

A. Contemplate the benefit of compassion and do a brief practice of mindfulness, equanimity, gratitude, and loving-kindness. Settle your mind into a meditation on your breath while imagining breathing kindness and thoughts of well-being into yourself imagined as a soft light, and then breathing out that light of kindness and well-being to others. You can return to this meditation periodically to refresh yourself should you feel overwhelmed at any point when contemplating the various forms of suffering others go through.

B. When settled, contemplate the following:

- Although I want only happiness and not to suffer, life is filled with difficulties and hardships.
- Others, just like me, want only happiness and not to suffer. Yet many face daily hunger, poverty, and homelessness.
- Many encounter conflicts, disrespect, living in fear, imprisonment, torture, abuse, or violence.
- Many experience sickness, frailties of body, and mental distress.
- Life is full of uncertainty and unpleasantness for all of us as we struggle to survive and thrive.
- If you feel a sense of compassion for yourself and others, focus on it for a while and sustain it. Think about how everyone is equal to you in not wanting to suffer, and about how wonderful it would be if everyone, everywhere could be free from suffering and its causes.

"Giving and taking" is a practice of imagining taking on hardships and giving away well-being.

- Desired effects of this practice:

  ° Counteracting excessive self-focus and fears
  ° Fostering exposure, empowerment in role as helper

A. Contemplate the benefit of giving and taking and do a brief practice of mindfulness, equanimity, gratitude, loving-kindness, and compassion.
B. When settled, contemplate the following:

  - My tendency to think only about my own needs limits my wish to develop my compassion and has other negative social, emotional, and health effects as well.
  - My wish to develop my compassion is based on understanding that to do so will strengthen my social and emotional well-being and my ability to help others. Therefore, I will try for a moment to consider the needs of others before my own.

    ° Imagine a future situation you face that is troubling you and picture your fears about it as being like a dark cloud in your chest.
    ° Now, with compassion, imagine inhaling the future situation in the form of light. As it enters your chest, it dispels the dark cloud of your fear and fills you with confidence, courage, and a sense of well-being.
    ° With loving-kindness, exhale that sense of well-being and confidence in the form of light to yourself in the future, imagining that it gives you confidence and the ability to overcome the troubling situation.
    ° Do the same visualization for someone you care about who is going through hardship.
    ° Do the same visualization for loved ones and friends.
    ° Do the same visualization, extending it to everyone, everywhere.

  - Rest in the visualization of everyone being freed from their suffering and filled with well-being, thinking how wonderful it would be if you could actually help others find happiness and freedom from suffering.

Activation takes compassion from a passive potential into an engaged expression.

- Desired effects of this practice:
  - ° Counteracting passivity
  - ° Fostering engagement in meaningful activities

A. Contemplate the benefit of activating your compassion and do a brief practice of mindfulness, equanimity, gratitude, kindness, compassion, and giving and taking.
B. When settled, contemplate the following:

  - Although I've imagined taking away the sufferings of myself and others, and then imagined us all filled with well-being, in reality the world is still full of suffering.
  - If I don't accept any responsibility for making this world a better place, then whose job is it?
  - If I want this world to improve, it is important that I do my part.
  - Generate and hold the thought, "It is my responsibility to improve the conditions of myself and others."

Goal-focused compassion involves the formulation of goals that can sustain and develop our commitment to a compassionate direction.

- Desired effects of this practice:
  - ° Counteracting a sense that life lacks meaning
  - ° Fostering a compassionate action and lifestyle, empowering, redirecting mental focus toward helping self and others

A. Contemplate the benefits of goal-focused compassion and do a brief practice of mindfulness together with a brief contemplation on the equanimity, gratitude, kindness, compassion, giving and taking, and activation exercises.
B. When settled, contemplate the following:

  - In order to sustain compassionate efforts over time, it is important to develop my internal capacities and begin to put my compassion into action.

- Take a moment to consider what internal qualities you want to make stronger and what direction in life is important to you.
- Set a goal to develop the qualities you identify as important in order to be of best help to yourself and others. Also consider what types of compassionate activities might be of interest to you.
- Hold your goals single-pointedly while thinking, "I will develop these capacities and enter into these activities in order to benefit myself and others."

Core Analytical Skills

Purpose: to turn back internal obstacles to compassion through analytical insight.

- Cognitive schema: patterns of concepts about reality that inform our judgments/reactions.
- Distortions in personal schema can occur based on our reactions to and interpretations of our unique experiences, thus affecting self-concept.

  - Overly negative/diminished sense of self can lead to feeling

    - worthless,
    - helpless,
    - hopeless.

  - This can sap motivation by exacerbating

    - depression,
    - anxiety,
    - avoidance.

  - Overly positive/inflated sense of self can lead to feeling

    - superior,
    - entitled,
    - invulnerable.

  - This can block compassion by exacerbating

    - inconsideration,

- self-indulgence,
- unrealistic expectations.
- Practicing the analytical core skills.
- After contemplating the rationale for the analytical core skills as described above and a brief practice of mindfulness, do a short review of the core compassion exercises.
- When settled into goal-focused compassion, contemplate the following:

  A. Identifying a cognitive distortion:

  - Within a calm and clear state of awareness, recall an incident that is troubling to you. Focus on your reactions to the situation, looking for how the situation affects your self-concept.
  - If you identify any distortion in self-concept, hold it clearly in mind.

  B. Analyzing the self-concept:

  - Ask yourself whether this concept of you is of mental or physical nature.
  - Mentally search for such a self within the various parts of your body and mind.
  - Recognizing that this concept is just that, a concept, allow it to dissolve along with the reactions it has aroused.

  C. Defining self-concept using compassionate insight:

  - Within the clarity of your awareness, recall your compassionate goal. Recall a time when you were living in accord with your core values and identify with that positive image of yourself, holding it clearly in mind for a while.
  - If wished, you can imagine that your compassionate goal takes the form of a healing, soothing ball of light in your chest.
  - As you focus on your compassionate goal, imagine the light gets brighter, filling your body with light and melting away all your internal obstacles to reaching your goal.

- Imagine that light going out from your pores, dispelling the problems of your loved ones, friends, acquaintances, and eventually, everyone, everywhere. Hold that image single-pointedly while identifying with your compassion and insight.

Notes

[1] Figley, C. R., & Nelson, T. (1989). Basic family therapy skills, I: Conceptualization and initial findings. *Journal of Marital and Family Therapy, 15*(4), 211-130. https://onlinelibrary.wiley.com/doi/abs/10.1111/j.1752-0606.1989.tb00820.x

[2] Elliott, R., Bohart, A. C., Watson, J. C., & Murphy, D. (2018). Therapist empathy and client outcome: An updated meta-analysis. *Psychotherapy, 55*(4), 399-410. http://dx.doi.org/10.1037/pst0000175

[3] Figley, C. R. (Ed.). (2002). *Treating compassion fatigue*, 1-2. Brunner-Routledge.

[4] Davis, M. H., Hull, J. G., Young, R. D., & Warren, G. G. (1987). Emotional reactions to dramatic film stimuli: The influence of cognitive and emotional empathy. *Journal of Personality and Social Psychology, 52*(1), 126-133. https://doi.apa.org/doiLanding?doi=10.1037%2F0022-3514.52.1.126

[5] Ricard, M., Wise, J., & Singer, P. (2016, October 19). Put your compassion into action. *Lion's Roar: Buddhist Wisdom for our Time.* https://www.lionsroar.com/put-your-compassion-into-action/

[6] See https://www.merriam-webster.com/dictionary/compassion.

[7] Hendriksen, E. (2018). How does that make you feel: A therapist on learning to empathize without burning out. *The Cut.* https://www.thecut.com/2018/01/a-therapist-on-learning-to-empathize-without-burning-out.html

[8] Ashar, Y. K., Andrews-Hanna, J. R., Dimidjian, S., & Wager, T. D. (2016). Towards a neuroscience of compassion: A brain systems-based model and research agenda. In J. D. Greene (Ed.), *Positive neuroscience* (pp. 1-27). Oxford University Press.

[9] de Waal, F. B. M. (2008). Putting the altruism back into altruism: The evolution of empathy. *Annual Review of Psychology, 59*, 279–300. https://doi.org/10.1146/annurev.psych.59.103006.093625. Also see Decety, J., & Jackson, P. L. (2004). The functional architecture of human empathy. *Behavioral and Cognitive Neuroscience Reviews, 3*(2), 71-100. https://doi.org/10.1177/1534582304267187; Fan, Y., Duncan, N. W., de Greck, M., & Northoff, G. (2011). Is there a core neural network in empathy? An fMRI based quantitative meta-analysis. *Neuroscience and Biobehavioral Reviews, 35*(3), 903-11. https://doi.org/10.1016/j.neubiorev.2010.10.009; Lamm, C., Decety, J., & Singer, T. (2010). Meta-analytic evidence for common and distinct neural networks associated with directly experienced pain and empathy for pain. *NeuroImage, 54*(3), 2492-2502. https://doi.org/10.1016/j.neuroimage.2010.10.014; Shamay-Tsoory, S.

G., Aharon-Peretz, J., & Perry, D. (2009). Two systems for empathy: A double dissociation between emotional and cognitive empathy in inferior frontal gyrus versus ventromedial prefrontal lesions. *Brain: A Journal of Neurology, 132*(Pt 3), 617-627. https://doi.org/10.1093/brain/awn279; Van Overwalle, F., & Baetens, K. (2009). Understanding others' actions and goals by mirror and mentalizing systems: A meta-analysis. *NeuroImage, 48*(3), 564-584. https://doi.org/doi:10.1016/j.neuroimage.2009.06.009; Zaki, J., & Ochsner, K. (2012). The neuroscience of empathy: Progress, pitfalls and promise. *Nature Neuroscience, 15*(5), 675-680. https://doi.org/doi:doi:10.1038/nn.3085

[10] Ibid.

[11] Ashar et al. (2016).

[12] Simon-Thomas, E. R. (2012). Three insights from the cutting edge of compassion research. *Greater Good Magazine.* https://greatergood.berkeley.edu/article/item/three_insights_from_the_cutting_edge_of_compassion_research

[13] Esch, T., & Stefano, G. B. (2011). The neurobiological link between compassion and love. *Medical Science Monitor, 17*(3), RA65-RA75. https://doi.org/10.12659/MSM.881441

[14] Condon, P., & Barrett, L. F. (2013). Conceptualizing and experiencing compassion. *Emotion, 13*(5), 817-821. https://doi.org/10.1037/a0033747

[15] Hart, S., & Hodson, V. K. (2004). *The compassionate classroom: Relationship based teaching and learning.* Puddle Dancer Press.

[16] Eldor, L., & Shoshani, A. (2016). Caring relationships in school staff: Exploring the link between compassion and teacher work engagement. *Teaching and Teacher Education, 59*, 126-136. https://www.sciencedirect.com/science/article/abs/pii/S0742051X16301135

[17] Decety, J., & Fotopoulou, A. (2015). Why empathy has a beneficial impact on others in medicine: Unifying theories. *Frontiers in Behavioral Neuroscience, 8*, 457. https://doi.org/10.3389/fnbeh.2014.00457

[18] Fogarty, L., Curbow, B., Wingard, J., McDonnell, K., & Somerfield, M. (1999). Can 40 seconds of compassion reduce patient anxiety? *Journal of Clinical Oncology, 17*(1), 371-379. https://doi.org/10.1200/JCO.1999.17.1.371

[19] van der Cingle, M. (2011). Compassion in care: A qualitative study of older people with a chronic disease and nurses. *Nursing Ethics, 18*(5), 672-685. https://doi.org/doi:10.1177/0969733011403556

[20] Black, W., & Living, R. (2004). Volunteerism as an occupation and its relationship to health and wellbeing. *British Journal of Occupational Therapy, 67*(12), 526-532.

[21] Beersdorf, W. (2017). *Compassion in law enforcement.* https://leb.fbi.gov/spotlights/leadership-spotlight-compassion-in-law-enforcement

[22] Killam, K. (2014). Building empathy in healthcare: A Q&A with Dr. Helen Riess of Harvard Medical School about her efforts to nurture empathy among health care workers. *Greater Good Magazine.* https://greatergood.berkeley.edu/article/item/building_empathy_in_healthcare

[23] Vitalie, T. (2018). *Top 10 firefighter traits.* http://www.fortwaynefiredepartment.org/career-opportunities/resources/top-10-firefighter-traits

[24] Figley, C. R. (Ed.). (1995). *Compassion fatigue: Coping with secondary traumatic stress disorder in those who treat the traumatized.* Brunner/Mazel.

[25] Mathieu, F. (2012). Compassion fatigue. In C. R. Figley (Ed.), *Encyclopedia of trauma* (pp. 137-139). Sage Publications. https://www.doi.org/10.4135/9781452218595.n46

[26] Ibid.

[27] Bride, B. (2012). Secondary traumatic stress. In C. R. Figley (Ed.), *Encyclopedia of trauma* (pp. 601-602). Sage Publications. https://www.doi.org/10.4135/9781452218595.n204

[28] Sartor, T. A. (2016). Vicarious trauma and its influence on self-efficacy. *Vistas Online.* https://www.counseling.org/docs/default-source/vistas/article_2721c024f16116603abcacff0000bee5e7.pdf?sfvrsn=6

[29] Pearlman, L. A. (2012). Vicarious trauma. In C. R. Figley (Ed.), *Encyclopedia of trauma* (pp. 783-786). Sage Publications. https://www.doi.org/10.4135/9781452218595.n271

[30] Sartor, T. A. (2016).

[31] Baker, T. E. (2012). Burnout. In C. R. Figley (Ed.), *Encyclopedia of trauma* (pp. 70-72). Sage Publications. https://www.doi.org/10.4135/9781452218595.n23

[32] Newell, J. M., & MacNeil, G. A. (2010). Professional burnout, vicarious trauma, secondary traumatic stress, and compassion fatigue: A review of theoretical terms, risk factors, and preventive methods for clinicians and researchers. *Best Practices in Mental Health: An International Journal, 6*(2), 57-68.

[33] Figley, C. R. (2002), 3-6.

[34] Flynn, J., & Gullatte, M. (2017). When compassionate care takes a turn toward fatigue—Compassion fatigue and its consequences for nurses. *MedPage Today.* https://www.medpagetoday.com/nursing/nursing/69366

[35] Ibid.

[36] Johnson, S, Donald, I., Taylor, P., Cooper, C., Cartwright, S., & Millet, C. (2005). The experience of work-related stress across occupations. *Journal of Managerial Psychology, 20*(2), 178-187. https://doi.org/10.1108/02683940510579803

[37] Ibid.

[38] Jaracz, M., Rosiak, I., Bertrand-Bucińska, A., Jaskulski, M., Nieżurawska, J., & Borkowska, A. (2017). Affective temperament, job stress and professional burnout in nurses and civil servants. *PloS One, 12*(6), e0176698. https://doi.org/10.1371/journal.pone.0176698

[39] Collins, S. (2008). Statutory social workers: Stress, job satisfaction, coping, social support and individual differences. *British Journal of Social Work, 38*(6), 1173-1193. https://doi.org/10.1093/bjsw/bcm047

[40] Rodolfo, K. (2000). What is homeostasis? *Scientific American.* https://www.scientificamerican.com/article/what-is-homeostasis/

[41] McEwen, B., & Sapolsky, R. (2006). Stress and your health. Journal of Clinical Endocrinology & Metabolism, *91*(2), E2. https://doi.org/10.1210/jcem.91.2.9994

[42] Miller, K. I., Stiff, J. B., & Ellis, B. H. (1988). Communication and empathy as precursors to burnout among human service workers. *Communication Monographs, 55*(9), 336–341. https://doi.org/10.1080/03637758809376171

[43] Ibid.

[44] See http://ccare.stanford.edu/research/wiki/compassion-definitions/emotion-resonance/

[45] Ibid.

[46] Wang, Y. T., Huang, G., Duke, G., & Yang, Y. (2017). Tai chi, yoga, and qigong as mind-body exercises. *Evidence-Based Complementary and Alternative Medicine, 2017.* https://doi.org/doi:10.1155/2017/8763915

[47] Moran, C. (2002). Humor as a moderator of compassion fatigue. In C. R. Figley (Ed.), *Treating compassion fatigue.* Brunner-Routledge.

[48] Saltsman, T. L., Seery, M. D., Ward, D. E., Radsvick, T. M., Panlilio, Z. A., Lamarche, V. M., & Kondrak, C. L. (2021). Facing the facets: No association between dispositional mindfulness facets and positive momentary stress responses during active stressors. *Personality & Social Psychology Bulletin, 47*(7), 1057-1070. https://doi.org/10.1177/0146167220956898

[49] American Psychiatric Association. (2013). *Diagnostic and statistical manual of mental disorders* (5th ed.) (*DSM–5*).

[50] I'd like to thank my colleague, Erika Neil, LCSW, for explaining this strategy to me.

[51] Gentry, J. E., Baranowski, A. E., & Dunning. K. (2002). ARP: The Accelerated Recovery Program (ARP) for compassion fatigue. In C. R. Figley (Ed.), *Treating compassion fatigue* (pp. 123-136). Brunner-Routledge.

[52] Tillman, J. G. (2019). When a patient dies by suicide. Association of American Medical Colleges. https://www.aamc.org/news-insights/when-patient-dies-suicide

[53] Vigil, N. H., Grant, A. R., Perez, O., Blust, R. N., Chikani, V., Vadeboncoeur, T. F., Spaite, D. W., & Bobrow, B. J. (2019). Death by suicide—The EMS profession compared to the general public. *Prehospital Emergency Care, 23*(3), 340-345. https://doi.org/10.1080/10903127.2018.1514090

[54] I want to acknowledge my friends and colleagues who helped me brainstorm this section, in alphabetical order: Peggy DiVincenzo, LPC, LMFT, Licensed Professional Counselor; Kimberly Hoskins, PsyD, Clinical Psychologist; Lorne Ladner, PhD, Clinical Psychologist; Erika Neil, LCSW, JD, Clinical Social Worker; and Eric Propst, PsyD, Clinical Psychologist.

[55] Kubler-Ross, E. (1969). *On death & dying.* Scribner.

[56] Lamia, M.C. (2011). Grief isn't something to get over: The notion that one "gets over it" is a myth. *Psychology Today.* https://www.psychologytoday.com/us/blog/intense-emotions-and-strong-feelings/201105/grief-isnt-something-get-over

[57] Tillman, J. G. (2019).

[58] Ibid.

59 Tedeschi, R. & Triplett, K. N. (2012). Spiritual intelligence and posttraumatic growth. In C. R. Figley (Ed.), *Encyclopedia of trauma* (pp. 649-651). Sage Publications. https://www.doi.org/10.4135/9781452218595.n222

60 Ibid.

61 Green Cross Standards of Care. https://greencross.org/about-gc/standards-of-care-guidelines/

62 Ibid.

63 Hilliard, J. (2019). The relationship between addiction and first responders. *Addiction Center.* https://www.addictioncenter.com/addiction/emergency-responders/

64 Ibid.

65 Ibid.

66 Ibid.

67 Abbot, C., Barber, E., Burke, B., Harvey, J., Newland, C., Rose, M., & Young, A. (2015). What's killing our medics? Ambulance Service Manager Program. *Reviving Responders.* http://www.revivingresponders.com/originalpaper

68 Bishopp, S. A., & Boots, D. P. (2014). General strain theory, exposure to violence, and suicide ideation among police officers: A gendered approach. *Journal of Criminal Justice, 42*(6), 538-548. https://doi.org/10.1016/j.jcrimjus.2014.09.007

69 SAMHSA (2018). *First responders: Behavioral health concerns, emergency response, and trauma. Disaster technical assistance center supplemental research bulletin.* https://www.hsdl.org/?abstract&did=813843

70 Bentley, M. A., Crawford, J. M., Wilkins, J. R., Fernandez, A. R., & Studnek, J. R. (2013). An assessment of depression, anxiety, and stress among nationally certified EMS professionals. *Prehospital Emergency Care, 17*(3), 330-338. https://doi.org/10.3109/10903127.2012.761307

71 Kramer, C. (2019). *Emergency responders learn tools to cope with trauma from the job.* Nexstar Broadcasting. https://www.mychamplainvalley.com/news/emergency-responders-learn-tools-to-cope-with-trauma-from-the-job/

72 Green Cross Standards of Care. https://greencross.org/about-gc/standards-of-care-guidelines/

73 Ibid.

74 Tynan, L. Signs you're in a toxic work environment and how to handle it. *TopResume.* https://www.topresume.com/career-advice/how-to-handle-toxic-work-environment

75 Jacobs, J. (2019). *Compassion in the workplace.* Pacific Prime. https://www.pacificprime.com/blog/compassion-in-the-workplace.html

76 Ibid.

77 Riley, R. (2019). Michigan kids are going to school traumatized—and teachers lack training, resources to help. *Detroit Free Press.* https://www.freep.com/in-depth/news/columnists/rochelle-riley/2019/12/13/special-education-trauma-kids-michigan-schools/3739003002/

[78] Epitropoulos, A. (2019). 10 signs of a toxic school culture. ASCD Education Update. http://www.ascd.org/publications/newsletters/education-update/sept19/vol61/num09/10-Signs-of-a-Toxic-School-Culture.aspx

[79] Lewis, S. Jesse Lewis Choose Love Movement. https://www.jesselewischoose love.org

[80] Emory University Center for Contemplative Science and Compassion-Based Ethics. https://seelearning.emory.edu

[81] These points were adapted based on an article by Nazareno, L., & Krafel, A. (2017). Taking care of ourselves and others: Creating a compassionate school. *Phi Delta Kappan.* https://kappanonline.org/nazareno-krafel-schools-kindness -compassion-taking-care-others/

[82] Jazaieri, H. (2018). Compassionate education from preschool to graduate school: Bringing a culture of compassion into the classroom. *Journal of Research in Innovative Teaching & Learning, 11*(1), 22-66. https://doi.org/10 .1108/JRIT-08-2017-0017

[83] Wolin, S., & Wolin, S. (1993). *The resilient self: How survivors of troubled families rise above adversity.* Villard Books.

[84] Ibid.

[85] For example, see Shapiro, C., Meyers, A., & Toner, C. (1996). *Strength-based, family-focused practice: A clinical guide from family justice.* https://www.families outside.org.uk/content/uploads/2011/02/family-justice-clinical-guide.pdf

[86] Patoni, L. (2012). Strengths-based approaches for working with individuals. *IRISS.* https://www.iriss.org.uk/resources/insights/strengths-based-approaches -working-individuals

[87] SAMHSA (2014). *A treatment improvement protocol: Trauma-informed care in behavioral health services.* https://www.integration.samhsa.gov/clinical -practice/SAMSA_TIP_Trauma.PDF

[88] Ibid.

[89] These modalities are reviewed more thoroughly in SAMHSA. (2019). *Enhancing motivation for change in substance abuse treatment.* https://store.sam hsa.gov/product/TIP-35-Enhancing-Motivation-for-Change-in-Substance -Use-Disorder-Treatment/PEP19-02-01-003

[90] Garland, E. L., Brintz, C. E., Hanley, A. W., Roseen, E. J., Atchley, R. M., Gaylord, S. A., Faurot, K. R., Yaffe, J., Fiander, M., & Keefe, F. J. (2020). Mind-body therapies for opioid-treated pain: A systematic review and meta-analysis. *JAMA Internal Medicine, 180*(1), 91-105. https://doi.org/10.1001/jamainternmed.2019.4917

[91] SAMHSA. (2019).

[92] Ibid.

[93.] National Association of Social Workers (NASW). (2017). *Code of ethics.* https://www.socialworkers.org/about/ethics/code-of-ethics/code-of-ethics -english

[94] American Psychiatric Association. (2017). Ethical principles of psychologists and code of ethics. https://www.apa.org/ethics/code/

[95] American Counseling Association. (2014). 2014 ACA Code of Ethics. https:// www.counseling.org/resources/aca-code-of-ethics.pdf

[96] National Education Association (NEA) (2019). *National Education Association code of ethics.* http://www.nea.org/home/30442.htm

[97] International Association of Chiefs of Police (IACP). (1957). *Law enforcement code of ethics.* https://www.theiacp.org/resources/law-enforcement-code -of-ethics

[98] Stringfellow, A. (2019, March 11). What is caregiver fatigue? *Senior Link.* https://www.seniorlink.com/blog/what-is-caregiver-fatigue

[99] Ladner, L. (2019). Personal communication.

[100] Ackerman, C. E. (2019). 28 benefits of gratitude & most significant research findings. *PositivePsychology.com.* https://positivepsychology.com/ benefits-gratitude-research-questions/

[101] Brody, D. (2019, December 16). 61% of bosses are bullies. Here's how that's about to change. *Forbes Magazine.* https://www.forbes.com/sites/denise brodey/2019/12/16/61-of-bosses-are-bullies-heres-how-thats-about-to-change #4efc5f40376e

[102] Jamie, G. (2017). *2017 WBI U.S. workplace bullying survey.* MAPE: Minnesota Association of Professional Employees. https://www.workplacebullying .org/wbiresearch/wbi-2017-survey/

[103] Sansone, R. A., & Sansone, L. A. (2015). Workplace bullying: A tale of adverse consequences. *Innovations in Clinical Neuroscience, 12*(1-2), 32-37.

[104] Ibid.

[105] Way, K. (2019). French executives found responsible for 35 employees' deaths by suicide. *Vice News.* https://www.vice.com/en_us/article/y3mzyb/france-telecom-orange-suicide-collective-moral-harassment?fbclid=IwAR3CdlnYT6 hitmnLxk_k1xmOmueqZOAFFn5AlzO0RSavXtr2yUx3I-c74Ng

[106] Sansone, R. A., & Sansone, L. A. (2015).

[107] Ariza-Montes, A., Muniz, N. M., Montero-Simó, M. J., & Araque-Padilla, R. A. (2013). Workplace bullying among healthcare workers. *International Journal of Environmental Research and Public Health, 10*(8), 3121-3139. https:// doi.org/10.3390/ijerph10083121

[108] Meissner, J. E. (1996). Nurses: Are we eating our young? *Nursing, 16*(3), 51-53.

[109] Ariza-Montes et al. (2013).

[110] The Joint Commission. (2016). Bullying has no place in healthcare. *Quick Safety, 24.* https://www.jointcommission.org/-/media/tjc/documents/newsletters/quick _safety_issue_24_june_2016pdf.pdf

[111] Hillis, K. (2013). *Bullying in law enforcement: End the silence.* Miller County Sheriff's Office SLES Session XLII. https://www.cji.edu/wp-content/ uploads/2019/04/bullyin-in-law-enforcement-end-the-silence.pdf

[112] Ibid.

[113] Brody, D. (2019). See also https://www.stopbullying.gov for anti-bullying strategies.

114 Wasilewski, M., & Olsen, A. (2018). *Understanding workplace bullying in the police subculture.* https://www.officer.com/training-careers/education/article/21020641/understanding-workplace-bullying-in-the-police-subculture

115 Hoel, H., & Giga, S. (2006). *Destructive interpersonal conflict in the workplace: The effectiveness of management interventions.* University of Manchester Institute of Science and Technology.

116 Whitaker, T. (2012). Social workers and workplace bullying: Perceptions, responses and implications. *Work, 42*(1), 115-123. https://doi.org/10.3233/WOR-2012-1335

117 Adapted from a list of strategies found in Sacawa, P. (2018).

118 Tedeschi, J., MD. (2019). Personal correspondence. Dr. Tedeschi kindly gave me permission to include his statements here. I have drawn out pertinent sections from what he wrote to me and slightly edited them. See also https://www.courant.com/business/hc-xpm-2012-03-29-hc-aetna-doctor-network-20120329-story.html, and https://youtu.be/L6tf1z5Nss4.

119 Jorge, M. (2019). The opioid crisis reflects larger big pharma norms. *Morning Consult.* https://morningconsult.com/opinions/opioid-crisis-reflects-larger-big-pharma-norms/. See also https://www.ncbi.nlm.nih.gov/pmc/articles/PMC6461324/.

120 Court, E., & Ramsey, L. (2019). Healthcare CEOs make as much as $26 million a year. Here's what the industry's top executives earned in 2018. *Business Insider.* https://www.businessinsider.com/pharma-and-healthcare-ceo-compensation-2018-2019-4

121 Rosenfeld, J. (2019). The rising price of insulin. *Medical Economics.* https://www.medicaleconomics.com/article/rising-price-insulin

122 Murphy, T. (2018). Cancer patients are twice as likely to declare bankruptcy. *Chicago Tribune.* https://www.chicagotribune.com/nation-world/ct-cancer-treatment-debt-20180522-story.html

123 Baranowsky, A. B. (2002). The silencing response in clinical practice: On the road to dialogue. In C. R. Finley (Ed.), *Treating compassion fatigue* (pp. 154-171). Brunner-Routledge.

124 Ibid.

125 Ibid.

126 Ibid.

127 Wee, D. F., & Myers, D. (2002a). Strategies for managing disaster mental health worker stress. In C. R. Finley (Ed.), *Treating compassion fatigue* (pp. 181-212). Brunner-Routledge.

128 Wee, D. F., & Myers, D. (2002b). Stress response of mental health workers following disaster: The Oklahoma City bombing. In C. R. Finley (Ed.), *Treating compassion fatigue* (pp. 57-84). Brunner-Routledge.

129 Ibid.

130 Ibid.

131 Wee, D. F., & Myers, D. (2002a).

132 Self-assessment tools for screenings can be found on pp. 27-31 of Figley Institute's (2012) *Workbook for CFE training on Compassion Fatigue.* http://

www.figleyinstitute.com/documents/Workbook_AMEDD_SanAntonio_2012July20_RevAugust2013.pdf

[133] SAMHSA. (2018). *Crisis Intervention Team (CIT) methods for using data to inform practice: A step-by-step guide.* https://store.samhsa.gov/product/Crisis-Intervention-Team-CIT-Methods-for-Using-Data-to-Inform-Practice/SMA18-5065

[134] For a more detailed breakdown of the above points, see Wee, D. F., & Myers, D. (2002a).

[135] SAMHSA. (2014). *Tips for disaster responders: Understanding compassion fatigue.* https://store.samhsa.gov/system/files/sma14-4869.pdf

[136] Kessler, R. C., Sonnega, A., Bromet, E., Hughes, M., & Nelson, C. B. (1995). Posttraumatic stress disorder in the National Comorbidity Survey. *Archives of General Psychiatry, 52*(12), 1048-1059. https://doi.org/10.1001/archpsyc.1995.03950240066012. Mentioned in Stamm, B. H. (2002). Measuring compassion satisfaction as well as fatigue: Developmental history of the compassion satisfaction and fatigue test. In C. R. Finley (Ed.), *Treating compassion fatigue* (pp. 107-122). Brunner-Routledge.

[137] King, L., King, D., Fairbank, J., Keane, T., & Adams, G. (1998). Resilience-recovery factors in post-traumatic stress disorder among female and male veterans: Hardiness, post war social support and additional stressful life events. *Journal of Personality and Social Psychology, 74*(2), 420–434. https://doi.org/10.1037//0022-3514.74.2.420

[138] Ibid.

[139] Stamm, B. H. (2002). Measuring compassion satisfaction as well as fatigue: Developmental history of the compassion satisfaction and fatigue test. In C. R. Finley (Ed.), *Treating compassion fatigue* (pp. 107-122). Brunner-Routledge.

[140] Vaish, A., Grossmann, T., & Woodward, A. (2008). Not all emotions are created equal: The negativity bias in social-emotional development. *Psychological Bulletin, 134*(3), 383-403. https://doi.org/doi:10.1037/0033-2909.134.3.383

[141] Pearlman, L. A., & McKay, L. (2008). *Understanding & addressing vicarious trauma.* Headington Institute. https://mutualaiddisasterreliefsite.files.wordpress.com/2017/04/vtmoduletemplate2_ready_v2_85791.pdf

[142] Ibid.

[143] Ibid.

[144] Ibid.

[145] Ibid.

[146] Ibid.

[147] Meichenbaum, D. (2007). *Self-care for trauma psychotherapists and caregivers: Individual, social and organizational interventions. Melissa Institute.* https://melissainstitute.org/wp-content/uploads/2016/12/SELF-CARE-FOR-TRAUMA-PSYCHOTHERAPISTS-AND-CAREGIVERS-changed-26.pdf

[148] Pearlman, L. A., & McKay, L. (2008).

[149] Ibid.

[150] Zaccari, A. (2017). *Vicarious trauma coping and self-care practices among trauma therapists.* Walden Dissertations and Doctoral Studies Collection,

Walden University. https://scholarworks.waldenu.edu/cgi/viewcontent.cgi?
article=5220&context=dissertations

[151] Becker, E. (1973). *The denial of death*. Free Press.

[152] I would like to acknowledge my friend and fellow social worker, Michael
Sanger, PhD, professor of social work at Valdosta State University, for providing the articles that helped me write this section.

[153] Rayburn, C. A. (2008). Clinical and pastoral issues and challenges in working
with the dying and their families. *Adultspan Journal, 7*(2), 94-108.

[154] Ibid.

[155] Peteet, J. R., Rodriguez, V. B., Herschkopf, M. D., McCarthy, A., Betts, J.,
Romo, S., & Murphy, J. M. (2016). Does a therapist's world view matter?
Journal of Religion and Health, 55(3), 1097–1106. https://doi.org/10.1007/
s10943-016-0208-9

[156] Ibid.

[157] Rayburn, C. A. (2008).

[158] Sermabeikian, P. (1994). Our clients, ourselves: The spiritual perspective and
social work practice. *Social Work, 39*(2), 178-183. https://doi.org/10.1093/
sw/39.2.178

[159] Hohn, K., McCoy, M., Ivey, D., Ude, P. U., & Praetorius, R. T. (2017). Integrating faith and practice: A qualitative study of staff motivations. *Social
Work & Christianity, 44*(4), 3-22.

[160] Solomon, S., Greenberg, J., & Pyszczynski, T. (2015). *The worm at the core*.
Random House.

[161] Geros-Willfond, K. N., Ivy, S. S., Montz., K., Bohan, S. E., & Torke, A. M.
(2016). Religion and spirituality in surrogate decision making for older
hospitalized adults. *Journal of Religious Health, 55*, 765-777. https://doi
.org/101007/s10943-015-0111-9

[162] Ibid.

[163] Solomon, S., Greenberg, J., & Pyszczynski, T. (2015).

[164] Kesebir, P., & Pyszczynski, T. (2011). The role of death in life: Existential
aspects of human motivation. *Oxford Handbook of Human Motivation*.
https://doi.org/10.1093/oxfordhb/9780195399820.013.0004

[165] Shpancer, N. (2020). Overcoming fear: The only way out is through. *Psychology
Today*. https://www.psychologytoday.com/us/blog/insight-therapy/201009/
overcoming-fear-the-only-way-out-is-through

[166] Nia, H. S., Lehto, R. H., Ebadi, A., & Peyrovi, H. (2016). Death anxiety
among nurses and health care professionals: A review article. *International
Journal of Community Based Nursing and Midwifery, 4*(1), 2-10.

References

Abbot, C., Barber, E., Burke, B., Harvey, J., Newland, C., Rose, M., & Young, A. (2015). What's killing our medics? Ambulance Service Manager Program. *Reviving Responders.* http://www.revivingresponders.com/originalpaper

Ackerman, C. E. (2019). 28 benefits of gratitude & most significant research findings. *PositivePsychology.com.* https://positivepsychology.com/benefits-gratitude-research-questions/

Aknin, L. B., Hamlin, J. K., & Dunn, E. W. (2012). Giving leads to happiness in young children. *Plos One, 7*(6), e39211. https://doi.org/10.1371/journal.pone.0039211

American Counseling Association. (2014). 2014 ACA Code of Ethics. https://www.counseling.org/resources/aca-code-of-ethics.pdf

American Psychiatric Association. (2013). *Diagnostic and statistical manual of mental disorders* (5th ed.) (*DSM-5*).

American Psychiatric Association. (2017). Ethical principles of psychologists and code of ethics. https://www.apa.org/ethics/code/

Anderson, E., & Hope, D. (2008). A review of the tripartite model for understanding the link between anxiety and depression in youth. *Clinical Psychology Review, 28*(2), 275-287. https://doi.org/10.1016/j.cpr.2007.05.004

Ariza-Montes, A., Muniz, N. M., Montero-Simó, M. J., & Araque-Padilla, R. A. (2013). Workplace bullying among healthcare workers. *International Journal of Environmental Research and Public Health, 10*(8), 3121-3139. https://doi.org/10.3390/ijerph10083121

Asanga, *Compendium of knowledge.* 2010. Quoted in Yongdzin Yeshe Gyentsen, *A necklace for the lucid: A clarification of the workings of the mind and mental factors.* (Vincent Montenegro, Trans.). Ganden Mountain Press.

Ashar, Y. K., Andrews-Hanna, J. R., Dimidjian, S., & Wager, T. D. (2016). Towards a neuroscience of compassion: A brain systems-based model and research agenda. In J. D. Greene (Ed.), *Positive neuroscience* (pp. 1-27). Oxford University Press.

Baker, T. E. (2012). Burnout. In C. R. Figley (Ed.), *Encyclopedia of trauma* (pp. 70-72). Sage Publications. https://www.doi.org/10.4135/9781452218595.n23

Baranowsky, A. B. (2002). The silencing response in clinical practice: On the road to dialogue. In C. R. Finley (Ed.), *Treating compassion fatigue* (pp. 154-171). Brunner-Routledge.

Barbara, M. (2016). *UnSelfie: Why empathetic kids succeed in our all-about-me world.* Touchstone.

Barefoot, J. C., Dahlstrom, W. G., & Williams, R. B. (1983). Hostility, CHD incidence, and total mortality: A 25-year follow-up study of 255 physicians. *Psychosomatic Medicine, 45*, 59-64.

Barnes, S., Brown, K. W., Krusemark, E., Campbell, W. K., & Rogge, R. D. (2007). The role of mindfulness in romantic relationship satisfaction and response to relationship stress. *Journal of Marital and Family Therapy, 33*(4), 482-500.

Becker, C. B., Darius, E., & Schaumberg, K. (2007). An analog study of patient preferences for exposure versus alternative treatments for posttraumatic stress disorder. *Behaviour Research and Therapy, 45*, 2861-2873.

Becker, E. (1973). *The denial of death.* Free Press.

Beckes, L., Conan, J. A., & Hasselmo, K. (2013). Familiarity promotes the blurring of self and other in the neural representation of threat. *Social Cognitive and Affective Neuroscience, 8*(6), 670-677. https://doi.org/10.1093/scan/nss046

Beersdorf, W. (2017). *Compassion in law enforcement.* https://leb.fbi.gov/spotlights/leadership-spotlight-compassion-in-law-enforcement

Benjet, C., Bromet, E., Karam, E. G., Kessler, R. C., McLaughlin, K. A., Ruscio, A. M., Shahly, V., Stein, D. J., Petukhova, M., Hill, E., Alonso, J., Atwoli, L., Bunting, B., Bruffaerts, R., Caldas-de-Almeida, J. M., de Girolamo, G., Florescu, S., Gureje, O., Huang, Y., … K. C. Koenen. (2015). The epidemiology of traumatic event exposure worldwide: Results from the World Mental Health Survey Consortium. *Psychological Medicine, 46*(2): 327-343. https://www.ncbi.nlm.nih.gov/pmc/articles/PMC4869975/

Bentley, M. A., Crawford, J. M., Wilkins, J. R., Fernandez, A. R., & Studnek, J. R. (2013). An assessment of depression, anxiety, and stress among nationally certified EMS professionals. *Prehospital Emergency Care, 17*(3), 330-338. https://doi.org/10.3109/10903127.2012.761307

Biglan, A., Flay, B. R., Embry, D. D., & Sandler, I. N. (2012). The critical role of nurturing environments for promoting human well-being. *American Psychologist, 67*(4): 257-271. https://www.ncbi.nlm.nih.gov/pmc/articles/PMC3621015/#!po=71.2766

Bishopp, S. A., & Boots, D. P. (2014). General strain theory, exposure to violence, and suicide ideation among police officers: A gendered approach. *Journal of Criminal Justice, 42*(6), 538-548. https://doi.org/10.1016/j.jcrimjus.2014.09.007

Bjork-James, S. (2017, November 27).What the latest FBI data do and do not tell us about hate crimes in the US. *The Conversation.* http://theconversation.com/what-the-latest-fbi-data-do-and-do-not-tell-us-about-hate-crimes-in-the-us-87561

Black, W., & Living, R. (2004). Volunteerism as an occupation and its relationship to health and wellbeing. *British Journal of Occupational Therapy, 67*(12), 526-532.

Bodhi, B. (2000). *A comprehensive manual of Abhidhamma: The philosophical psychology of Buddhism.* Buddhist Publication Society Pariyatti Editions.

Bögels, S., Hoogstad, B., van Dun, L., de Schutter, S., & Restifo, K. (2008). Mindfulness training for adolescents with externalizing disorders and their parents. *Behavioral and Cognitive Psychotherapy, 36,* 193-209.

Bono, G., McCullough, M. E., & Root, L. M. (2008). Forgiveness, feeling connected to others, and well-being: Two longitudinal studies. *Personality and Social Psychology Bulletin, 34,* 182-195.

Borreli, L. (2014). Human brain hardwired for acts of kindness, as vagus nerve activated during empathy. *Medical Daily.* https://www.medicaldaily.com/human-brain-hardwired-acts-kindness-vagus-nerve-activated-during-empathy-313020

Boyce, B. (2011, February 28). The healing power of mindfulness: Mindfulness: What it does, how to do it, why it works—A discussion with a distinguished panel of experts. *Mindful: Healthy Mind, Healthy Life.* https://www.mindful.org/the-healing-power-of-mindfulness/

Boyer, A. (2013, January 21). Cognitive restructuring: Six ways to do cognitive restructuring. *Psychology Today.* https://www.psychologytoday.com/us/blog/in-practice/201301/cognitive-restructuring

Brandt, A. (2016, July 1). 4 reasons why you should embrace your anger. *Psychology Today.* https://www.psychologytoday.com/us/blog/mindful-anger/201606/4-reasons-why-you-should-embrace-your-anger

Bride, B. (2012). Secondary traumatic stress. In C. R. Figley (Ed.), *Encyclopedia of trauma* (pp. 601-602). Sage Publications. https://www.doi.org/10.4135/9781452218595.n204

Brody, D. (2019, December 16). 61% of bosses are bullies. Here's how that's about to change. *Forbes Magazine.* https://www.forbes.com/sites/denisebrodey/2019/12/16/61-of-bosses-are-bullies-heres-how-thats-about-to-change/#4efc5f40376e

Buchanan, T. W. (2007). Retrieval of emotional memories. *Psychological Bulletin, 133*(5), 761-779. https://www.ncbi.nlm.nih.gov/pmc/articles/PMC2265099/#!po=6.00000

Bushman, B. J., & Baumeister, R. F. (1998). Threatened egotism, narcissism, self-esteem, and direct and displaced aggression: Does self-love or self-hate lead to violence? *Journal of Personality and Social Psychology, 75*(1), 219-229. https://doi.org/10.1037/0022-3514.75.1.219

Calderon, A., Ahern, T. H., & Pruzinsky. T. (2018). Can we change our mind about caring for others? The neuroscience of systematic compassion training. In L. Stevens & C. C. Woodruff (Eds.), *The neuroscience of empathy, compassion and self-compassion* (pp. 213-234). Academic Press.

Cardozo, B. L., Kaiser, R., Gotway, C. A., & Agani, F. (2003). Mental health, social functioning, and feelings of hatred and revenge of Kosovar Albanians one year after the war in Kosovo. *Journal of Traumatic Stress, 16*, 351-360.

Chen, J. (2018, July 26). For life's big questions, Tibetan Buddhist monks and nuns try a scientific approach. *Stat News.* https://www.statnews.com/2018/07/26/tibetan-buddhist-monks-and-nuns-try-a-scientific-approach/

Chopra, Deepak. (2015). The health benefits of practicing compassion. *Huffington Post.* https://www.huffingtonpost.com/deepak-chopra/the-health-benefits-of--pr_b_7586440.html

Collins, S. (2008). Statutory social workers: Stress, job satisfaction, coping, social support and individual differences. *British Journal of Social Work, 38*(6), 1173-1193. https://doi.org/10.1093/bjsw/bcm047

Condon, P., & Barrett, L. F. (2013). Conceptualizing and experiencing compassion. *Emotion, 13*(5), 817-821. https://doi.org/10.1037/a0033747

Condon, P., & Makransky, J. (2019, November 20). Recovering the relational starting point of compassion training: A foundation for sustainable and inclusive care. *Perspectives on Psychological Science.* https://doi.org/10.31231/osf.io/dmxj7

Court, E., & Ramsey, L. (2019). Healthcare CEOs make as much as $26 million a year. Here's what the industry's top executives earned in 2018. *Business Insider.* https://www.businessinsider.com/pharma-and-healthcare-ceo-compensation-2018-2019-4

Dalai Lama XIV. (2005). *The universe in a single atom: The convergence of science and spirituality.* Morgan Road Books.

Dalai Lama XIV. (2012). http://philosiblog.com/2012/01/29/it-is-important-that -when-pursing-our-own-self-interest-we-should-be-wise-selfish-and-not -foolish-selfish/

Davidson, R., Kabat-Zinn, J., Schumacher, J., Rosenkranz, M., Muller, D., Santorelli, S. F., Urbanowski, F., Harrington, A., Bonus, K., & Sheridan, J. F. (2003). Alterations in brain and immune function produced by mindfulness meditation. *Psychosomatic Medicine, 65*(4), 564-570.

Davis, M. H., Hull, J. G., Young, R. D., & Warren, G. G. (1987). Emotional reactions to dramatic film stimuli: The influence of cognitive and emotional empathy. *Journal of Personality and Social Psychology, 52*(1), 126-133. https://doi .apa.org/doiLanding?doi=10.1037%2F0022-3514.52.1.126

Decety, J., & Fotopoulou, A. (2015). Why empathy has a beneficial impact on others in medicine: Unifying theories. *Frontiers in Behavioral Neuroscience, 8,* 457. https://doi.org/10.3389/fnbeh.2014.00457

Decety, J., & Jackson, P. L. (2004). The functional architecture of human empathy. *Behavioral and Cognitive Neuroscience Reviews, 3*(2), 71-100. https://doi .org/10.1177/1534582304267187

Desbordes, G., Gard, T., Hoge, E. A., Hölzel, B. K., Kerr, C., Lazar, S. W., Olendzki, A., & Vago, D. R. (2014). Moving beyond mindfulness: Defining equanimity as an outcome measure in meditation and contemplative research. *Mindfulness, 6,* 356-372. https://doi.org/10.1007/s12671-013-0269-8

de Waal, F. B. M. (2008). Putting the altruism back into altruism: The evolution of empathy. *Annual Review of Psychology, 59,* 279-300. https://doi.org/10.1146/ annurev.psych.59.103006.093625

Dingfelder, S. F. (2011, February). Reflecting on narcissism: Are young people more self-obsessed than ever before? *Monitor on Psychology, 42*(2), 64. https://www.apa.org/monitor/2011/02/narcissism

Eldor, L., & Shoshani, A. (2016). Caring relationships in school staff: Exploring the link between compassion and teacher work engagement. *Teaching and Teacher Education, 59,* 126-136. https://www.sciencedirect.com/science/ article/abs/pii/S0742051X16301135

Elliott, R., Bohart, A. C., Watson, J. C., & Murphy, D. (2018). Therapist empathy and client outcome: An updated meta-analysis. *Psychotherapy, 55*(4), 399-410. http://dx.doi.org/10.1037/pst0000175

Emmons, R. A., & McCullough, M. E. (2003). Counting blessings versus burdens: An experimental investigation of gratitude and subjective well-being in daily life. *Journal of Personality and Social Psychology, 84*(2), 377-389. https://doi .apa.org/doiLanding?doi=10.1037%2F0022-3514.84.2.377

Emory University Center for Contemplative Science and Compassion-Based Ethics. https://seelearning.emory.edu

Epitropoulos, A. (2019). 10 signs of a toxic school culture. ASCD Education Update. http://www.ascd.org/publications/newsletters/education-update/ sept19/vol61/num09/10-Signs-of-a-Toxic-School-Culture.aspx

Epstein, Y. M. (1981). Crowding stress and human behavior. *Journal of Social Issues, 37*(1), 137. https://spssi.onlinelibrary.wiley.com/doi/ abs/10.1111/j.1540-4560.1981.tb01060.x

Esch, T., & Stefano, G. B. (2011). The neurobiological link between compassion and love. *Medical Science Monitor, 17*(3), RA65-RA75. https://doi.org/ 10.12659/MSM.881441

Fan, Y., Duncan, N. W., de Greck, M., & Northoff, G. (2011). Is there a core neural network in empathy? An fMRI based quantitative meta-analysis. *Neuroscience and Biobehavioral Reviews, 35*(3), 903-11. https://doi.org/10.1016/j.neubiorev.2010.10.009

Figley, C. R. (Ed.). (1995). *Compassion fatigue: Coping with secondary traumatic stress disorder in those who treat the traumatized.* Brunner/Mazel.

Figley, C. R. (Ed.) (2002). *Treating Compassion Fatigue.* Brunner-Routledge.

Figley, C. R., & Nelson, T. (1989). Basic family therapy skills, I: Conceptualization and initial findings. *Journal of Marital and Family Therapy, 15*(4), 349-365. https://onlinelibrary.wiley.com/doi/abs/10.1111/j.1752-0606.1989.tb00820.x

Figley Institute. (2012). *Workbook for CFE training on Compassion Fatigue.* http://www.figleyinstitute.com/documents/Workbook_AMEDD_San Antonio_2012July20_RevAugust2013.pdf

Flynn, J., & Gullatte, M. (2017). When compassionate care takes a turn toward fatigue—Compassion fatigue and its consequences for nurses. *MedPage Today.* https://www.medpagetoday.com/nursing/nursing/69366

Foa, E. B., Hembree, E. A., Cahill, S. P., Rauch, S. A., Riggs, D. S., Feeny, N. C., & Yadin, E. (2005). Randomized trial of prolonged exposure for posttraumatic stress disorder with and without cognitive restructuring: outcome at academic and community clinics. *Journal of Consulting and Clinical Psychology, 73*(5), 953-964. https://doi.org/10.1037/0022-006X.73.5.953

Foa, E. B., Zoellner, L. A., Feeny, N. C., Hembree, E. A., & Alvarez-Conrad, J. (2002). Does imaginal exposure exacerbate PTSD symptoms? *Journal of Consulting and Clinical Psychology, 70*(4), 1022-1028. https://doi.org/10.1037//0022-006x.70.4.1022

Fogarty, L., Curbow, B., Wingard, J., McDonnell, K., & Somerfield, M. (1999). Can 40 seconds of compassion reduce patient anxiety? *Journal of Clinical Oncology, 17*(1), 371-379. https://doi.org/10.1200/JCO.1999.17.1.371

Frankl, V. (1959). *Man's search for meaning.* Beacon Press.

Fredrickson, B. L. (2013). *Love 2.0: Creating happiness and health in moments of connection.* Hudson Street Press.

Garland, E. L., Brintz, C. E., Hanley, A. W., Roseen, E. J., Atchley, R. M., Gaylord, S. A., Faurot, K. R., Yaffe, J., Fiander, M., & Keefe, F. J. (2020). Mind-body therapies for opioid-treated pain: A systematic review and meta-analysis. *JAMA Internal Medicine, 180*(1), 91-105. https://doi.org/10.1001/jamainternmed.2019.4917

Gentry, J. E., Baranowski, A. E., & Dunning. K. (2002). ARP: The Accelerated Recovery Program (ARP) for compassion fatigue. In C. R. Figley (Ed.), *Treating compassion fatigue* (pp. 123-136). Brunner-Routledge.

Germain, C. B., & Gitterman, A. (1980). *The life model of social work practice.* Columbia University Press.

Germer, C., & Neff, K. (2014). *Mindful self-compassion handouts.* UCSD Center for Mindfulness, Mindfulness-Based Professional Training Institute.

Geros-Willfond, K. N., Ivy, S. S., Montz., K., Bohan, S. E., & Torke, A. M. (2016). Religion and spirituality in surrogate decision making for older hospitalized adults. *Journal of Religious Health, 55,* 765-777. https://doi.org/101007/s10943-015-0111-9

Glaser, R., Rice, J., Speicher, C., Stout, J. C., & Kiecolt-Glaser, J. K. (1986). Stress depresses interferon production by leukocytes concomitant with a decrease in natural killer cell activity. *Behavioral Neuroscience, 100*(5), 675-678. https:// doi.org/10.1037//0735-7044.100.5.675

Glasser, M., Kolvin, I., Campbell, D., Glasser, A., Leitch, I., & Farrelly, S. (2001). Cycle of child sexual abuse: Links between being a victim and becoming a perpetrator. *British Journal of Psychiatry, 179,* 482-497. https://doi.org/10.1192/ bjp.179.6.482

Goodman, R., Hunt, C., Pruzinsky, T., & Hurley, W. (2015). *Brief mindfulness-based compassion training: A multi-method approach to assessing positive psychological outcomes and potential barriers to future practice among therapist trainees.* Unpublished grant proposal.

Goodman, R. D., Hurley, W., Pruzinsky, T., & Rietschel, C. H. (2016, April). Development of COMPASS: Mindfulness-based compassion training research. Paper presented at the meeting of the American Counseling Association, Montréal, QC.

Grant, A. M., & Gino, F. (2010). A little thanks goes a long way: Explaining why gratitude expressions motivate prosocial behavior. *Journal of Personality and Social Psychology, 98*(6), 946-955. https://doi.org/10.1037/a0017935

Green Cross Standards of Care. https://greencross.org/about-gc/standards-of-care -guidelines/

Gungthang Rinpoche the Third, Venerable Konchok Tenpai Dronme. (2012). *The water and wood shastras* (Y. Khedrup and W. Hurley, Trans. from the Tibetan). Karuna Publications.

Gyatso, P. (1997). *The autobiography of a Tibetan monk.* Harvill Press.

Gyeltsen, Losang Chokyi, the Fourth Panchen Lama. (1997). *The Gelek/Kagyu tradition of Mahamudra* (A. Berzin & H. H. the Dalai Lama, Trans.). Snow Lion.

Hadash, Y., Segev, N., Tanay, G., Goldstein, P., & Bernstein, A. (2016). The decoupling model of equanimity: Theory, measurement, and test in a mindfulness intervention. *Mindfulness, 7*(5), 1214-1226. https://doi.org/10.1007/ s12671-016-0564-2

Hanh, Thich Nhat. http://famousquotefrom.com/thich-nhat-hanh/

Hamilton, D. R. (2011). 5 Beneficial Side Effects of Kindness. *Huffington Post.* https://www.huffingtonpost.com/david-r-hamilton-phd/kindness-benefits _b_869537.html

Hart, S., & Hodson, V. K. (2004). *The compassionate classroom: Relationship based teaching and learning.* Puddle Dancer Press.

Hayes, S. C., Strosahl, K. D., & Wilson, K. G. (2012). *Acceptance and commitment therapy: The process and practice of mindful change* (2nd ed.). Guilford Press.

Hendriksen, E. (2018). How does that make you feel: A therapist on learning to empathize without burning out. *The Cut.* https://www.thecut.com/2018/01/a-- therapist-on-learning-to-empathize-without-burning-out.html

Herman, J. L. (2005). Justice from the victim's perspective. *Violence against Women, 11*(5), 571-602. https://doi.org/10.1177/1077801205274450

Hilliard, J. (2019). The relationship between addiction and first responders. *Addiction Center.* https://www.addictioncenter.com/addiction/emergency -responders/

Hillis, K. (2013). *Bullying in law enforcement: End the silence.* Miller County Sheriff's Office SLES Session XLII. https://www.cji.edu/wp-content/ uploads/2019/04/bullyin-in-law-enforcement-end-the-silence.pdf

Hoel, H., & Giga, S. (2006). *Destructive interpersonal conflict in the workplace: The effectiveness of management interventions.* University of Manchester Institute of Science and Technology.

Hohn, K., McCoy, M., Ivey, D., Ude, P. U., & Praetorius, R. T. (2017). Integrating faith and practice: A qualitative study of staff motivations. *Social Work & Christianity, 44*(4), 3-22.

The Honey Foundation. *Kindness research and info: More research and case studies about the impact of kindness and compassion.* https://www.honeyfoundation.org/research-info/

Howell, E. F. (2014). Ferenczi's concept of identification with the aggressor: Understanding dissociative structure with interacting victim and abuser self-states. *American Journal of Psychoanalysis, 74*(1), 48-59. https://doi.org/10.1057/ajp.2013.40

Hunt, C., Goodman, R. D., Hilert, A. J., Hurley, W., & Hill, C. E. (2020, November). Assessing the effects of mindfulness and compassion-based, pre-session centering for therapists. Poster presented at the annual Mind and Life Contemplative Research Conference.

Hunt, C. A., Goodman, R. D., Hilert, A. J., Hurley, W., & Hill, C. E. (2021). A mindfulness-based compassion workshop and pre-session preparation to enhance therapist effectiveness in psychotherapy: A pilot study. *Counselling Psychology Quarterly.* https://www.tandfonline.com/doi/full/10.1080/09515070.2021.1895724

Hunt, C., Goodman, R. D., Hurley, W. C, Pruzinsky, T., Hilert, A., & Hill, C. (2015). *Assessing the effects of a mindfulness workshop and pre-session centering exercises for therapists: A pilot study.* Unpublished.

Hurley, R. (2019). *Celebrating the richness of reality: The life and art of Wilson Hurley.* Fresco Books.

Hurley, W. (2014). Enhancing a positive school climate with Compassion and Analytical Selective-Focus Skills (COMPASS). *IISTE Journal of Education.* http://www.iiste.org/Journals/index.php/JEP/article/view/11589

Hurley, W., Farfalla, J., & Pless, V. (2020, August). Fighting compassion fatigue during public health epidemics. *ASTHO Brief, Exploring critical issues in state and territorial public health.* https://astho.org/ASTHOBriefs/Fighting-Compassion-Fatigue-During-Public-Health-Epidemics/

International Association of Chiefs of Police (IACP). (1957). *Law enforcement code of ethics.* https://www.theiacp.org/resources/law-enforcement-code-of-ethics

Jacobs, J. (2019). *Compassion in the workplace.* Pacific Prime. https://www.pacificprime.com/blog/compassion-in-the-workplace.html

Jaffe, E. (2011). The complicated psychology of revenge. *Association for Psychological Science.* https://www.psychologicalscience.org/observer/the-complicated-psychology-of-revenge

James, W. (1890). *The principles of psychology* (Vol. 1). Henry Holt and Company.

Jamie, G. (2017). *2017 WBI U.S. Workplace bullying survey.* MAPE: Minnesota Association of Professional Employees. https://www.workplacebullying.org/wbiresearch/wbi-2017-survey/

Jampa, Gyumed Khensur Lobsang. (2013). *The easy path, Illuminating the First Panchen Lama's secret instructions* (L. Ladner, Ed.). Wisdom Publications.

Jaracz, M., Rosiak, I., Bertrand-Bucińska, A., Jaskulski, M., Nieżurawska, J., & Borkowska, A. (2017). Affective temperament, job stress and professional burnout in nurses and civil servants. *PloS One, 12*(6), e0176698. https://doi.org/10.1371/journal.pone.0176698

Jauk, E., & Kaufman, S. B. (2018). The higher the score, the darker the core: The nonlinear association between grandiose and vulnerable narcissism. *Frontiers in Psychology, 9,* 1305. https://doi.org/10.3389/fpsyg.2018.01305

Jazaieri, H. (2018). Compassionate education from preschool to graduate school: Bringing a culture of compassion into the classroom. *Journal of Research in Innovative Teaching & Learning, 11*(1), 22-66. https://doi.org/10.1108/JRIT-08-2017-0017

Jazaieri, H., Jinpa, G., McGonigal, K., Rosenberg, E. L., Finkelstein, J., Simon-Thomas, E., & Goldin, P. R. (2013). Enhancing compassion: A randomized controlled trial of a compassion cultivation training program. *Journal of Happiness Studies, 14*(4), 1113-1126. https://doi.org/10.1007/s10902-012-9373-z

Jazaieri, H., McGonigal, K., Jinpa, T., Doty, J. R., Gross, J. J., & Goldin, P. R. (2014). A randomized controlled trial of compassion cultivation training: Effects on mindfulness, affect, and emotion regulation. *Motivation and Emotion, 38*(1), 23-35. https://doi.org/10.1007/s11031-013-9368-z

Johnson, S., Donald, I., Taylor, P., Cooper, C., Cartwright, S., & Millet, C. (2005). The experience of work-related stress across occupations. *Journal of Managerial Psychology, 20*(2), 178-187. https://doi.org/10.1108/02683940510579803

Joiner, T. (2017, August). Mindfulness would be good for you. If you weren't so selfish. *Washington Post.* https://www.washingtonpost.com/outlook/mindfulness-would-be-good-for-you-if-it-werent-all-just-hype/2017/08/24/b97d0220-76e2-11e7-9eac-d56bd5568db8_story.html

The Joint Commission. (2016). Bullying has no place in healthcare. *Quick Safety, 24.* https://www.jointcommission.org/-/media/tjc/documents/newsletters/quick_safety_issue_24_june_2016pdf.pdf.

Jorge, M. (2019). The opioid crisis reflects larger big pharma norms. *Morning Consult.* https://morningconsult.com/opinions/opioid-crisis-reflects-larger-big-pharma-norms/

Jung, C. G. (1964). *Civilization in transition* (R. F. C. Hull, Trans.). Routledge & Kegan Paul.

Kabat-Zinn, J., Massion, A., Kristeller, J., Peterson, L., Fletcher, K., Pbert, L., Lenderking, W. R., & Santorelli, S. (1992). Effectiveness of a meditation-based stress reduction program in the treatment of anxiety disorders. *American Journal of Psychiatry, 149*(7), 936-943. https://doi.org/10.1176/ajp.149.7.936

Kashdan, T. (2011). The problem with happiness. *Huffington Post.* https://www.huffingtonpost.com/todd-kashdan/whats-wrong-with-happines_b_740518.html

Kasser, T., Cohn, S., Kanner, A. D., & Ryan, R. M. (2007). Some costs of American corporate capitalism: A psychological exploration of value and goal conflicts. *Psychological Inquiry, 18*(1), 1-22. https://doi.org/10.1080/10478400701386579

Kawachi, I., Sparrow, D., Spiro, A. 3rd, Vokonas, P., & Weiss, S. T. (1996). A prospective study of anger and coronary heart disease. The normative aging study. *Circulation, 94*(9), 2090-2095. https://doi.org/10.1161/01.cir.94.9.2090

Kensinger, Elizabeth A. (2009). Remembering the details: Effects of emotion. *Emotion Review, 1*(2), 99-113. https://doi.org/10.1177/1754073908100432

Kernberg, O. F. (1975). *Borderline conditions and pathological narcissism.* Jason Aronson.

Kesebir, P., & Pyszczynski, T. (2011). The role of death in life: Existential aspects of human motivation. *Oxford Handbook of Human Motivation.* https://doi .org/10.1093/oxfordhb/9780195399820.013.0004

Kessler, R. C., Sonnega, A., Bromet, E., Hughes, M., & Nelson, C. B. (1995). Posttraumatic stress disorder in the National Comorbidity Survey. *Archives of General Psychiatry, 52*(12), 1048-1059. https://doi.org/10.1001/ archpsyc.1995.03950240066012

Khedrup, Thubten. (2008). *Memories of life in Lhasa under Chinese rule* (Matthew Akester, Trans.). Columbia University Press.

Killam, K. (2014). Building empathy in healthcare: A Q&A with Dr. Helen Riess of Harvard Medical School about her efforts to nurture empathy among health care workers. *Greater Good Magazine.* https://greatergood.berkeley .edu/article/item/building_empathy_in_healthcare

King, L., King, D., Fairbank, J., Keane, T., & Adams, G. (1998). Resilience-recovery factors in post-traumatic stress disorder among female and male veterans: Hardiness, post war social support and additional stressful life events. *Journal of Personality and Social Psychology, 74*(2), 420-434. https://doi .org/10.1037//0022-3514.74.2.420

Kobau, R., Sniezek, J., Zack, M. M., Lucas, R. E., & Burns A. (2010). Well-being assessment: An evaluation of well-being scales for public health and population estimates of well-being among US adults. *Health and Well-Being, 2*(3), 272-297. https://doi.org/10.1111/j.1758-0854.2010.01035.x

Koenig, J. (2012). *The dictionary of obscure sorrows.* YouTube. https://youtu.be/ AkoML0_FiV4.

Konrath, S., & Bonadonna, J. P. (2014). Physiological and health-related correlates of the narcissistic personality. In A. Besser (Ed.), *Psychology of Narcissism.* Nova Science Publishers.

Kornfield, J. (2000, February). The practice of forgiveness. *Spirit Rock Meditation Center Newsletter.*

Kramer, C. (2019). *Emergency responders learn tools to cope with trauma from the job.* Nexstar Broadcasting. https://www.mychamplainvalley.com/news/ emergency-responders-learn-tools-to-cope-with-trauma-from-the-job/

Kroger, J. (2017). Identity formation in adolescence and adulthood. *Social Psychology Online.* https://doi.org/10.1093/acrefore/9780190236557.013.54

Kubler-Ross, E. (1969). *On death & dying.* Scribner.

Ladner, L. (2004). *The lost art of compassion: Discovering the practice of happiness in the meeting of Buddhism and psychology.* HarperCollins.

Lambert, N. M., & Fincham, F. D. (2011). Expressing gratitude to a partner leads to more relationship maintenance behavior. *Emotion, 11*(1), 52-60. https:// doi.org/10.1037/a0021557

Lamia, M.C. (2011). Grief isn't something to get over: The notion that one "gets over it" is a myth. *Psychology Today.* https://www.psychology-today.com/us/blog/intense-emotions-and-strong-feelings/201105/grief -isnt-something-get-over

Lamm, C., Decety, J., & Singer, T. (2010). Meta-analytic evidence for common and distinct neural networks associated with directly experienced pain and empathy for pain. *NeuroImage, 54*(3), 2492-2502. https://doi.org/10.1016/j .neuroimage.2010.10.014

The Lancet. (2015, June 8). Over 95% of the world's population has health problems, with over a third having more than five ailments. *ScienceDaily.* https:// www.sciencedaily.com/releases/2015/06/150608081753.htm

Langri Tangpa Dorje Seng-ge, Geshe. (1998). Quoted in *The essence of Mahayana Lojong Practice: A commentary to Geshe Langri Tangpa's mind training in eight verses,* by Sermey Khensur Lobsang Tharchin. Mahayana Sutra and Tantra Press.

Laozi, & Mitchell, S. (1988). *Tao te ching: A new English version.* Harper & Row.

Lazar, S. W., Kerr, C. E., Wasserman, R. H., Gray, J. R., Greve, D. N., Treadway, M. T., McGarvey, M., Quinn, B. T., Dusek, J. A., Benson, H., Rauch, S. L., Moore, C. I., & Fischl, B. (2005). Meditation experience is associated with increased cortical thickness. *NeuroReport, 16*(17), 1893-1897. Cited in *Brief summary of mindfulness research* by G. Flaxman & L. Flook. http://marc.ucla .edu/workfiles/pdfs/MARC-mindfulness-research-summary.pdf.

Leahy, R. L. (1997). Introduction. In *Practicing cognitive therapy: A guide to interventions.* Jason Aronson. http://cognitivetherapynyc.com/docs/arosnonintro .pdf

Levine, Saul, MD, (2003). Psychological and social aspects of resilience: A synthesis of risks and resources. *Dialogues in Clinical Neuroscience, 5*(3), 273-280. https://doi.org/10.31887/DCNS.2003.5.3/slevine

Lewis, S. (2013). *Nurturing, healing love.* Hay House. See also https://chooselovemovement.org/.

Lichfield, G. (2015, April). The science of near-death experiences: Empirically investigating brushes with the afterlife. *The Atlantic.* https://www.theatlantic.com/ magazine/archive/2015/04/the-science-of-near-death-experiences/386231/

Lindahl, J. R., Fisher, N. E., Cooper, D. J., Rosen, R. K., & Britton, W. B. (2017). The varieties of contemplative experience: A mixed-methods study of meditation-related challenges in Western Buddhists. *PloS One, 12*(5), e0176239. https:// doi.org/10.1371/journal.pone.0176239

Linehan, M. M., Schmidt, H., 3rd, Dimeff, L. A., Craft, J. C., Kanter, J., & Comtois, K. A. (1999). Dialectical behavior therapy for patients with borderline personality disorder and drug-dependence. *American Journal on Addictions, 8*(4), 279-292. https://doi.org/10.1080/105504999305686

Louis, B. (2015). *The difference sameness makes: Racial recognition and the "narcissism of minor differences."* Sage Publications. http://journals.sagepub.com/ doi/abs/10.1177/1468796805054960.

Lutz, A., Brefczynski-Lewis, J., Johnstone, T., & Davidson, R. J. (2008). Regulation of the neural circuitry of emotion by compassion meditation: Effects of meditative expertise. *PLoS One, 3*(3), 1-10. Cited in *Brief summary of mindfulness research* by G. Flaxman & L. Flook. http://marc.ucla.edu/workfiles/ pdfs/MARC-mindfulness-research-summary.pdf

Lyubomirsky, S., & Nolem-Hoeksema, S. (1995). Effects on self-focused rumination on negative thinking and interpersonal problem solving. *Journal of Personality and Social Psychology, 69*(1), 176-190. https://doi.org/ 10.1037//0022-3514.69.1.176

Marcia, J., & Josselson, R. (2013). Eriksonian personality research and its implications for psychotherapy. *Journal of Personality, 81*(6), 617-629. https://doi.org/10.1111/jopy.12014

Mascaro, J. S., Rilling, J. K., Negi, L., & Raison, C. L. (2013). Compassion meditation enhances empathic accuracy and related neural activity. *Social Cognitive and Affective Neuroscience, 8*(1), 48-55. https://doi.org/10.1093/scan/nss095

Mathieu, F. (2012). Compassion fatigue. In C. R. Figley (Ed.), *Encyclopedia of trauma* (pp. 137-139). Sage Publications. https://www.doi.org/10.4135/9781452218595.n46

Mautz, S. Science says "Random Acts of Kindness" week has astonishing health benefits. *Inc.* https://www.inc.com/scott-mautz/science-says-random-acts-of-kindness-week-has-astonishing-health-benefits.html.

McClure, A. C., Tanski, S. E., Kingsbury, J., Gerrard, M., & Sargent, J. D. (2010). Characteristics associated with low self-esteem among US adolescents. *Academic Pediatrics, 10*(4), 238-244.e2. https://doi.org/10.1016/j.acap.2010.03.007

McEwen, B., & Sapolsky, R. (2006). Stress and your health. *Journal of Clinical Endocrinology & Metabolism, 91*(2), E2. https://doi.org/10.1210/jcem.91.2.9994

Meichenbaum, D. (2007, May 4). *Self-care for trauma psychotherapists and caregivers: Individual, social and organizational interventions.* Melissa Institute. https://melissainstitute.org/wp-content/uploads/2016/12/SELF-CARE-FOR-TRAUMA-PSYCHOTHERAPISTS-AND-CAREGIVERS-changed-26.pdf

Meissner, J. E. (1996). Nurses: Are we eating our young? *Nursing, 16*(3), 51-53.

Miller, K. I., Stiff, J. B., & Ellis, B. H. (1988). Communication and empathy as precursors to burnout among human service workers. *Communication Monographs, 55*(9), 336-341. https://doi.org/10.1080/03637758809376171

Miller, W. R., & Rollnick, S. (2013). *Motivational interviewing: Helping people change.* Guilford Press.

Mindfulness Academy. *The benefits of patience.* http://mindfulnessacademyuk.org/the-benefits-of-patience/

Moberly, N. J., & Watkins, E. (2008). Ruminative self-focus and negative affect. *Journal of Abnormal Psychology, 117*(2), 314-323. https://doi.org/10.1037/0021-843X.117.2.314

Moran, C. (2002). Humor as a moderator of compassion fatigue. In C. R. Figley (Ed.), *Treating compassion fatigue.* Brunner-Routledge.

Murphy, T. (2018). Cancer patients are twice as likely to declare bankruptcy. *Chicago Tribune.* https://www.chicagotribune.com/nation-world/ct-cancer-treatment-debt-20180522-story.html

Musselman, D. L., Tomer, A., Manatunga, A. K., Knight, B. T., Porter, M. R., Kasey, S., Marzec, U., Harker, L. A., & Nemeroff, C. B. (1996). Exaggerated platelet reactivity in major depression. *American Journal of Psychiatry, 153*(10), 1313-1317. https://doi.org/10.1176/ajp.153.10.1313

National Association of Social Workers (NASW). (2017) *Code of ethics..* https://www.socialworkers.org/about/ethics/code-of-ethics/code-of-ethics-english

National Education Association (NEA) (2019). *National Education Association code of ethics.* http://www.nea.org/home/30442.htm

Nazareno, L., & Krafel, A. (2017). Taking care of ourselves and others: Creating a compassionate school. *Phi Delta Kappan.* https://kappanonline.org/nazareno-krafel-schools-kindness-compassion-taking-care-others/

Neff, K. D., & Germer, C. K. (2013). A pilot study and randomized controlled trial of the mindful self-compassion program. *Journal of Clinical Psychology, 69,* 28-44. https://doi.org/10.1002/jclp.21923

Newell, J. M., & MacNeil, G. A. (2010). Professional burnout, vicarious trauma, secondary traumatic stress, and compassion fatigue: A review of theoretical terms, risk factors, and preventive methods for clinicians and researchers. *Best Practices in Mental Health: An International Journal, 6*(2), 57-68.

Nia, H. S., Lehto, R. H., Ebadi, A., & Peyrovi, H. (2016). Death anxiety among nurses and health care professionals: A review article. *International Journal of Community Based Nursing and Midwifery, 4*(1), 2-10.

Nolen-Hoeksema, S., Wisco, B. E., & Lyubomirsky, S. (2008). Rethinking rumination. *Perspectives on Psychological Science, 3*(5), 400-424. https://doi.org/10.1111/j.1745-6924.2008.00088.x

Norton, P. J., & Price, E. C. (2007). A meta-analytic review of adult cognitive-behavioral treatment outcome across the anxiety disorders. *Journal of Nervous and Mental Disease, 195*(6), 521-531. https://doi.org/10.1097/01.nmd.0000253843.70149.9a

O'Donnell, E. (2013, May 10). Micro-utopia, anyone? Fredrickson describes nourishing power of small, positive moments. *NIH Record.* https://nihrecord.nih.gov/newsletters/2013/05_10_2013/story3.htm.

Orenstein, David, (2017, May 24). Study documents range of challenging meditation experiences. *News from Brown.* https://news.brown.edu/articles/2017/05/experiences

Pace, T. W., Negi, L. T., Sivilli, T. I., Issa, M. J., Cole, S. P., Adame, D. D., & Raison, C. L. (2010). Innate immune, neuroendocrine and behavioral responses to psychosocial stress do not predict subsequent compassion meditation practice time. *Psychoneuroendocrinology, 35*(2), 310-315. https://doi.org/10.1016/j.psyneuen.2009.06.008

Patoni, L. (2012). Strengths-based approaches for working with individuals. *IRISS.*https://www.iriss.org.uk/resources/insights/strengths-based-approaches-working-individuals

Pearlman, L. A. (2012). Vicarious trauma. In C. R. Figley (Ed.). *Encyclopedia of trauma* (pp. 783-786). Sage Publications. https://www.doi.org/10.4135/9781452218595.n271

Pearlman, L. A., & McCay, L. (2008). *Understanding & addressing vicarious trauma.* Headington Institute. https://mutualaiddisasterreliefsite.files.wordpress.com/2017/04/vtmoduletemplate2_ready_v2_85791.pdf

Peikoff, L. (1993). *Objectivism: The philosophy of Ayn Rand.* Meridian.

Pellegrino, B. (2012). *Evaluating the mindfulness-based and cognitive-behavior therapy for anger management program.* Philadelphia College of Osteopathic Medicine. http://digitalcommons.pcom.edu/cgi/viewcontent.cgi?article=1232&context=psychology_dissertations.

Peteet, J. R., Rodriguez, V. B., Herschkopf, M. D., McCarthy, A., Betts, J., Romo, S., & Murphy, J. M. (2016). Does a therapist's world view matter? *Journal of Religion and Health, 55*(3), 1097-1106. https://doi.org/10.1007/s10943-016-0208-9

Positive Psychology Program. *The benefits of gratitude: 28 questions answered thanks to gratitude research.* https://positivepsychologyprogram.com/benefits-gratitude-research-questions/#benefits.

Potter-Efron, R. T. (1994). *Angry all the time: An emergency guide to anger control.* New Harbinger Press.

Pruzinsky, T., & Hurley, W. (2013, September 22). *COMPASS* [PowerPoint slides].

Rand, A., & Branden, N. (1964). *The virtue of selfishness: A new concept of egoism.* New American Library.

Random Acts of Kindness. Kindness health facts. https://www.dartmouth.edu/wellness/emotional/rakhealthfacts.pdf

Random Acts of Kindness Foundation. Did you know there are scientifically proven benefits of being kind? https://www.randomactsofkindness.org/the-science-of-kindness

Rayburn, C. A. (2008). Clinical and pastoral issues and challenges in working with the dying and their families. *Adultspan Journal, 7*(2), 94-108.

Reddy, S. D., Negi, L., Dodson-Lavelle, B., Ozawa-de Silva, B., Pace, T. W., Cole, S. P., Raison, L. W., & Craighead, L. W. (2012). Cognitive-based compassion training: A promising prevention strategy for at-risk adolescents. *Journal of Child and Family Studies, 22*(2), 219-230. https://link.springer.com/article/10.1007/s10826-012-9571-7

Reynolds, S. (2011, August 2). Happy brain, happy life. *Psychology Today.* https://www.psychologytoday.com/us/blog/prime-your-gray-cells/201108/happy-brain-happy-life.

Ricard, M., Wise, J., & Singer, P. (2016, October 19). Put your compassion into action. *Lion's Roar: Buddhist Wisdom for our Time.* https://www.lionsroar.com/put-your-compassion-into-action/

Riley, R. (2019). Michigan kids are going to school traumatized—and teachers lack training, resources to help. *Detroit Free Press.* https://www.freep.com/in-depth/news/columnists/rochelle-riley/2019/12/13/special-education-trauma-kids-michigan-schools/3739003002/

Rodolfo, K. (2000). What is homeostasis? *Scientific American.* https://www.scientificamerican.com/article/what-is-homeostasis/

Rosenfeld, J. (2019). The rising price of insulin. *Medical Economics.* https://www.medicaleconomics.com/article/rising-price-insulin

Rubak, S., Sandbaek, A., Lauritzen, T., & Christensen, B. (2005). Motivational interviewing: A systematic review and meta-analysis. *British Journal of General Practice, 55*(513), 305-312.

Ryan, R. M., & Deci, E. L. (2000). Self-determination theory and the facilitation of intrinsic motivation, social development, and well-being. *American Psychologist, 55*, 68-78. https://dx.doi.org/10.1037/0003-066X.55.1.68

Saltsman, T. L., Seery, M. D., Ward, D. E., Radsvick, T. M., Panlilio, Z. A., Lamarche, V. M., & Kondrak, C. L. (2021). Facing the facets: No association between dispositional mindfulness facets and positive momentary stress responses during active stressors. *Personality & Social Psychology Bulletin, 47*(7), 1057-1070. https://doi.org/10.1177/0146167220956898

SAMHSA. (2014). *Tips for disaster responders: Understanding compassion fatigue.* https://store.samhsa.gov/system/files/sma14-4869.pdf

SAMHSA. (2014). *A treatment improvement protocol: Trauma-informed care in behavioral health services.* https://www.integration.samhsa.gov/clinical-practice/SAMSA_TIP_Trauma.PDF

SAMHSA. (2018). *Crisis Intervention Team (CIT) methods for using data to inform practice: A step-by-step guide.* https://store.samhsa.gov/product/Crisis-Intervention-Team-CIT-Methods-for-Using-Data-to-Inform-Practice/SMA18-5065

SAMHSA. (2018). *First responders: Behavioral health concerns, emergency response, and trauma. Disaster technical assistance center supplemental research bulletin.* https://www.hsdl.org/?abstract&did=813843

SAMHSA. (2019). *Enhancing motivation for change in substance abuse treatment.* https://store.samhsa.gov/product/TIP-35-Enhancing-Motivation-for-Change-in-Substance-Use-Disorder-Treatment/PEP19-02-01-003

Sansone, R. A., & Sansone, L. A. (2010). Gratitude and well being: The benefits of appreciation. *Psychiatry, 7*(11), 18-22.

Sansone, R. A., & Sansone, L. A. (2015). Workplace bullying: A tale of adverse consequences. *Innovations in Clinical Neuroscience, 12*(1-2), 32-37.

Santideva, A. (1979). *A guide to the Bodhisattva's way of life* (Stephen Batchelor, Trans.). Library of Tibetan Works and Archives.

Sartor, T. A. (2016). Vicarious trauma and its influence on self-efficacy. *Vistas Online.* https://www.counseling.org/docs/default-source/vistas/article_2721c-024f16116603abcacff0000bee5e7.pdf?sfvrsn=6

Saunders, J. J. (2001). *History of the Mongol conquests.* University of Pennsylvania Press. (Original work published 1972)

Scherwitz, L., Graham, L. E., Grandits, G., Buehler, J., & Billings, J. (1986). Self-involvement and coronary heart disease incidence in the multiple risk factor intervention trial. *Psychosomatic Medicine, 48*(3-4), 187-199.

Schumann, K., & Ross, M. (2010). The benefits, costs, and paradox of revenge. *Social and Personality Psychology Compass 4*(12), 1193-1205. https://onlinelibrary.wiley.com/doi/abs/10.1111/j.1751-9004.2010.00322.x

Semple, R., Reid, E., & Miller, L. (2005). Treating anxiety with mindfulness: An open trial of mindfulness training for anxious children. *Journal of Cognitive Psychotherapy, 19*(4), 379-392. Cited in Brief Summary of Mindfulness Research by G. Flaxman and L. Flook. http://marc.ucla.edu/workfiles/pdfs/MARC-mindfulness-research-summary.pdf

Seppala, E. (2013, July 24). Compassionate mind, healthy body. *Greater Good Magazine.* https://greatergood.berkeley.edu/article/item/compassionate_mind_healthy_body

Seppala, E. Top 10 scientific benefits of compassion. *Charter for Compassion.* https://charterforcompassion.org/defining-and-understanding-compassion/top-10-scientific-benefits-of-compassion

Sermabeikian, P. (1994). Our clients, ourselves: The spiritual perspective and social work practice. *Social Work, 39*(2), 178-183. https://doi.org/10.1093/sw/39.2.178

Shamay-Tsoory, S. G., Aharon-Peretz, J., & Perry, D. (2009). Two systems for empathy: A double dissociation between emotional and cognitive empathy in inferior frontal gyrus versus ventromedial prefrontal lesions. *Brain: A Journal of Neurology, 132*(Pt 3), 617-627. https://doi.org/10.1093/brain/awn279

Shapiro, C., Meyers, A., & Toner, C. (1996). *Strength-based, family-focused practice: A clinical guide from family justice.* https://www.familiesoutside.org.uk/content/uploads/2011/02/family-justice-clinical-guide.pdf

Sharma, M. K., Sharma, M. P., & Marimuthu, P. (2016). Mindfulness-based program for management of aggression among youth: A follow-up study. *Indian Journal of Psychological Medicine, 38*(3), 213-216. https://doi.org/10.4103/0253-7176.183087

Shiah, Y. J. (2016). From self to nonself: The nonself theory. *Frontiers in Psychology, 7,* 124. https://doi.org/10.3389/fpsyg.2016.00124

Shoham, A., Hadash, Y., & Bernstein, A. (2018). Examining the decoupling model of equanimity in mindfulness training: An intensive experience sampling study. *Clinical Psychological Science, 6*(5), 704-720. https://doi.org/10.1177/2167702618770446

Shonin, E., & Van Gordon, W. (2013). Can mindfulness meditation induce psychotic episodes? http://www.edoshoninarchive.com/PDFs/20131226_Shonin_VanGordon.pdf

Shpancer, N. (2020). Overcoming fear: The only way out is through. *Psychology Today.* https://www.psychologytoday.com/us/blog/insight-therapy/201009/overcoming-fear-the-only-way-out-is-through

Simon-Thomas, E. R. (2012). Three insights from the cutting edge of compassion research. *Greater Good Magazine.* https://greatergood.berkeley.edu/article/item/three_insights_from_the_cutting_edge_of_compassion_research.

Singh, N. N., Lancioni, E., Winton, A. S. W., Fisher, B. C., Wahler, R. G., Mcaleavey, K., Singh, J., & Sabaawi, M. (2006). Mindful parenting decreases aggression, noncompliance, and self-injury in children with autism. *Journal of Emotional and Behavioral Disorders, 14*(3), 169-177. https://doi.org/10.1177/10634266060140030401

Singh, N. N., Lancioni, G. E., Winton, A. S., Singh, J., Curtis, W. J., Wahler, R. G., & McAleavey, K. M. (2007). Mindful parenting decreases aggression and increases social behavior in children with developmental disabilities. *Behavior Modification, 31*(6), 749-771. https://doi.org/10.1177/0145445507300924

Smith, E. E. (January 19, 2013). There's more to life than being happy: Meaning comes from more complex things than being happy. *The Atlantic.* https://www.theatlantic.com/health/archive/2013/01/theres-more-to-life-than-being-happy/266805/

Solomon, S., Greenberg, J., & Pyszczynski, T. (2015). *The worm at the core.* Random House.

Speer, M. E., Bhanji, J. P., & Delgado, M. R. (2014). Savoring the past: Positive memories evoke value representations in the striatum. *Neuron, 84*(4), 847-856. https://doi.org/10.1016/j.neuron.2014.09.028

Spiegel, D. (1996). Psychological distress and disease course for women with breast cancer: One answer, many questions. *Journal of the National Cancer Institute, 88*(10), 629-631. https://doi.org/10.1093/jnci/88.10.629

Staicu, M. L., & Cuţov, M. (2010). Anger and health risk behaviors. *Journal of Medicine and Life, 3*(4), 372-375.

Stamm, B. H. (2002). Measuring compassion satisfaction as well as fatigue: Developmental history of the compassion satisfaction and fatigue test. In C. R. Finley (Ed.), *Treating compassion fatigue* (pp. 107-122). Brunner-Routledge.

Stringfellow, A. (2019, March 11). What is caregiver fatigue? *Senior Link*. https:// www.seniorlink.com/blog/what-is-caregiver-fatigue

Suttie, J. (2016, January 25). What doesn't kill you makes you kinder. *Greater Good Magazine*. https://greatergood.berkeley.edu/article/item/ what_doesnt_kill_you_makes_you_kinder

Suttie, J. (2018). How to find your purpose in midlife. *Greater Good Magazine*. https://greatergood.berkeley.edu/article/item/how_to_find_your_purpose _in_midlife

Tamborski, M., Brown, R. P., & Chowning, K. (2012). Self-serving bias or simply serving the self? Evidence for a dimensional approach to narcissism. *Personality and Individual Differences*, *52*(8), 942-946. https://doi.org/10.1016/j .paid.2012.01.030

Tang, Y. Y., Ma, Y., Wang, J., Fan, Y., Feng, S., Lu, Q., Yu, Q., Sui, D., Rothbart, M. K., Fan, M., & Posner, M. I. (2007). Short-term meditation training improves attention and self-regulation. *Proceedings of the National Academy of Sciences*, *104*(43), 17152-17156. https://doi.org/10.1073/pnas.0707678104

Teasdale, J. D., Segal, Z. V., Williams, J. M., Ridgeway, V. A., Soulsby, J. M., & Lau, M. A. (2000). Prevention of relapse/recurrence in major depression by mindfulness-based cognitive therapy. *Journal of Consulting and Clinical Psychology*, *68*(4), 615-623. https://doi.org/10.1037//0022-006x.68.4.615

Tedeschi, R. & Triplett, K. N. (2012). Spiritual intelligence and posttraumatic growth. In C. R. Figley (Ed.), *Encyclopedia of trauma* (pp. 649-651). Sage Publications. https://www.doi.org/10.4135/9781452218595.n222

Tend Academy. *What is compassion fatigue?* http://www.tendacademy.ca/what-is -compassion-fatigue/

Tharchin, Geshe Lobsang, (1979). *The logic and debate tradition of India, Tibet, and Mongolia*. Rashi Gempil Ling.

Tharchin, Sermey Khensur Lobsang. (1999). *Achieving Bodhicitta: Instructions of two great lineages combined into a unique system of eleven categories*. Mahayana Sutra and Tantra Press.

Thayer, B. A. *Considering population and war: A critical and neglected aspect of conflict studies*. https://www.ncbi.nlm.nih.gov/pmc/articles/PMC2781832/

Tillman, J. G. (2019). When a patient dies by suicide. Association of American Medical Colleges. https://www.aamc.org/news-insights/when-patient-dies-suicide

Tolin, D. F. (2010). Is cognitive-behavioral therapy more effective than other therapies? A meta-analytic review. *Clinical Psychology Review*, *30*(6), 710-720. https://doi.org/10.1016/j.cpr.2010.05.003

Tynan, L. Signs you're in a toxic work environment and how to handle it. *TopResume*. https://www.topresume.com/career-advice/how-to-handle-toxic-work -environment

Ueda, M. (1995). *Basho and his interpreters*. Stanford University Press.

University of Virginia School of Medicine. *Children who report memories of previous lives*. https://med.virginia.edu/perceptual-studies/our-research/ children-who-report-memories-of-previous-lives/

Vaish, A., Grossmann, T., & Woodward, A. (2008). Not all emotions are created equal: The negativity bias in social-emotional development. *Psychological Bulletin*, *134*(3), 383-403. https://doi.org/doi:10.1037/0033-2909.134.3.383

van der Cingle, M. (2011). Compassion in care: A qualitative study of older people with a chronic disease and nurses. *Nursing Ethics, 18*(5), 672-685. https://doi.org/doi:10.1177/0969733011403556

Van Overwalle, F., & Baetens, K. (2009). Understanding others' actions and goals by mirror and mentalizing systems: A meta-analysis. *NeuroImage, 48*(3), 564-84. https://doi.org/doi:10.1016/j.neuroimage.2009.06.009

Vassilopoulos, S. P. (2008). Social anxiety and ruminative self-focus. June, *Journal of Anxiety Disorders, 22*(5), 860-867. https://doi.org/10.1016/j.janxdis.2007.08.012

Vigil, N. H., Grant, A. R., Perez, O., Blust, R. N., Chikani, V., Vadeboncoeur, T. F., Spaite, D. W., & Bobrow, B. J. (2019). Death by suicide—The EMS profession compared to the general public. *Prehospital Emergency Care, 23*(3), 340-345. https://doi.org/10.1080/10903127.2018.1514090

Vitalie, T. (2018). *Top 10 firefighter traits.* http://www.fortwaynefiredepartment.org/career-opportunities/resources/top-10-firefighter-traits

Wang, Y. T., Huang, G., Duke, G., & Yang, Y. (2017). Tai chi, yoga, and qigong as mind-body exercises. *Evidence-Based Complementary and Alternative Medicine, 2017.* https://doi.org/doi:10.1155/2017/8763915

Wasilewski, M., & Olsen, A. (2018). *Understanding workplace bullying in the police subculture.* https://www.officer.com/training-careers/education/article/21020641/understanding-workplace-bullying-in-the-police-subculture

Way, K. (2019). French executives found responsible for 35 employees' deaths by suicide. *Vice News.* https://www.vice.com/en_us/article/y3mzyb/france-telecom-orange-suicide-collective-moral-harassment?fbclid=IwAR3CdlnYT6hitmnLxk_k1xmOmueqZOAFFn5AlzO0RSavXtr2yUx3I-c74Ng

Weber, J. (2017). Mindfulness is not enough: Why equanimity holds the key to compassion. *Mindfulness & Compassion, 2*(2), 149-158. https://doi.org/10.1016/j.mincom.2017.09.004

Wee, D. F., Myers, D. (2002a). Strategies for managing disaster mental health worker stress. In C. R. Finley (Ed.), *Treating compassion fatigue* (pp. 181-212). Brunner-Routledge.

Wee, D. F., & Myers, D. (2002b). Stress response of mental health workers following disaster: The Oklahoma City bombing. In C. R. Finley (Ed.), *Treating compassion fatigue* (pp. 57-84). Brunner-Routledge.

Weiner, S. J., & Auster, S. (2007). From empathy to caring: Defining the ideal approach to a healing relationship. *Yale Journal of Biology and Medicine, 80*(3), 123-130, https://www.ncbi.nlm.nih.gov/pmc/articles/PMC2248287/

Whitaker, T. (2012). Social workers and workplace bullying: Perceptions, responses and implications. *Work, 42*(1), 115-123. https://doi.org/10.3233/WOR-2012-1335

Williams, S. (1868). The old astronomer. In *Twilight hours* (p. 69). Strahan & Co.

Wisdom Library. *Definitions of Karuna.* https://www.wisdomlib.org/definition/karuna

Wolin, S., & Wolin, S. (1993). *The resilient self: How survivors of troubled families rise above adversity.* Villard Books.

Wong J., & Brown J. (2017, June 6). How gratitude changes your brain. *Greater Good Magazine.* https://greatergood.berkeley.edu/article/item/how_gratitude_changes_you_and_your_brain

Yu, R. (2006). Stress potentiates decision biases: A stress induced deliberation-to-intuition (SIDI) model. *Neurobiology of Stress, 3*, 83-95. https://doi.org/10.1016/j.ynstr.2015.12.006

Zaccari, A. (2017). *Vicarious trauma coping and self-care practices among trauma therapists.* Walden Dissertations and Doctoral Studies Collection, Walden University. https://scholarworks.waldenu.edu/cgi/viewcontent.cgi?article=5220&context=dissertations

Zaki, J., & Ochsner, K. (2012). The neuroscience of empathy: Progress, pitfalls and promise. *Nature Neuroscience, 15*(5), 675-680. https://doi.org/doi:doi:10.1038/nn.3085

Ziegler, E. H. (2011, October 20). Gratitude as an antidote to aggression. University of Kentucky College of Arts and Sciences: *Psychology.* https://psychology.as.uky.edu/gratitude-antidote-aggression.

Index

in giving and taking exercise, 117-18
kindness exercises and, 84, 92
mindfulness, beginning exercises with, 28,
30, 169
motivation for the day, helping to set, 174
tough times, integrating exercises into,
152-59
visualization as part of, 115, 147
Compendium of Higher Knowledge
(Asanga), 58

Dalai Lama, vii, 5, 85
compassionate heart, on the need for,
111-12
"wise selfish" joke, 44, 45, 51n7
SEE learning developed under the
guidance of, 184
damage model of treatment, 186
Deck, Edward L., 36
de-fusion process, 21
Dialectical Behavioral Therapy (DBT), 21

Ellis, Beth Hartman, 172-73
empathy, 31, 45, 47, 62, 111, 133
adversity, as a response to, 84-85
cognitive empathy, 97, 168-69
compassion and, 2, 103, 105, 140
in COMPASS program, 9, 45, 104
distortions in self-concept as blocking,
13-14
empathic children, 47
gratitude as linked to, 68
in the workplace, 99, 169-70, 177
"Enhancing a Positive School Climate with
Compassion and Analytical Selective-
Focus Skills (COMPASS)," 8-9
equanimity, 58, 60, 62, 190, 200
contemplation of, 101, 135, 191
courage, making easier, 73-74
defining and describing, 13, 57
equanimity exercises, 63-64, 93, 214, 216
evenness and balance, encouraging, 56,
63, 67, 79
mindful equanimity, 191, 204
practice of, 75, 106, 119, 128, 215, 217,
218, 219
resonating with expression of, 142, 152
Erickson, Erik, 111, 129-30, 132, 160

Figley, Charles, 170
Frankl, Viktor, 22
Fredrickson, Barbara, 89

generativity, 132, 133

Genghis Khan, 79
giving and taking, 13, 109, 113, 218
in challenging situations, 199-201
in COMPASS program, 115, 117-18, 151
contemplation of, 119, 128, 135, 219
in "exchanging self for others" tradition,
110-12
"inhale the suffering" concept and,
115-16
internal equilibrium, helping to regain,
155, 204
goal-focused compassion, 13, 129, 133
contemplations on, 135-36, 149-50
practice of, 142-43, 219, 221
realistic expectations for, 131
gratitude, 13, 67, 133, 184, 204
appreciation, opening the heart in, 79
benefits of being grateful, 68-69
in COMPASS program, 62, 72, 93, 104
contemplations on, 101, 106, 128,
217, 219
defining and describing, 71-72, 215
expressions of gratitude, 68, 182
helping without expecting gratitude,
157, 159
gratitude practice, 75, 135
of caregivers, 191-92, 195, 200, 207
desired effects of showing gratitude, 215-16
equanimity practice and, 73, 93, 216
generating gratitude, 70, 184, 195, 200
in giving and taking exercises, 119, 218
Green Cross Standards of Humane Practice
of Self Care, 31, 182

Hanh, Thich Nhat, 68
Hayes, Stephen C., 123-24
Hunt, Carly, 9
Hypothalamic-Pituitary-Adrenal (HPA)
Axis, 19, 25

identical resonance, 173
insight. *See* compassionate insight

Jesse Lewis Choose Love Movement, 18, 184
Jobs, Steve, 70
Joiner, Thomas, 43
Jung, Carl Gustav, 80, 139

Kabat-Zinn, Jon, 23, 29
Kernberg, Otto, 111
Kesebir, Pelin, 213
kindness, 13, 81, 85
anger, responding to, 86-87
benefits of showing kindness, 45, 46, 50

Made in the USA
Middletown, DE
04 February 2022

60476591R00148